# THE HOOKER

# THE HANDYMAN

# AND

# WHAT THE PARROT SAW

## Patricia Harman

WALDORF PUBLISHING

Published by Waldorf Publishing
2140 Hall Johnson Road
#102-345
Grapevine, Texas 76051
www.WaldorfPublishing.com

The Hooker,
The Handyman and What the Parrot Saw

ISBN: 978-1-64316-637-7
Library of Congress Control Number: 2018943874

Copyright © 2019

*Dedicated to the people in my life who have shown me more love and support than I had any right to deserve or expect; my son Sam who gives meaning to my life, my Aunt Pat from whom I inherited my spirit of adventure, my family, The Breakfast Club, my law enforcement family, and to the people of AH & PWC for whom it was my privilege to serve as a law enforcement officer.*

# Table of Contents

*Chapter 1*
**Let's Just Call It Fiction**


Sergeant Charlotte "Charlie" Cavanaugh of the Landon City, Virginia, Police Department busily tapped away on her laptop. She had just returned home from her shift, but a police investigator's work was never really done. That was especially true after she made the rank of sergeant.

Home was her one-bedroom apartment in the heart of Landon, Virginia only twenty minutes from her beloved ocean in the off season. During the hot summer months, it could take forty minutes to an hour to get to the beach and she cursed every beach bag toting, sun screen wearing, ice-cream eating tourist along the way for the delay. Charlie's apartment wasn't especially upscale but on a cop's salary and still reeling from the financial devastation that comes from a middle-class divorce, it was the best she could do. The furnishings were warm and comfortable and the art and accents spoke of her love for the sea, the only true constant in her life. The sea, movies, and her work. It was all she had. All she was. A faded sign over her bedroom door read TAKE ME TO THE OCEAN. One day she would spend eternity there. On her loneliest nights she longed for it. She was tired. Tired of surviving. Tired of the inhumanity she watched people inflict on one another, especially on those they "loved." She prayed no one would ever love her that much again. She had had enough of that to last ten lifetimes. I love you and goodbye were synonymous her world.

The last few months had been particularly challenging for Charlie. Two homicides had rocked her sleepy town. Even more disturbing was that the fact that the two murders had been linked to two of her old cases when she was assigned as a detective to the "kiddy crimes." Pedophile cases.

Before making sergeant, she worked kiddy crimes for two long, heart breaking years. The two recently dead pedophiles appeared to have no apparent connection to each other than the depravity of their souls and the fact that she had been the detective that worked both of the cases. Charlie fretted as she studied the reports stored on her issued laptop. There has to be some kind of a connection. The molesters' crimes connected them, that was clear; but how were they tied to each other?

She asked her mentor, Officer Mike Thompson for some insight but all she got was his usual retort: "So, the suits can't connect the dots huh? What a shocker."

It was his typical response to anything involving detectives. Officer Mike Thompson a.k.a. "Thompson" was a life-long patrol officer and a street cop's street cop. He despised all police officers who *sold out* to specialty units like detective, motor officer or K9 or, God forbid and most offensive of all, supervisor.

"Worthless as tits on a boar hog," he would mutter. A lot of cops felt the same way he did, that only patrol officers were "real cops." He was right though. Patrol was the best time she ever had on the job. It was where the rubber met the road. Roll call. Pursuits. Talking car to car at two in the morning. That was the good stuff. But every family has a price and patrol duty came with a hefty bill. There are some things you cannot un-see. These traumas stay with an officer forever. Like all patrol officers sometimes Charlie's number would come up and one of these calls would be hers. It was the price she had to pay to be a part of this family. Three in particular fell into the "things she wished she had never seen" category.

Two brothers were drag racing each other side by side southbound on the main drag of Landon at 80 mph. Charlie was driving northbound in her police cruiser. It was a nice day and she had her window down and her arm hanging out. The brother in the outside lane saw the police cruiser first and hit the brakes causing him to swerve and tap the other vehicle sending the old Plymouth Fury careening into the oncoming lane. It was headed straight for Charlie's cruiser. She instinctively swerved, avoiding the missile by inches as it hurtled past her and hit the Chevy behind her head-on. The Chevy's driver, Diane Lagento, never saw it coming and never felt a thing. That's what Charlie would tell Diane's mother and she prayed it was true. Diane was single, like Charlie. She was Charlie's age, build, hair color, and height. She loved her mother and her cat. She was going to school to be a physical therapist and on that day she died instantly and all her dreams died with her. All Charlie could do was helplessly watch in the rearview mirror as the two vehicles exploded against each other and went airborne. Charlie never heard the impact of the collision, but she should have. The head-on was a combined speed of 120 mph according to the telltale tap of the speedometer needles on their respective dials. Diane's speedometer tapped at 45 mph, the other car at 75 mph but Charlie didn't hear a thing even though her window was open, and she was only a few yards away when they hit. The mind's capacity to manage trauma is truly remarkable and that was her first taste of it. Even all these years later Charlie couldn't drive through that stretch of road without whispering her name, and recalling how she looked upside down in her Chevy, suspended by her useless seatbelt. Her index finger had been ripped off and lay on the roof lining of the inverted car but there was surprisingly little blood. She just imploded and there was no sound.

The second "thing she wished she had never seen" happened when a small plane went down in front of her. Charlie was sitting in her police cruiser writing a report in an empty parking lot when she heard a very low flying private plane overhead. She watched in disbelief as it clipped the trees of a wooded area adjacent to the shopping center, caught on fire and tore into pieces. She saw the smoke rising from the woods and reported it to dispatch and headed into the woods on foot. She couldn't wait for the heroes, the fire department; she had to search for survivors. As she trekked to the site, dispatch reported to her by radio that a nearby private airport tower was reporting a MAY DAY of a small aircraft occupied by four adults and a baby. Oh God please don't let me find the baby, she prayed. Additional officers and the fire department arrived and she could hear them in the distance when she came upon a charred man sitting by a stream. At least she thought it was a man. All of his skin was gone. He was charred and pink and veiny and conscious. He didn't appear to be in any pain.

"Have you found the baby?" he asked, his skeletal eyeballs wide with concern.

"No. Not yet. Help is on the way."

"Am I going to die?" he asked as he continued to penetrate her with his wide eyes.

"Yes Sir. Make your peace." He died before the last word left her mouth. When her backup officer got to her,

Charlie was praying. "Come on kid," her backup said. "The heroes will deal with him. Come away."

But the worst . . . the worst of the worst was the Mary Jane Klasky case.

These were the scars that were assigned to her for eternity. The price she paid to belong to something important. She couldn't drive through the site of the accident without whispering Diane's name or smelling anti-freeze. She couldn't see a small plane without hearing his words. "Did you find the baby? Am I going to die?". And Mary Jane Klasky . . . she would never recover from. Ever.

*Chapter 2*
**Mary Jane Klasky**

As Charlie closed her laptop and stood up to stretch, she tried desperately to block out thoughts of the FBI agent that had been thrust upon her this morning. As she started the unloading process, she could not shake him. Shoes, handcuffs, firearm, cuffs, pants, shirt—she felt ten pounds lighter. She sat down on the bed and closed her eyes. Determined to block him out she let her thoughts wander to Mary Jane Klasky, as she often did when she was stressed. Just last week about a half-hour into her morning pile of paperwork, the bouncy blond teen had appeared in Charlie's office and plopped into the chair popping her gum.

"Hey Officer Cavanaugh," she said chewing like a cow. "What's shakin'?"

"Ms. Mary Jane Klasky," Charlie smiled. "Hey sweetie. How did you get up here? I'm really swamped, kiddo, and you know I'm not Officer Cavanaugh any-more. You can call me Charlie or Sergeant but my title isn't Officer. That's for the real police." She winked at the teen. "Now I'm mostly just a paper-pusher." Charlie sighed and motioned to the mess on her desk.

Mary Jane was the victim in Charlie's very first child molestation case. Charlie wasn't a sergeant at the time, or even a detective; she was a patrol officer, a road dog, and she had only been on the street a short time. She had responded as backup to a call for a domestic dispute at the Klasky house. Mary Jane's house. It was violent and a neighbor had called after hearing the commotion. Mrs. Klasky was sporting the early signs of what was going to be a nasty black eye and Mr. Klasky was drunk and belligerent. The wife refused to say what he had done to her, saying that she fell. Without the wife's statement or a witness, they would not be able to make an arrest. Charlie was the back-up officer so she let the primary officer, Fred Miller, who was many years her senior, take the lead. Charlie stood watch over the drunken Mr. Klasky while Officer Miller took the wife into another room and tried to get her to talk. Miller returned with the wife and shook his head 'no' at Charlie.

"Okay Mr. and Mrs. Klasky, we'll be going then. Let's try to keep it down okay?" Officer Miller said as he nodded toward the door at Charlie. Charlie knew she should keep her mouth shut and follow Miller out but something churning in her gut was keeping her feet glued to the floor.

"Is there anyone else at home?" she blurted impulsively at Mrs. Klasky. The parents shot each other a look. "Don't look at him! Look at me! I asked you a question! Who else is home?" Charlie was as surprised by her assertiveness as was Officer Miller.

"Our daughter. M-Mary Jane . . . she's twelve . . ." she said with a stutter, glancing up the stairs and then looking nervously at her husband. Miller made a jerking motion with his head up the stairs and Charlie lit up the stairs while Miller waited with the punchee and the puncher, who was raising slurred objections about needing a warrant to be in his house.

"Mary Jane?" Charlie called as she opened the door to the only room with a light on. Inside sat a frail blond angel clutching a pillow, her eyes red from crying. "Hi there, Sweetie," Charlie said softly and got down on one knee. The girl looked so much younger than twelve.

"My name is Charlotte and I'm a police officer. Are you okay?" The girl nodded but didn't speak. "Is it okay if I sit down with you for a minute?" Mary Jane nodded again and moved over to make room on her small bed. "Scary night, huh?" And again the girl nodded. "Hey, don't you talk? You do have teeth, don't you? Oh no, were you born without teeth? That's terrible!" The girl giggled a little. "Oh wait! You do have teeth! Oh, thank goodness!" Charlie smiled.

"Do you know why I am here tonight Mary Jane?"

"My parents?"

Charlie nodded and tightened her lips.

"Sometimes parents argue and that's okay. All parents argue once in a while, but if they hit, then it's not okay. Right?" Mary Jane nodded in agreement. "I need to know if that happened tonight. Did someone get hit tonight?" Mary Jane shrugged and looked at the floor. "This is really important sweetie. Did someone hit someone else tonight?" The girl shrugged again. Charlie decided to try a different approach. "Do you know what your parents were fighting about, Mary Jane?" The girl shot a quick look to the nightstand and then looked at the floor and shrugged again. Charlie looked at the nightstand and the blood began to leave her head.

A bottle of KY Jelly was laying in the open nightstand drawer.

*KY Jelly? What the hell was sexual lubricant doing in a twelve-year-old's nightstand?* The nightstand drawer was opened enough that Charlie could see the partial cover of an adult magazine inside the drawer. Charlie felt her chest tighten and she struggled to breathe. She closed her eyes and willed herself to stay calm for the child's sake. When she opened her eyes the girl was staring at her, wide-eyed. Charlie took a breath. She had no idea what she was going to say—she just started talking.

"Do you know why I became a police officer Mary Jane? To protect people who were being hurt by other people. To save them Mary Jane, so that they couldn't be hurt anymore." The girl's tears started to pool. "You don't have to say anything Mary Jane, just nod okay? Is someone hurting you?" The child nodded 'yes.' "Is your father hurting you?" The child nodded again and started to sob.

"I can stop him, Mary Jane." Charlie hugged the girl. "I will stop him," Charlie said, her own tears starting to fall. Charlie got her game face back on and called Officer Miller to the top of the stairs, gave him a quick briefing and asked him to call CPS and keep the parents downstairs while she waited with the girl.

Child Protective Services arrived with an active file on the Klasky family started by Mary Jane's school. All the signs of potential abuse were there but neither the mother nor the victim would break their silence for fear of the wrath it would bring. Following the CPS preliminary evaluation, Paul Klasky was arrested for domestic assault to get him out of the house. It would never stick without the wife's cooperation but it got him out of there for the night and gave them a shot. Once he was gone, Charlie went to work on the wife and got a consensual search of Mary Jane's room in under thirty minutes, in spite of Officer Miller's suggestion that they wait for the detectives and a search warrant.

Mrs. Klasky spun a woe-is-me tale of mental and physical abuse, a one-income household and true love, until the alcohol "got ahold" of her husband. She said she only suspected her husband was raping their preteen daughter; she wasn't positive, and she did stop him tonight and had the black eye to prove it.

*Well wasn't she the fucking hero?* Charlie wanted to throw up. She wanted to kill Mary Jane's mother almost as much as she wanted to kill the drunken molesting father.

By the time the suits arrived, Charlie had completed the search of Mary Jane's room which included numerous adult magazines which her father used as visual aids to show his daughter what he wanted her to do. The bottle of KY Charlie spotted on the nightstand was one of many. The other discarded bottles of KY were located behind the bed. She also found a stash of airline bottles of alcohol Paul Klasky used to impair his child. The worst discovery of all was found under the girl's mattress—a diary detailing a year and a half of sexual abuse at the hands of her father in heartbreaking detail.

Dear diary, tonight Daddy made me . . .

The responding detective and Operations Lt. Gerald Grisolm, who would later become Charlie's CID captain, weren't exactly thrilled with the overzealous rookie patrol officer, but on the other hand she did seem to have all of her bases covered so the Lt. let her run with the case and was there to help her with the details. As the case unfolded Charlie learned a few things.

She learned she wanted to be a detective, in spite of her mentor's strict no-suits policy.

She learned that in order to save a victim of molestation at the hands of a family member, you must first destroy that child's family with an arrest.

It was a Catch-22 that Charlie was unprepared for and it hit her hard. Lt. Grisolm did what he could to prepare Charlie for the harsh reality of working a molestation case, but he was promoted to captain shortly after the Klasky case and transferred, leaving Charlie pretty much on her own. Captain Grisolm always felt bad about not being there for Charlie when things went sideways. He knew he couldn't explain to her the madness in moving an innocent child from one room in hell to another and telling them you were "saving them." That was the reality and Charlie had to learn it on her own. There was no other way.

The case did make one thing clear to Charlie, the storybooks are bullshit. This was something her own childhood and Nicholas Cage had already taught her. She just didn't know that it was true for so many others until she became a police officer.

Charlie made Virginia Circuit Court history when she used Mary Jane's diary to convict Paul Klasky without using the direct testimony of his traumatized daughter. In the year that led up to the court date, Mrs. Klasky committed suicide and Mary Jane was passed back and forth from family members to foster care and back again as the highly publicized trial drew near. The state secured a fifty-four-year sentence for the forty-one-year-old Klasky. He would never see the light of day. None of them would.

*Chapter 3*
**Carneys—Small Hands**

Whenever Charlie saw Mary Jane, now blossoming into a beautiful young lady, she felt obliged to spend time with her after all she had been through, but now was not the time. Charlie was so overwhelmed. Mercifully, Mary Jane's visit was brief and soon Charlie was back at it, but still not finished when her workout partner and lead detective Clint McCallister was ready to punch out that night and head to the gym. She would have to pass.

"Peace out!" he had yelled as he walked past her office. "Going to Amy's after."

She regretted passing on the work out. Clint didn't need it but she sure did. Charlie Cavanaugh was not built for police work. She was tough and smart, but she was small; very small with small features, and the small hands of a carnival worker. Carneys . . . small hands, smell like cabbage as Mike Myers would say.

Thankfully, she entered police work at a time when gender and size no longer mattered. At least it didn't matter as much as it once had. The addition of pepper spray and TASERs, props to the Smith brothers of TASER, were great levelers of the playing field. The weapon of the future—Thomas A. Swift's Electric Rifle, coined in the early 1970's by inventor Jack Cover, after the fictional character created by Edward Stratemeyer in 1910. The TASER had saved her bacon more than once and that of a suspect she might have otherwise had to shoot. On most occasions, her diminutive size worked to her advantage rather than to her detriment. There wasn't a whole lot of glory in beating up a 5'4" 118-pound female police officer.

Unlike too many of her male counterparts, Charlie would rather talk her perps down than bash their skulls. "Just because you have the authority, doesn't mean you have the right," her mentor would say. On the rare occasion when she could feel herself about to lose her temper and was tempted to hold the trigger on her TASER a few seconds too long, she could detect a hint of Thompson's cigar smoke that would bring her back down. Her mentor loved a good cigar ("good" being code for *cheap*) and Charlie loved him for it and for so much more.

Charlie had a love affair with the Constitution that not all of her fellow officers understood or embraced. Protect, serve, and enforce; in that order. That was how she thought a public servant should behave. It was about public service, not power.

When Charlie was promoted from patrol officer to detective and started working child molestation cases, civility and professionalism became scarce resources. She wanted to kill the bastards she dealt with for what they had done. For the innocence lost and for the lives altered in a way that no judge, jury, or prison sentence could ever undo. Charlie could see it in their little eyes; shock, betrayal, confusion, pain. Their eyes all looked the same. In her darkest hours in her bed at night as she slept, it was the eyes of these children that stared back at her . . . just before the train would come.

Unfortunately, plea bargaining was a way of life for kiddy crime cases. Actually, plea bargaining is a necessary part of any kind of policing. Occasionally, John Q. Public gets a hair up their butt and tries to eliminate plea bargaining from the criminal justice system. Big mistake. In the case of kiddy touchers, plea bargaining protects victims. It saves the child from reliving the trauma on the stand and saves the parents from hearing it. It also lowers the threshold for guilt. Beyond a reasonable doubt is a pretty high benchmark to hit, and plea bargaining allows for justice to be served even if every box isn't checked. It also cuts the backlog on cases by as much as sixty percent. Having to try every case would raise the cost of the criminal justice system in a way that would have taxpayers dumping tea. It's necessary. The downside is, especially when prosecuting pedophiles, they don't get enough jail time. As was the case with the two dead pedophiles from Charlie's old cases.

As a police sergeant in Major Crimes, Charlie wasn't taking cases to court anymore but she was still trying to protect the predator from the prey. There was just a lot more to it now. There were personnel to manage—all men. There were reports to review, evaluations to write, vacations to approve, and mental health to monitor. It was exhausting. Charlie never really wanted to be promoted. She liked the front lines.

"You take their stripes, you gotta take their shit," Thompson would caution.

When the promotion was offered, however, she accepted. But this left little room for anything else in her life. Truth be told, there wasn't really anything else in her life anyway and never really had been. Charlie was a freak. No one seemed to fit with her. To say she had less than a traditional upbringing would be an understatement, and as for her introduction to sex—unconventional is a word that leaps. Charlie's brother Tom was in and out mental health facilities in Georgia and her stepsisters lived in California where they had both attended college and built lives. Real lives. She loved them, but she was not like them and not close to them. Charlie was single. Divorced actually, but she preferred to say single. Everyone else that really meant something to her was gone. Her parents were gone. Cancer took them both. Her husband, a.k.a. The Plaintiff, was gone, but not gone enough. They still worked for the same police department though mercifully at different stations. Charlie had been alone most of her life but it wasn't something she liked to think about.

What she had left was Moses, Thompson's talks-too-damn-much parrot, her job, her love of the sea, her movies, and her internet buddy, AJ. AJ was a headless, bodiless pretend boyfriend—words on a page. But his words meant so much to her. He meant so much to her.

*Chapter 4*
**AJ**

**AJ101-789: Hi Angel. How was your shift to-night?**

VABlueAngel: Better now that I am home and you are here waiting for me. ☺

**AJ101-789: It's what I live for.**

VABlueAngel: Me too. I've become so attached to you and yet you are a zillion-miles away . . . or may-be you're not lol. Actually, you could end up being my crazy Aunt Pat! Honestly though AJ, I don't know how I would have gotten through the last year without you. Those fucking kiddy cases nearly buried me. I'm so grateful.

**AJ101-789: Language ☹ Tell me about your day . . .**

VABlueAngel: Sorry. I really am trying but you know that a sewer mouth and police work go hand in hand. What does AJ stand for?

**AJ101-789: That has been my experience as well but you are better than that.**

He typed, ignoring the question she knew he could not answer.

VABlueAngel: ☺ I love how you look after me AJ. It's been a long time since anyone has. Okay, I told you about the two homicides of the pedophiles right? Well, there's been a development. Federal "help" was brought in.

**AJ101-789 Uh-oh.**

VABlueAngel: Right?! While I understand that a potential serial killer is very unusual for a small agency to deal with, I really resent the fact that a fed is being foisted on my team when I don't need and didn't ask for help. We are all seasoned investigators. Many of my detectives have worked for much larger agencies and we are perfectly capable of working a serial. He's FBI. He's flipping FBI, AJ. FEDERAL BUREAU OF IDIOTS. FEDERAL BUREAU OF INTUITION. FEDERAL BUREAU OF INJUSTICE. He's apparently assigned to a regional major crimes task force in D.C., and since they can apparently afford to spare him (I'll just bet) I'm going to be stuck with him. The chief said, via my captain, that we are to give him "every consideration" while he assists us. Thanks for the vote of confidence Chief. I have my best guy at the helm. Clint McCallister knows his stuff, he really does. He's not much for tact but I guess that's what I'm here for. So now I am going to have to be the buffer between Clint and the fed. This guy is as arrogant as any fed I've ever met and it's annoying as hell. He also has kind of a command presence about him that is a tad unnerving. Maybe that's why he's arrogant but it's going to be no fun trying to keep him in check. I'm not sure but he seems to get off on tuning me up. Like he is making fun of me or laughing at me or something? Am I rambling?

Charlie and AJ's paths had crossed when he sent her an email with suggested corrections to a post Charlie made on the police department's public relations website about some child molestation legislation for which she was seeking community support. His unsolicited "corrections" had infuriated her until she learned he was serving in the military overseas and bored to tears. He told her he had been a police officer before 9-11, but quit his agency and signed up with the military just one month after the attacks, to defend his country.

His love of country and duty struck at Charlie's heart. He said he had a military assignment that, very much like police work, consisted of days and weeks of boredom, followed by moments of pure terror. He could never provide specifics however, and the closer they became, the more grateful she was not to know the kind of danger he was in. He told her he spent his downtime looking at police websites and starting up conversations with officers who might share their "war stories" with him to break the monotony.

AJ didn't know that Sergeant C. M. Cavanaugh was a woman but after her blazing email in response to his "corrections," he researched her and found a photo. One look and his heart was gone. It was her department file photo. She was smirking at the camera like she had a secret. It was clear she was tickled to be photographed in a police uniform. She looked like a kid playing dress up. Huge brown eyes and pulled back shiny brown hair and that little smirk. She was up to something. It took weeks for AJ to engage her fully, but charming a woman was not difficult for him.

**AJ101-789: Yes, you are rambling. Is he single?**
VABlueAngel: How should I know?
**AJ101-789: Answer the question. Is he single?**
VABlueAngel: No ring.
**AJ101-789: Ahhh**
VABlueAngel: Here we go.
**AJ101-789: He's attracted to you. He's interested. That's why he's pulling your pigtails.**
VABlueAngel: Oh for Christ's sake AJ, you think

EVERYONE is interested in me!

**AJ101-789: I've seen your picture. You have an enchanting smile and hauntingly beautiful eyes—it is an indefensible combination kiddo. You're beautiful and smart as hell. I also know your heart—also beautiful. I have no idea what kind of insane man would let you go, but I thank God for your ex's lack of judgment and character—otherwise you might not be in my life.**

VABlueAngel: Maybe I am not the angel you think me to be AJ. Have you ever thought of that? I was, after all, fired from my marriage. In your life, AJ? Words on a page? I don't know anything about you. I don't even know what branch of the service you are in—you just popped on my screen. Can you believe it's been over a year? How old are you anyway?

**AJ101-789: It's been fifteen months and yes Charlie, you are in my life. You keep me going over here and you know me better than any woman ever has. I know that's crazy but it's true. I've never shared myself with anyone like I have with you.**

VABlueAngel: Oh . . . okay—just as long as there is no pressure. LOL

**AJ101-789: I realize that this is little more than a fantasy relationship to you and that I cannot expect fidelity from you on any level, but I need you to know my feelings for you are very real. They are life-sustaining in this depressing and endless hell hole. That being said, I also realize I have to be fair. I have no idea how many years it will be like this given my position and you have far too much to offer to spend your nights alone, but until a man appears who is deserving of your affection, your trust, and your gifts, please**

**consider me a viable alternative.**

VABlueAngel: You are so much more than an "alternative." You seem to be able to look into my soul. You comfort me, encourage me, and make me feel far less lonely. Oh crap! AJ, I'm being called back in to work. I'm sorry. I have to go.

**AJ101-789: I understand Angel. Watch your six.**

Charlie sighed as she looked for her gun. She had only been home for an hour and had only been talking to AJ for twenty minutes. Chats with AJ usually lasted anywhere from thirty minutes to two hours but they always ended the same way . . . with a smile. Her nights—his mornings. She got re-dressed in her black pants, her beige shell blouse, and her black blazer, handcuff case in the back, cell phone in the front, firearm on her side. She checked her look in the mirror. She was attractive—she guessed. The plaintiff had told her on their third date that she was cute. He went on to explain that an attractive woman's looks fell into one of four categories: stunning, beautiful, pretty, and cute . . . and Charlie was "cute." Cute was a fair description. Charlie had never considered herself pretty; she would never be beautiful, and she would damn sure never be stunning. This she accepted without self-incrimination on most days.

His assessment of her, however, probably should have been a clue.

A clue that he was an asshole.

*Chapter 5*
**Closer**


*Closer* by Nine Inch Nails began to pound in his ears. That feeling was coming on. It was half terror, half exhilaration and the most intense phase of his slow and inevitable descent. "*You let me violate you . . .*"

It was time. Time to get close to her. He wanted it more than he had ever wanted anything in his life, though he had never allowed himself to want for much. He learned early in life that he was not worthy. Some people were chosen to live worthy, if ordinary, lives. He had been jealous of those people for as long as he could remember. He was broken alright, but that was okay. More than okay. It allowed him to know what she needed. The broken call to the broken. Kindred spirits. The threat still existed, however, that she might be repulsed by the real him so he would just keep that little secret to himself. Everyone has secrets after all.

He sighed and rubbed his temples. It had been too long. Watching scum die was amazing theater.

They weren't victims, he told himself. They were predators. His only regret was that there wouldn't be time to terrorize them first, but the boy would never allow that. The boy had every justification to watch their kind suffer, but even after all he had been through it just wasn't in him. This had concerned him at first, but he was confident that he still had the upper hand and always would. After all, he was the one who saved the boy.

*Chapter 6*
**Fucking Fed**

The call back into work involved a body that had been found in a dumpster at the Landon Mall. The twenty-something multi-pierced vape manager hit the dumpster with a flashlight before tossing in the garbage bag and instead of finding the usual raccoon, she found a body. As Charlie made the drive from her apartment to Landon Mall her mind now resisted all attempts at distraction. Another dead body meant she was forced to deal with the recent memory of the meddling Fed. When she had arrived at work that morning he was standing in her office, looking at the plaques and awards that hung on her *I love me* wall behind her desk.

"Sergeant Over-Achiever, I presume," he mused in a friendly manner that she wasn't sure reflected sincerity or condescension. He was being too familiar and in response she had pulled back her shoulders and raised her chin as she proceeded to size up the stranger. He's a cop—she figured that straight away. Not exactly a stretch to conclude given that someone had let him into the station, upstairs to the Criminal Investigations Division, and into her office, where he was now standing unescorted. That could only happen with credentials.

He was a damn good-looking cop. Tall with a frame that suggested a lot of upper body muscle underneath his coat. He had thick brown hair, with waves that rivaled a perfect high tide. His eyes were deep brown and intense and she found herself staring at them, into them. Everything about him was massive and strong. He had a square head and a strong jaw with a dimple in his chin, and was dressed in a tailored long black cashmere coat that had to have cost a fortune. Pretention thy name is Fed.

Charlie hated that her first thought when meeting an attractive man was his marital status, what he looked like naked, and if he might be interested in her, usually in that order. It made her feel like such a guy. "Cat got your tongue Sergeant Cavanaugh?" he prodded as his eyes lit up like a child who had a secret he was just bursting to tell.

"Have we met?" she asked as she brushed past him and set her things down on her desk. Damn. He smelled good, too. Really good.

"No, but we're about to. Special Agent Jake Adams, FBI." He stretched out his hand while flashing a dangerously seductive smile that threatened to take her breath away. Charlie became immediately flustered and felt herself blush. She quickly looked down and adjusted some papers on her desk that didn't need adjusting before shaking his hand. His hand was massive and manicured. A metro-sexual. Charlie couldn't decide if she was impressed or repulsed.

She tried desperately not to look, but she couldn't help herself—he wasn't wearing a wedding ring. *No Charlie!* She admonished herself. No more cops. Ever. She glanced at her own hands as she accepted his handshake. Damn. She needed a manicure herself. She guessed he was in his late thirties or early forties. He took her hand into his giant mitt. It was soft and warm and it swallowed her tiny fingers. He held on longer than he should have and stared down into her eyes, which immediately clenched her stomach into a knot.

"Have a seat Agent . . . Ahrens?" Charlie said, pretending to forget his name as she motioned toward one of the two chairs opposite her desk.

"Adams. Please call me Jake." He smiled again and reached into his pocket for his credentials.

"Not necessary Agent, everything about you says FBI."

"I think I've just been insulted," he said with feigned indignation, the corners of his mouth suppressing a smile.

"Not as far as you know. Now what can I do for you?" Her eyes narrowed as she leaned forward.

"Well . . . I'm detached to a regional task force . . ." he began.

*Oh no*, Charlie thought. *Damn it Chief, don't do this to me.* She fought hard to make sure that her face revealed nothing.

". . . so I've been sent to assist you on what our behavior folks at Quantico think may be a serial killer."

"Two homicides do not make it a serial, Agent . . . ummmm . . ."

"Adams." He grinned, completely aware that she was trying to make him insignificant. Okay Beautiful. Got it. You're in charge. *This is going to be fun*, he thought.

Jake sat back and took her in for a moment. She looked determined and headstrong. Beautiful chestnut colored hair with the slightest and most perfect hint of red. God, he loved redheads. He guessed her to be maybe thirty, thirty-one-years-old. Her bangs fell into her face, partially obstructing the biggest pair of brown eyes he had ever seen. Her brown shiny mane fell past her shoulders with the sides held back by two ornate clips. Not a typical look for a police supervisor but attractive nonetheless. Quite a combination he thought—fire wrapped in cloud. It suggested a vulnerability Jake Adams rarely glimpsed in female law enforcement officers. Jake knew this was going to be tricky, being an outsider always is, but this was unexpected. He was completely enchanted. *Oh well*, Jake thought. He was sure there was a better than average chance she couldn't shoot or drive worth a damn—few female officers he knew could and that was always a turn off. At that moment he caught a glimpse of the sharp shooter award on her wall. *Holy fucking hot*. Jesus, if she could drive, he was a goner. Aware that she was staring at him and waiting for a response he said, "Actually Sergeant Cavanaugh, if it is the same killer, a serial it does make," he said mimicking her speech pattern.

Charlie sighed and said, "Okay Adams, let's put our cards on the table." She flopped her hands on her desk in resignation. "You have to know that bringing a federal agent in on a local crime is not going to go over well with my crew. It suggests we need your help to solve this case, which we most certainly do not."

Even as she protested, she knew that probably wasn't entirely true. Homicides of any kind were not commonplace in Landon, Virginia. Landon usually had two to five homicides a year. In addition, the Landon PD would peripherally assist with Virginia Beach's eight to ten homicides each year, but that was about it. Landon's homicides were usually domestic killings, gang related, or an occasional robbery gone sideway. It was only March and as of this Federal-sabotage meeting, Landon now had two recent and open murders on the books. The investigations for both cases had gone ice cold.

"Umm, I hate to point out the obvious Charlotte, but they are unsolved." The way he said her name sent a shockwave through her gut and unfortunately through her pelvis as well. He said it like a whisper, Charlotte . . . There was such familiarity to it. It was as if he had said her name a hundred times before. *What the hell was this? Sexual attraction?* Clearly it had been too long since she had been laid, she thought. *Stop acting like a girl Charlie.*

She shook her head and regrouped.

"Sergeant," she said.

"I beg your pardon?"

"I would appreciate it if you would address me as Sergeant," she said firmly.

"I see." He leaned forward in the chair and pierced her with his glassy brown eyes as punishment for her assertion, "and I would appreciate it if you would address me as Jake, Sergeant."

*Shit!* Calling her Sergeant was having the same effect. *Oh, this is bad.*

Their eyes locked across the desk and she didn't hear or see Captain Grisolm standing in the doorway. "Everything okay here?" he asked, sensing the tension.

Charlie blinked and turned her attention toward the captain and involuntarily jutted out her bottom lip. "Good morning, Sir," she said, brusquely.

"Hey, come on Charlie, don't give me that face. I just found out this morning." He waved the letter from the Task Force at her. "The chief said we are to give our guest here every consideration. He is here to help us out. I was just coming to tell you about it but it looks like someone beat me to the punch. Agent Adams I presume? Welcome to Landon. I can't tell you how pleased we are to be getting some Federal mutual aid on this."

The captain's tendency to worship Feds and the alphabet soup of agencies they worked for was well known at the Landon PD. As the story goes, the captain had wanted to be an FBI agent since he was kid watching Dragnet. Though he had no interest in accounting, he did have an affinity for it and majored in it at William and Mary because he knew that most FBI agents were either lawyers or accountants. He met his wife, a freshman, during his senior year of college and fell madly in love. His wife was from Landon and had no intention of traveling the globe with a federal agent but said she could handle being a police wife if he wanted to adjust his life-long dream and become a local officer instead of an FBI agent. He acquiesced but it left him overly enamored of the fabulous Feds. He thought they hung the moon.

"Please, call me Jake," Adams said as he stood up to shake the captain's hand. Jake hesitated briefly, having difficulty pulling his eyes away from the most adorable pout he had ever seen on a police sergeant. "I'm very pleased to have been given this opportunity to assist, Sir. Things at the Task Force have been slow. I don't do slow," he scowled.

"Well, then working for the FBI must be a daily dose of hell," Charlie quipped. Both men ignored her and she suddenly felt like a bratty kid sister out with her brother's friends.

"Well, that could work in your favor Jake. Charlie here has the stamina of three officers. I'll be surprised if you can keep up with her," the captain said, proudly.

"Is that so? No worries Captain, I'll keep up," Jake said, shooting a mischievous look Charlie's way.

Charlie felt herself blushing and was humiliated by her reaction. She stood up and said assertively, "If you boys are finished with your misogynistic banter, I've got two unsolved homicides to work on." She pushed her way between them suddenly needing to escape from her own office, which had gotten far too small. Her backside brushed against the hot fed as she squeezed by, sending hackles up across the back of her neck.

"I'll assign him to McCallister," she said dismissively as she bolted for the door.

"Hmmm," the captain said, stopping her in her tracks. "You think that's such a good idea, Charlie?" She turned around to face the captain, her eyes pleading. She knew his comment was more of a decision than a question. "I was thinking it would be better if he partnered up with you instead of Clint. I would be more comfortable with that." The ground underneath her suddenly felt very tentative. Charlie opened her mouth to object but the captain was shaking the Fed's hand and exiting her office before she could protest further.

Jake looked at Charlie and shrugged. "Guess it's you and me kid," he smiled. "I mean hey, come on it's not like I'll be here fulltime. I'll be splitting my time between here and Virginia Beach, so you'll have to share me with Mike Kerns at the VBPD," he grinned, with the self-importance that is so typical of Feds, she thought.

"You know him?" he asked.

The only thing she could remember about Mike Kerns is that she attended a defensive tactics class with him and that his butt looked really good in black BDUs.

"We've crossed paths a few times in training."

Jake was downright giddy that he was going to be paired with this feisty ball of fire. He had no intention of sleeping with her. He didn't think so anyway. He hadn't really thought his plan through that far. But, if he had to be in Landon, having some eye candy and a worthy sparring partner would certainly make the assignment more interesting. The truth was he didn't have to be there, but this was turning out to be a much better decision than he had imagined.

Charlie could see the wheels turning in his head. She set her jaw, rolled her eyes, and walked out of the office. "Well, I better get over to see Captain Kerns at the Beach so I'll see you same time tomorrow?" he called to her. She ignored him, and continued to walk away; fuming, worried, and excited. This was a complication she did not need. Not now.

*Chapter 7*
**Terminal Bliss**

Death Star's "Terminal Bliss" was almost too dark, even for him. Too close to the nerve. "The cry that she made was the cry of a dying child . . ." He could handle it, he decided. He grinned, closed his eyes, and sipped his Lagavulin.

Three down. He would savor each and every one. He reached for the Saran Wrap and tore off a small piece. It was a show of defiance. He twisted it in his fingers and then quickly threw it on the floor as if it had caught fire in his hand. He growled at his weakness and dropped his head to his hands. He regained control of himself by remembering the joy of his most recent execution. Even the dumpster where he left the body was too good for that monster. Fuck him. Fuck them all.

*Chapter 8*
**Grecko**

Charlie hated being called back in to work as soon as she got home. Call-outs were part of the job but she actually preferred being summoned in the middle of the night rather than as soon as she got home. It unnerved her and set her on edge. She needed her decompression time. At least she hoped that's what was setting her on edge.

She desperately tried to block the fact that Jake Adams had taken up residence in her head all day. She hated that she had to cut off AJ when they were having such a nice chat. She needed to vent more about the meddling Fed, but AJ was sweet about her rambling. It's one of the things she missed most when her ex turned her world upside down—having someone to talk to when she got home at night. It's something couples take so much for granted. Another beating heart.

"Watch your six," AJ had typed to her. Charlie loved that AJ knew police talk. It meant watch your back. Your front being twelve o'clock, your back being six o'clock. It was a military expression that cops had made their own. Their job was far more dangerous than that of a cop, but like firefighters, their enemy was known; definitive. At least that was true until 9/11. Most of the time cops don't know who the enemy is until they are being shot at or sucker punched because until that fateful moment, cops are there to "help."

Charlie arrived on the scene behind the Landon Mall and gathered her necessities.

She parked her cruiser and nodded to the patrol officer on the perimeter. The officer lifted up the crime scene tape so she could walk underneath it. For reasons unknown but universal, anytime crime scene tape is strung up the words always seem to be upside down.

"Cold enough for you, Officer Predzin?" she asked as she smiled at the rookie.

"Yes ma'am," the chiseled officer grinned and blew cold air smoke from his mouth. Charlie immediately sensed the tension on the crime scene. Senior Detective Clint McCallister was marching toward her with purpose and she didn't need to wonder what it was about. She couldn't see the fed anywhere in view but she knew from Clint's gait that Jake Adams must be on the scene throwing his federal weight around.

"I know Clint. I know," she said raising a hand.

"What the fuck, Charlie?"

"Brief me first, then I'll deal with him. What do we have?"

Clint McCallister was a seasoned detective and gave Charlie's rank its due respect but she knew not to run roughshod over him. He was too good at what he did and she was a street cop at heart, not a white shirt. Right or wrong, Clint was as much her friend as her subordinate.

"Okay, Sarge," he said with a sigh and took out his notebook from his back pocket. "The DOA is a John Doe at the moment, but I got a feeling he's going to be just like the last two. Maybe Alex Jordan. The dumpster reeks of bleach." *Like the last two . . .* The words rang in her ears. Clint's mouth was moving but all Charlie could hear was a loud buzzing. *Like the last two*, she thought as her stomach gave an unappreciated tumble.

Charlie shivered but it wasn't from the cold night air. It all started a few weeks earlier when a known sex offender, Jerome Jenkins, had been murdered. Jerome Jenkin's family had come home from a school play that the father/sex offender was not permitted to attend because he wasn't allowed within two hundred yards of a school. The family found him smothered in the bathtub, apparently mid-bath. His head was encased in what was left of the plastic wrap. He was doused in hydrochloric acid and DRT—dead right there. The acid had melted the plastic and most of his face. Charlie could not imagine what it was like for one of the family members to discover him. What Charlie saw that day left an impression. Even though the body was presumed to be Jerome Jenkins there was no way in hell he could positively be identified by facial recognition. Grecko, the primary CSI, definitely had his hands full.

Charlie knew the drill. The Crime Scene Investigator (CSI) after responding to a crime scene would conduct an initial assessment, followed by making a game plan for the starting point. The crime scene would then be diagrammed and photographed. Each item of evidence would then be located, measured, and noted on the diagram before being collected and packaged. Depending on the nature of the evidence the CSI may process it for fingerprints at the scene; however, if the item has what appears to be blood, it is packaged and sent to the laboratory for processing. The CSI golden rule: If it's not documented it did not happen. It was imperative that prior to photographing the crime scene that nothing be added, i.e. police processing gear, measuring tape, etc. If something causes the scene to be altered and the defense locates it in a photograph the evidence can be disqualified. A single piece of fiber has been enough to convict someone of a crime. It would be disastrous to have that piece of fiber excluded as evidence due to a rookie mistake. That's why a slick sleeve like Grecko, though not a supervisor, was in charge at major crime scenes.

Charlie recalled that awful day on the Jerome Jenkins crime scene. She volunteered to follow Grecko during his initial walk through. Cops are notorious for a bad sense of humor, but CSIs were the worst. Charlie remembered when Grecko crossed the threshold of the front door "the smell" hit him. He had turned around to face Charlie with half a smile and said, "Barbeque anyone?" Charlie knew exactly what he was referring to. Burnt flesh has a tendency to put off a very specific aroma. Several nights she had nightmares of a man with three-quarters of his face missing and screaming for help. Jerome Jenkins died a slow and extremely painful death as the acid burned his face.

When Charlie was on the scene of the Jerome Jenkins homicide she couldn't help but wonder how a man like Jenkins got to keep his family. His house was a perfectly appointed piece of American Pie, circa Donna Reed. There were carefully selected decorative accents and family pictures showing the happy couple and their two adorable boys. This man was a pervert and a criminal of the highest and most perverse order but was still living the dream. She didn't get it. Her ex had left her for being "distant" and for "not needing" him. This perv was a scout leader who had raped three of his eleven preteen scouts and still had his family intact. It blew her mind.

She was certain it was closer to seven of the boys but she could only get three to turn on him. Brave little boys. Brave parents. Jerome Jenkins only got a few months in jail because the parents of the boys agreed to a plea deal to keep their boys from having to testify.

Charlotte understood their position but she was sure she could have put him away for years and it wrenched her gut to know that he was still out there. Though the sex offender status, she hoped, would keep him from being in positions of trust with other kids. The hydrochloric acid certainly would.

The killer had started by covering Jenkins' mouth with the plastic wrap and then continued down to his neck where the wrap had been pulled especially tight. Then it went around and around until the murder victim just had one big cellophane head which the killer then melted with the acid. No forced entry into the home, no sign of a struggle, no defense wounds. It was as if the victim just sat there quietly while his killer smothered him. She wondered if he was dead before the acid started to melt his face.

Charlie had lots of questions. A man is sitting in a bathtub—his hands and arms are not restrained. So, why was there no thrashing of water on the tub walls or floors? Why does a man sit quietly while his head and face are being wrapped? "Personally, if someone was wrapping my head and my arms were free, I would have done everything in my power to poke a hole in it, but that's just me," Grecko said, thinking out loud. She hoped the medical examiner would be able to find something after a thorough examination of the body of the victim.

Victim. It was hard for Charlie to think of this molester as a victim, but the penalty for molesting a child was not death, even if it should be. Charlie never understood how a sex offender, who wasn't allowed near schools, playgrounds, or ballfields was allowed to be around his OWN children as long as they weren't the ones he molested. *Just give him time,* she thought.

The second homicide was Dilbert Reigns. No chance of him becoming anything but a perv with such a name. He was the handyman the five-year-old's mother had hired to do some work around the house after her husband took off with a skanky stripper. *Was there any other kind?* The stripper smelled money when she met the husband/father on a business trip to Las Vegas and neither of them had any guilt about him leaving his family to fend for themselves.

Eventually Dilbert, the handyman, would offer to look after the little boy while she ran errands. What single mother could resist such an offer? When the child started refusing to eat popsicles and would cry at the sight of one, his mother took him to a shrink, who eventually determined that Dilbert Reigns referred to his penis as a Popsicle while he repeatedly molested the boy. The judge did not find the therapist's testimony credible, saying he felt like she had led the child.

Dilbert Reigns was found in similar fashion, head cocooned in plastic wrap in the basement of an apartment complex where he was working. Grecko was pissed that the minimal evidence left behind at the Jerome Jenkins homicide was leading to nowhere. When he got the call for the Dilbert Reigns homicide he had hoped the plastic wrap would be in one piece and not melted. If it was in one piece, he had a chance to locate physical evidence which could lead to a possible suspect. Melted plastic wrap as physical evidence was worthless, except circumstantially linking the M.O. to other scenes. So much for DNA, fingerprints, or even fracture-matching the wrap back to the roll box it came from. Grecko was only able to determine that plastic wrap was used and that acid was added to disfigure the victim's face and destroy the crime scene.

On the previous crime scene, the victim's face had been swabbed and sent to the lab on the off-chance that they might identify the brand of acid used. Just to be thorough, Grecko bagged the hands of the deceased even though there was no sign of a struggle in either case. Once at the morgue, the fingernails would be scraped in the hopes foreign DNA might be found.

Reigns, unlike Jenkins, was found on a basement concrete floor and not sitting in water. That meant a chance that physical evidence was left behind. According to Locard's Exchange Principle: Anyone who enters a crime scene will bring in and leave behind physical evidence, and a person who leaves a crime scene will leave with physical evidence related to the scene. Both can be used for forensic evidence. There was a good chance that foreign hairs, fiber, or touch DNA could be located on Reigns and the surrounding concrete floor. It was apparent whomever was orchestrating the homicides was intelligent and maybe even experienced. Grecko could not take the chance of missing the smallest of details. He even broke out the Alternate Light Source Unit in an attempt to find footwear impressions left on the concrete. The ALSU is an excellent tool for locating fibers and any other physical evidence left behind.

The first suspect in a possible retaliation homicide case like this is the dead offender's victims. Victims of violent crime store up a lot of anger. They are not only angry at the molester but at the adults who loved them but failed to protect them. Sometimes they are angrier at the latter, though there is hardly anything less fair to a parent who truly had no idea what was happening. It can boil inside them for years, turning them into a ticking time bomb that usually manifests itself into drug abuse, alcoholism, depression, or in the cruelest twist of all—imitation.

Occasionally, a victim will go after the molester to exact their revenge, but this wasn't the case here. These were relatively recent cases and the victims were still very young. Strike one.

The next likely suspect the police would consider would be someone from the victim's family—a parent or sibling—but weeks of investigation had cleared all of the family members in both cases. Strike two.

Then of course there was always the possibility that the two killings had nothing to do with the fact that these two men were molesters and that the crimes were totally random . . . but that left investigators with no motive. Strike three.

People don't kill for no reason. There is always a reason. Greed. Need. Lust. Anger. There's always a reason. There were dots and they had to be connected. Charlie was good making those connections, for other people. Not so much for herself.

Charlie liked being a detective, no doubt much to the chagrin of her mentor Mike Thompson.

Suits! She could hear him saying, using his pet name for "useless detectives."

Charlotte was immediately assigned to Crimes Against Children upon making detective. She was one of only three female detectives at the time. One female was on maternity leave and the other had announced that she would be following suit in the coming year "God willing." *Damn split-tails* she could hear Thompson grouse. Well, at least they didn't have to worry about maternity leave with Charlie. That ship had sailed, for now. Fucking plaintiff.

*That's the problem with trusting your life to some-one else*, she thought. She wondered what a person is supposed to do when someone decides they are no longer interested in the life you have built with them. What do you do then? You have this idea in your head about how your life is going to be and then maybe someone gets sick or killed in a car accident or visits one of the Twin Towers on the wrong day. The surviving person will be devastated and sad for a very long time and their life will never be the same but they will probably recover. What if those same people said, *I CHOOSE for this to happen rather than be with you. I CHOOSE to leave you on your own out here to fend for yourself for the rest of your life after I promised to protect you. After I said I loved you. After I pledged my life to you.* Charlie likened it to a homicide. Your life taken away. Gone. Poof. In the wind. You have no say. Your home, your best friend, your routine, half your income, half your family—gone. By choice. Their choice. It's a homicide without a punishment or even a criminal code to cover it. Sure. Dump your family. You deserve to be happy even at the cost of destroying another human being. YOU are more important—save yourself. Your partner is not important.

Charlie sighed. She hated when she ended up down this rabbit hole. That's why she took the promotion to detective. That's why she applied for the police SCUBA diving team. That's why she took the promotion to sergeant. Keep moving. Thompson always said a moving target is harder to hit.

Don't think about it. Don't think about it. Don't think about it. *I'm fine.*

Charlie was selected to take over a hefty caseload

consisting solely of child molesters. Captain Grisolm had warned her that they were the worst of the worst. Charlie had no idea that Landon had so many pervs.

"It's a combination of things really," the captain explained, "we have a high residential population and the schools are educating kids about Chester the Molester so they are reporting it more and the economy is in the toilet which leads to stress which makes it difficult for sex offenders to control their shit." It made sense. The captain was Sigmund freaking Freud. The captain preferred female detectives in kiddy crimes because their closure rate was higher in terms of confessions from the molesters, and they were better at getting traumatized kids to talk.

Charlie had difficulty believing that she was worthy of making detective after the hand life had dealt her, but she knew she was a good detective. It was one of the few true foundations in her life. She was good at this job.

The average tenure of an officer before being promoted sergeant was twelve-fourteen years but being a female gave Charlie an edge.

"Sometimes having a vagina comes in handy," Thompson would say when he was waxing philosophical.

There were only fourteen female officers total out of a police force of a hundred, so the promotion of females when they did well on the promotion test was expected, unless the females were gay—that was another story. After all, your sex life has everything to do with your competence and your ability to lead. Doesn't it? Idiots.

Charlotte remained in investigations after her promotion. New supervisors were always rotated back to patrol first following their promotion, usually the midnight shift in one of the two district stations so they could learn their craft at a slower pace, but Captain Grisolm had pressured Chief Sullivan to leave Charlie in investigations where she could also continue to help with molestation cases if needed.

"*Like the last two,*" Clint McCallister's words were still resonating in her ears.

"Sarge! You're not even listening to me!" Clint whined forcing Charlie's wandering mind back to the Landon Mall crime scene.

"Sorry, Clint," she pointed to her head and blinked, "just processing."

Clint rolled his eyes. "Well, are you going to do anything about this or not?"

Charlie sighed. "Where is he?" she asked, unable to see the Fed.

"Right there!" Clint said, indignantly pointing to Grecko.

Randy Grecko was a weird little "Poindexter" looking guy who definitely put the "P" in pocket protector. He was short with thinning hair and glasses too big for his face but he was good at what he did. He also had a little crush on Charlie, which meant her evidence would always get processed quickly.

Sometimes having a vagina really does come in handy.

Clint waived a hand in Grecko's direction. "I don't know what the hell that little propeller head is doing over there but he gave me two minutes to look at the body and now he's taped it off and he won't let me anywhere near the damn dumpster. That guy gives me the creeps! Fucking Count Dracula," Clint said and shivered dramatically.

*I guess Jake Adams isn't here after all,* Charlie thought, surprised at her disappointment.

"Come on. I'll talk to him. I want to get a look at the John Doe. Is his face visible?"

"What face?" Clint quipped.

*Cops are sick.*

*Chapter 9*
## Are There Maggots on My Phone?

Charlie headed toward the dumpster with Clint on her heels. She was relieved that Adams wasn't on scene. *What was his first name again? Oh yeah, Jake.*

Who was she kidding? She remembered his name. Jake Adams. She remembered everything about him; the way he looked, the way he smelled, and the way those damned eyes bore right through her.

Being hot was one thing, but this was her sandbox and the fucking fed was an interloper. She was not going to let him affect her tomorrow morning, the way he had affected her today. God, how Charlie hated acting like a girl. *Damn split-tail!* she could hear Thompson saying. *Shut up Thompson.*

Charlie spoke to Grecko and he invited her and only her into the inner perimeter. "You may take a look at the head but that's it. Take a picture if you want but then get out of my scene."

"Ma'am," he added after a pause.

"Yes Sir," she responded saluting him. Charlie approached the dumpster and as she began to climb up, she affirmed why she was not a CSI. Dumpster diving is the worst. No one wants to do it. Well, no one sane. It is one of the most disgusting jobs ever, ranking right up there with fishing out corpses floating in water, bloated bodies left in ninety-degree homes, and skin slippage on a dead body. Charlie wasn't sure whether the aroma she was getting a whiff of was the trash, the body, the chemicals, or all three. Her nose was telling her something was off . . . different. *Bleach, I'm smelling bleach,* she thought to herself. She took one look at her personal attire and decided maybe she should leave this for Grecko. "Hey Grecko, how 'bout doing a gal a favor and snapping a pic with my cellphone? Is that bleach I'm smelling?"

Grecko had been standing back just to observe what Charlie was going to actually do and how she was going to do it. "I thought you'd never ask, Sarge. By all means hand me your phone and yes, the one distinct odor seems to be bleach."

Charlie handed him the phone. Grecko brought over a heavy-duty milk crate to stand on. He peered over the top of the dumpster and snapped two photos for Charlie. "I got one pic of the head and another showing the positioning of the body. Hope this cures your curiosity Sarge and anyone else's," he rolled his eyes toward Clint.

Before retrieving the phone from Grecko's hand Charlie said, "Please check it and tell me there are no maggots on my phone."

Grecko brushed off his coveralls pretending maggots were on him and chuckled, "No. No maggots. The body appears to be fresh. Not enough time for the maggots to begin their feast, but the rodents have. By the way, you'll see from the photos that this body is different. Plastic wrap, but no acid."

Clint was peering over Charlie's shoulder as she slid the two photographs back and forth on her phone screen. "Clint, I can feel you literally breathing down my neck. Think you're close enough?"

"Sorry Sarge, I just wanted to take a look-see. Why doesn't this guy have half his face eaten away by acid? Changing it up? Copycat? Hmmm."

"You mean why the change in M.O.? Don't know. Hey Grecko. Have you found anything indicative of acid?"

"Sorry, from what I can see through the plastic wrap our vic's face is kinda in one piece . . . not burned off; however, the odor of bleach is very strong. I'm thinking the perp changed up his M.O., or the bleach was already here, or this dump is not related to the other two bodies but the plastic wrap makes that a stretch." Grecko scratched the top of his head, "Maybe a copycat since we never released info about the acid."

Charlie bumped into Clint after turning around to head back to the cruiser. "God damn it, Clint! Must you literally be on top of me? Keep this shit up and you'll find yourself walking at least ten paces behind my six." While walking back to the car she continued to study the facial photo. Her gut was kicking in and Clint was distracting her. Before getting into her cruiser Charlie peered over the roof and yelled to Grecko, "Do you need me to have food sent or do you have enough to choose from where you are?"

From the bellow of the dumpster came his response. "Funny Sarge. You and your sidekick should take your act on the road."

Clint and Charlie left the scene to conduct their own research. If this body is connected to the other cases, that made three homicides. Three related homicides equaled a serial killer. Adams was right.

Grecko continued with his photographs. There can never be too many photos. Sometimes the naked eye will miss what the camera lens will see. If the CSI is unable to recreate the crime scene exactly, credibility is shot and so is the case.

Once Grecko decided it was time to get down and dirty, a passion of his for reasons passing understanding, he put on a Tyvek suit and booties along with double layered rubber gloves. A dumpster is a breeding ground for, well, everything. He knew every step he made and every level he searched may contain a syringe needle or worse. Charlie notified the state medical examiner as they must be notified and permission must be granted before a body can be moved. A dead body is the property of the medical examiner's office. As a result, Grecko's job had become a little easier. They all agreed that they would wait for the M.E.

Within ninety minutes the state M.E. arrived driving the mortuary van. Grecko had already packaged the hands with paper bags to protect any evidence in or around the hand and fingernails and M.E. Ronnie Rogers, nodded in approval.

Thankfully, the dead body was fresh or there may have been unsavory repercussions as the two men loaded the body into the black vinyl body bag positioned on a gurney. The body would then be taken to the ME's office for the autopsy. At the autopsy Grecko and McCallister would be in attendance. They would need to wear Tyvek suits and eye protection while the M.E. weighed and measured the body and would take additional photographs. The plastic wrap would be removed and packaged and handed over to Grecko for chain of custody and lab submission. Blood samples would be taken and the outside of the body examined carefully for anything that may have contributed to the cause of death. Complicated shit. *We have so many boxes to check it's amazing we ever win a case,* Charlie thought.

It was late when Charlie arrived home for the second time. As always, Thompson's parrot and beloved alter ego was there waiting to greet her. "Fucking suits!"

the parrot squawked. "Hi Moses," Charlie grinned at the feather covered wise-ass. The bird was annoying as hell and had a vocabulary that would rival most sailors but the bird was one of Thompson's most prized possessions along with his 1955 primer gray Chevrolet POS. Coming home to the bird of her mentor wasn't the same thing as coming home to someone waiting for her but it was better than coming home to an empty apartment.

In spite of being out so late on the call, Charlie was determined to beat the fed to her office the next morning arriving at eight twenty-five just to be sure, only to find him sitting in her office, self-satisfied and smirking with two cups of Starbucks coffee.

"I guess we can agree now that we do in fact have a serial?" he asked rhetorically as he handed her one of the cups. She glared at him, sighed, tried not to smile, and took the coffee with a shake of her head. He grinned back. She sat down at her desk and they sat quietly drinking their coffee and staring at each other, both oddly comfortable in the silence.

"I guess you'd like a briefing on the homicide last night?"

"Whatever you think Sergeant. It's your sandbox."

As he said it his eyes danced. Her sandbox? Had she said that to him yesterday? Or had she only thought it? She gave him the rundown on Dumpster Doe: "We're pretty sure the John Doe is a perp from a molestation case I worked last year. Like the other two homicides, this guy barely got a slap on the wrist because the victim was too young to testify."

"How young?" Jake asked, his face hardening.

"Eleven months old," she said without blinking.

"Jesus," Jake ran his hand through his hair.

Charlie remained impassive. "He died from an internal infection four months later but the medical examiner's office and the DA said they didn't have enough to prove a connection to the repeated rapes."

Jake held up a hand. "One minute."

"Too much for you, Agent?"

He shot daggers at her with his eyes. "I've never worked Crimes Against Children, Sergeant. I just asked for one minute."

"Of-of course," she stuttered, feeling like a superior shit. She was a complete phony. Two years of working these fucked up cases hadn't hardened her in the least. If Jake Adams wasn't sitting right in front of her she could have easily burst into tears over what Alex Jordon had done to that baby.

Charlie spoke softly. "I'm sorry. I don't mean to come across as jaded. It's just that, well, if you shed one tear, you'll shed a thousand . . . so the trick is to never let yourself shed that first one." Her eyes teared up in spite of her words.

Their eyes locked. They communicated without speaking; held each other up without touching and kept each other from crossing over. He held her stare until she was steady. She nodded to him, letting him know that she had it under control and thanking him for the support. He nodded back in understanding. It was as if they were partners who had worked a hundred horrific scenes together. "Thank you," they both said to each other at the same time.

"Would you mind if I looked at the case files from the first two homicides?"

"Sure. Let me get them for you," she said taking a deep breath to steady herself. She went to Clint's desk to look for the two homicide case files. As usual, Clint's desk looked like a grenade had exploded on it. She moved a few files around and suddenly felt Jake's presence behind her. Silent but undeniable. She felt her face flush, knowing without turning around that Adams was standing behind her and she started to ramble. "I know this looks bad," she said apologizing for Clint's desk without addressing Adams directly.

"My senior detective, Clint McCallister, actually knows where everything is. I don't, but he does. I forgot my secret decoder ring today so I'm having some difficulty," she quipped as she continued to look through the sea of papers and files. Out of the corner of her eye she was pleased to see that she had gotten a grin out of him. *Good. He was coming down too.* She was completely mesmerized by his mouth. His lips were full and just the right size for his large square face and dimpled chin. Not like "a little butt" chin, just the tiniest cutest little point right in the middle. His mouth seemed to be in a perpetual half smile, like a golden retriever. She located the files and turned to see him still grinning at her.

"What?"

Jake tightened his lips, raised his eyebrows, and shook his head. Still grinning, he followed her back to her office. Jake knew he was having an effect on her. She was flustered and rambling. This was his power over women and he used it well and on many occasions, but now there was a twist; she was having an effect on him too. He wasn't used to this and though he was allowing himself a few moments of pleasure in it, he was not particularly amused.

"There's a conference room there to the right," she motioned. "You can spread out in there."

"Will you be joining me?"

"I've already read them from stem to stern Adams, and I've got payroll time sheets to do," she said meeting his disappointed eyes. Golden retriever eyes. *Damn.*

"Oh, come on, I'll get you set up."

When she opened the door to the conference room there were six detectives huddled around the conference table including senior detective Clint McCallister. They all had investigative case files in their hands.

"I'll trade you one burglary for two robberies," the short detective with the pointy nose was saying to Clint.

"No way!" Clint squealed, incredulous, "You don't even have any suspects! I've got video on both these mopes. It's just a matter of time before I close both these cases with arrests."

"But those are small-time Mom and Pop robberies," the short detective countered, "this is a high-profile burglary. Think of the press. You'll get all the glory!" he said, knowing Clint's affinity for press. Charlie watched as Clint lit up at the thought of a photo op. God how she hated pretty policemen. Paging Hollywood.

"Gentlemen," she said sternly, "You know, I don't just throw a dart when deciding to whom a case will be assigned. I actually have a fairly complex . . ." and they all chimed in; "complex methodology for case assignment designed to tap your strengths and maximize case closure," then they burst out laughing. Charlie couldn't suppress her laugh; a laugh that almost brought Jake Adams to his knees.

"Oh, you've heard that one. Get out, you knuckleheads, I need this room. McCallister, don't you have an autopsy to get to?"

They continued to snicker and snort as they grabbed

their case files and filed out one by one. They smiled as they passed their sergeant and gave the once over to the unidentified preppy-man beside her.

A short legged, hobbit-sized detective glanced back at the tall stranger and then whispered to Clint, "If my head were that far from my feet, I don't think I could walk." Clint chuckled, rolled his eyes, and tried to ignore the hair standing up on the back of his neck.

Jake knew what Charlie was doing, and he did not take the bait. He was not going to give her the satisfaction of addressing the fact that she did not introduce him to her men. *You're in charge. Jesus, I get it,* he thought, exasperated. Finally, he started to relax a little. He reminded himself that all female officers are control freaks. It was good that he caught on to this early so he wouldn't get pulled further under her spell.

Jake Adams was very good at wresting control from those who felt the need to be in charge, especially women. Women who had no idea that, from a very primal place, the last thing they truly wanted was to be in charge. He knew that what they really wanted was to surrender. Charlie was just like the others. Prettier maybe, smarter and more enchanting but she was just more of the same. He could handle this. He could handle her.

Just then Officer Heather Hinson slinked down the hallway, making a beeline for the new stud in the bull pen. Heather was the agency's Crime Prevention Officer. She spent all of five minutes working the street, eighteen months by police standards, before the chief tapped her for the cushy P.R. assignment because of how good she would look on camera. Upon her arrival, all of the detectives immediately stopped in their tracks, each of them trying to pull in their stomachs and stand a little taller like a scene out of Caddy Shack. Charlie suddenly felt invisible, as she always did in Heather's presence. Heather was petite, thin, blond, and stunning and man did she know it. *Her stunning . . . me cute. Got it.*

"I heard we had a federal agent in the house," she cooed, "Officer Heather Hinson," she said, batting her eyes and offering her downward hand as if she were royalty.

"Nice to meet you," Jake nodded toward her without making direct eye contact, taking her hand, or giving her his name.

"Sarge, you coming?" he smiled at Charlie as he moved his massive frame through the door and into the conference room without looking back at Heather.

"Oh, well, guess you guys are busy, huh? All this murder and mystery!" Heather said and giggled nervously as she scampered away, clearly unnerved at being ignored. As the other detectives locked their eyes on her departing scamper, Clint sidled up to Charlie and said discreetly, "Close your mouth Sarge, you look like you're missing a chromosome."

"Did you see that Clint? She had no effect on him. What the fuck?"

"She always has an effect on me. Yum. Yum," Clint growled. Charlie stomped on his foot.

"Ow! How the hell should I know? I guess he's either gay or in love," Clint said with a shrug.

"Hmmm," Charlie said, absentmindedly as she entered the conference room.

Charlie settled Jake into the conference room where he remained for the next two hours reviewing the cases. She blew off the few questions from Clint about why his case files were being reviewed by the "pretty boy with the high dollar wardrobe" by reminding him that he had an autopsy to attend to and a report to write from last night, but she knew that Clint knew. Fucking fed.

*Chapter 10*
**The Anchor**


At noon Charlie started to wonder why Jake Adams had not returned to her office to dazzle her with his brilliant over-educated Federal insight. Maybe he reviewed the files and left? She wondered, as a pang of disappointment washed over her. She finally couldn't stand not knowing and casually walked by the conference room with a stack of paperwork where she could see he was repackaging the two case files.

"Sergeant Cavanaugh," he called to her. She drew a quick breath.

"Thank you for accommodating me," he smiled appreciatively and handed the case files back to her. "Look Sarge, I know this is going to be . . . delicate," he said, "let's get some lunch so we can talk some more."

"I don't usually eat lunch," she replied without making eye contact as she took the files from him and walked them back to Clint's unmanned desk. When she returned to her office she found Jake sitting there waiting for her and looking determined. Charlie sat down at her desk and tried to look bored. She was still puzzled over his disinterest in Hot Pants Heather but was trying to play it cool.

"So Super Fed, what do you think?" she smiled a tight smile.

Jake got up, walked around her desk, yanked her chair out and said, "I'll tell you what I think. I think you shouldn't skip lunch Sergeant. Let's go. Now."

"Fine," she said, trying hard not to look as rattled as she felt. She grabbed her police radio and coat. "I'll drive and you're buying."

"Yes ma'am," he grinned.

Charlie drove them to her favorite restaurant, hating herself for wanting to impress him. She ran the first traffic light as it turned from yellow to red, calling it "pink," tailgated the slow drivers that wouldn't move out of the left lane and "California rolled" three stop signs.

*Jesus,* Jake thought, *I know the car is unmarked but there is still a spotlight on it. It still looks like a police car.* Charlie was a lousy driver. *Thank God*, he thought. She may be adorable, smart, and a crack shot, but she can't drive worth a shit. That helped.

The Anchor was an institution in Landon. A U.S. Navy themed restaurant owned and operated by genuine American hero, Colonel Frank Fortune. Thompson had introduced her to the frequent cop stop and she had been coming here ever since. Eleven years now.

"How long have you been coming here?" he asked, reading her thoughts again.

"Over a decade," she said proudly. She loved the familiarity of the Anchor and the way Colonel Fortune always made such a fuss over her. When they arrived, Jake rushed past her to open the door. *Well that was nice*, she thought.

"Sergeant Cavanaugh herself!" the colonel exclaimed as she walked in. The colonel looked distinguished and debonair as always in his blue blazer and off-white turtleneck sweater. He greeted Charlie with a huge hug that made Jake frown and raised his temperature a few degrees. *Turn her loose,* he thought involuntarily and tried to control the fire he knew was lighting in his eyes.

Charlie flashed a smile she reserved only for Colonel Fortune. "Colonel, it's always so nice to see you." She beamed in the colonel's presence. Her eyes were soft and sparkling. *Wow*, Jake thought, *what he wouldn't give to be on the receiving end of that smile.*

"Colonel this is FBI Agent Jake Adams. He's been detailed to the PD so you might be seeing him around a bit."

"Ahh, the serial," the colonel said gravely. *Geez. Everybody had an opinion on this case.*

"Well, welcome aboard Agent and I do hope you will come and see us often while you are in town. Where are you staying Sir?"

Jake looked uncomfortable for a moment and then said, "I'm, uh, over at the Radisson on Langley."

Charlie frowned.

"Hmm. I guess the Feds really know how to take care of their people," the colonel chided.

"That's six blocks from my apartment," Charlie said to no one in particular. "And the most expensive hotel in Landon."

"Well, I guess you two will be carpooling then," the colonel said, winking at Charlie. "Traffic in this town is a nightmare, Agent, especially in the summer when everyone heads for the beach. Let me show you to your table."

Jake was visibly moved by all of the medals and glass encased weapons and photos of the colonel with famous politicians, war heroes, and even movie stars that adorned the walls of The Anchor. As they sat down at their table, Jake looked upward and noticed the hundreds of police patches that covered the vaulted ceiling.

"This is quite a place," Jake remarked.

"He's quite a man," Charlie said softly.

Jake couldn't believe how Charlie had transformed

since entering the restaurant. She was demure and child-like in the colonel's presence. Jake was mesmerized.

"Please excuse me, but the tax payer in me is just a tad put off. The Radisson?" *That was quick. The sergeant was back.*

Jake held up his hand before she could expound. "Not all things are what they appear Sergeant." Talk about your understatements, he thought, darkly. "Head-quarters gives me a lodging stipend and I can either fully cover a room at the Comfort Inn or I can add to it out of my own pocket and stay someplace nice. I prefer the latter."

When she eyed him suspiciously, clearly unsatisfied by his answer, he continued, "Look, it's just me. No wife, no kids, I don't travel or have any expensive hobbies or fetishes so this is how I like to spend my money." He regretted that he brought up the *no wife and kids* part, having meant to keep her guessing on that one. He wanted to make her ask, intrigued by how she might broach the subject.

"Fetishes?" Charlie raised an eyebrow and smiled, breaking the tension. She blushed. Jake laughed and shrugged his shoulders. God she was getting to him.

Charlie momentarily felt sadness for him. Could he possibly be as alone as she was? Could anyone? She wondered if men handled loneliness differently than women. Perhaps they even enjoyed it. *Lucky bastards.*

"I'm sorry Jake. Yes, of course that makes perfect sense." A sudden pang of shame drove her to change the subject. "You know, I'm actually glad you dragged me out for lunch. I have been meaning to come see him for weeks," her eyes softened and her voice warmed as she spoke of her sadness and affection for the man. For the first time, maybe ever, Jake felt a tug at his heart instead of his nether region.

"Colonel Fortune's wife passed away in early January and I haven't seen him since the funeral," Charlie confessed. "I don't know what has kept me at such a distance. I adore this man. He's like a father to me. It's all just so sad. They were a team. He looks good though," she mused quietly, as though talking to herself. The waiter took their orders and the colonel stopped by to make sure they were being well looked after.

"Absolutely," she said smiling her colonel-only smile. "How are feeling Sir? You look well. How are you adjusting without your Addie?"

The colonel glanced at Jake, and Charlie immediately regretted asking him such a personal question in front of a stranger. *Why did she always have to be the bull in the damn china shop?*

The colonel, ever gracious, smiled and responded with his trademark charm, wit, and class. Rubbing his chin, he said, "Well Charlotte, my dear, after sixty-two years in captivity, adjustment is an understatement, but I find that I am managing better than I expected thanks to friends and family. Of course, I worry what it will be like a few months down the road when all the kind notes and visits stop, but as long as I have this place, I know I will never be alone and I know she will always be close by." He nodded to his wife's picture on the massive mahogany bar. Then, to Jake he winked and said, "And as long as beautiful, single women like Charlotte keep coming here, I'll be young forever."

Charlie cringed. *Oh my God Colonel, no matchmaking. Good looking and good FOR me are not the same thing.* She knew the colonel hated that she was alone and that he thought her ex, who was too cowardly to cross the threshold of The Anchor since the split, was a world class putz, but this was not the time, nor the man.

Jake was drinking in the softer side of Sergeant Charlotte Cavanaugh and loving it. She was letting him in. Maybe not on purpose, but she was letting him in just the same. They ordered their meals and Jake assumed the next topic of discussion would be the cases at hand, but he was wrong.

"So, what is your story Agent Adams? Sorry, Jake," she corrected herself and smiled at him.

"Funny, I was just about to ask you the same thing."

"I asked you first," she said grinning. He looked a little lost for a moment and she was worried she had done it again.

Stand by for breaking china.

He hesitated. "It's not a happy story."

Charlie nodded, her face encouraging him to continue. He imagined she had used this technique on many people from whom she was trying to extract information, and that she probably got what she wanted. Resistance was futile so he continued, cautiously. "I grew up in Santa Cruz, California; I'm an only child and my parents died when I was sixteen years old." He said it matter-of-factly like he was describing the death of a childhood pet.

"What? Both of them? Together?"

Jake shrugged. "It is what it is. October 17, 1989. A 6.9 earthquake hit the Oakland and San Francisco areas of California where we lived. My parents were driving on a bridge when it collapsed during the quake. Sixty-four people were killed that day, including my parents."

Charlie was speechless, so he continued. "I had stayed late at school that day. I had detention for doing something stupid. They were on their way to pick me up when they were killed."

"Is that true?" she asked, quietly. He raised his head to let her see his eyes and she immediately felt awful. *Hook, line, and sinker,* he thought. Women love a tortured a man. He was almost disappointed at how easily she bought his story. "I'm so sorry Jake. Jesus, maybe I have been a cop too long. This job can make a person so cynical." The story was bullshit, but the pain in his eyes was real. Jake had in fact lost both his parents on that day in 1989 but an earthquake was more palatable than the truth. He didn't like people judging his misguided parents, which he knew would be the case if he told the real story. The earthquake happened the same day they died so he always associated it with their death. It somehow made it less of a lie. He didn't mind seeing sympathy in someone's eyes, but not pity. Pity was something he simply could not bear.

"So, then what happened? Who took care of you?"

Jake wanted to take her in his arms right then and there. The tough side of this woman was attractive, but the soft side of her was irresistible. *Easy Jake. Female cops are bad. Female cops are bad*, he chided himself.

"Jake? Who took care of you?" she repeated.

"Umm . . ." he stumbled, lost in her eyes. "My uh, my mother was estranged from her sister at the time of their death but she was the only relative I had so CPS tracked her down. She told Child Protective Services she would leave her family in Nevada and move to Santa Cruz to live with me in my parent's house until I graduated seven months later. Two days after graduation she emancipated me and asked me for some money. From her perspective she was owed something for being inconvenienced."

Jake rolled his eyes and made air quotation marks. "She handed me off to a lawyer who explained the facts of life quick and dirty. He also asked me for money and then he sent me on my way."

Charlie shook her head in horror. "Then what?"

"Then? Then I survived." He shrugged. "My parents were fairly well off. I spent eight years bumming around before I finally grew up enough to realize the money wasn't going to last forever. I bought my way into UCLA, graduated, applied to the Bureau."

"Wow. That's quite a story," she said, hoping he would catch the movie line reference from My Cousin Vinny, but figuring that was too much to expect. He couldn't possibly be this good looking, this smart, and be able to quote movie lines. She shook her head as she processed the circumstances of his parent's demise, still slightly suspicious, but then realized that her own story was equally fucked up.

"It could have been worse," he said.

"How?"

"They could have been poor."

She looked at him like he was crazy and they both busted out laughing.

*Cops are sick.*

*Chapter 11*
**My Cousin Vinny**


"Your turn now," he said narrowing his eyes.

"Well, clearly, I should have told my story first. Now my story isn't interesting at all." They both laughed.

*Why am I so comfortable?* They both thought at the same moment. For two traumatized and mostly hollow human beings, they were connecting in a way that simply did not make sense to either of them. They talked through lunch, through dessert, and into their fourth cup of coffee, until the colonel finally interrupted. "I hate to break this up kids but we actually closed the restaurant an hour ago." Charlie looked at her watch in alarm. It was 3:30. She looked around and realized the place was completely empty and she blushed.

"They only serve lunch?" Jake whispered.

"No. They are open from noon to 2:30 for lunch and then they reopen at 5:00 for dinner so the colonel can have his afternoon nap." She stood up to hug the colonel and handed Jake the check. "I'm so sorry Colonel," Charlie apologized. "It's this case." She made wide eyes at the colonel and with her back to Jake she mouthed "Stop." The colonel's eyes danced mischievously. Charlie rolled her eyes, hugged him, and headed for the car while Jake took care of the check.

Once they were both back in the car, they sat quietly for a minute as it warmed up. She turned in her seat to face him. "Thank you for lunch Jake, I'm sorry for giving you such a hard time this morning."

"I understand Charlie. I mean, Sergeant," he smiled warmly. "I know this is a tough position for you to be in."

Charlie's eyes softened. "Jake. You can call me Charlie away from the office. I just meant, you know, around the guys, Sergeant is more appropriate."

"I'm just here to help, Charlie," he said quietly. Then as if his hand was detached from his body he watched as it reached up and tucked a loose strand of hair behind her ear. She stared at him, mouth partially open and breathing audibly.

"My Cousin Vinny."

"What?" she asked, snapping out of her trance.

"'That's quite a story' is a line from My Cousin Vinny."

"Holy shit," she said out loud putting the car into drive. "Buckle up, Agent." After the drive to the restaurant, she didn't have to tell him twice.

When they got back to the station, Jake headed for his car saying that he had taken up enough of her time but would see her in the morning. *Thank God*, she thought, realizing that she still had a ton of work on her desk. She no sooner sat down at her desk and got started on the first report, when Clint appeared in her doorway.

"How was the autopsy? Any surprises?"

"Where the hell have you been?" he demanded in a tone that caused her to put her pen down and raise a warning eyebrow at him. There was always a fine line of familiarity where Clint was concerned that had to be managed.

"You're the subordinate. I'm the boss. These are the facts and they are not in dispute," she said eyeing Clint playfully.

Clint grinned. "Oh! Oh! Oh! Wait! A Few Good Men!" he blurted.

"Who said it?"

"Uhhh, wait. The Six Degrees guy! Bacon! Kevin Bacon!"

"And the character he played?"

"Oh, come on Sarge! Jeez! Um . . . Jack . . . his name was Jack . . . damn!" he said slapping his hand on his leg.

"Ross. Captain Jack Ross." She said smiling triumphantly. "Amateur."

"Damn Sarge! I was close to pulling it!"

"Like hell you were," she laughed and pointed to the chair in front of her.

"What's on your mind, Night Rider?" Night Rider was her pet name for Clint because he liked working nights. It was a term of endearment. She leaned back in her chair and stretched her arms over her head, making it difficult for Clint to concentrate.

"Nothing," he lied. "I just asked where you've been."

"The Anchor."

"You took Preppy McFed to The Anchor?" he asked, looking and sounding hurt.

"Look Clint, the captain, in his infinite wisdom," she said as she made a dramatic sweep of her hand, "has not only assigned this guy to our serial but to me personally, so don't hump my leg about this. Don't we have enough to deal with? We had to review the case."

"Okay," he said with a pout. "Are we working out or what?"

"Ugh," she grunted. "I'm not used to eating lunch. Let me let this settle a little?" She put a hand on her stomach.

"Hey fine with me, you're the one that said the extra twenty CID pounds were making you look like a fire hydrant! I'm just sayin'!" he said as he walked away.

"Just give me an hour, dickhead," she shouted.

"I'll be at Amy's after."

"Beer only Clint!" she shouted after him. "Clint! Did you copy that, Night Rider?"

Clint was one of those weird-as-shit alcoholics. He could drink beer with no problem, but the hard stuff made him crazy, dark and addicted and he had to steer clear of it. Charlie had helped him out of a very deep hole and she was committed to making sure he didn't return to Wonderland.

Charlie finally wrapped it up at around nine p.m. and headed back to her apartment feeling surprisingly chipper. She thought about her long lunch with Jake and laughed to herself when she remembered Clint calling him Preppy McFed. *Clint's funny.* She couldn't shake how Jake's eyes looked when he talked about losing his parents. She felt an ache in her gut over all he must have gone through. Then she remembered him pushing her hair behind her ear. *What the hell was that about?* A shiver ran through her body. *Good shiver or bad shiver?* Usually she could tell, but not this time. Both? *Jesus, what a day.*

## Chapter 12
**The Stakeout**

The killer was feeling benevolent. Benevolence always came in the form of Pearl Jam's "Black." He desperately tried to remember what it felt like to love. *To be loved? No. That, he had never known, but had he loved? Maybe. He hadn't killed her. If that wasn't love, he didn't know what was. She wanted to come inside but he couldn't let her. Not knowing protected her. He protected her. Ungrateful bitch. She didn't understand. "Distant, closed off, secretive, cryptic." No, these were not words of love. She did not love him. Perhaps he should have killed her. The next one would pay the price for her insolence.*

Charlie sat in Captain Grisolm's office arguing with him. The captain was used to this. "Seriously Captain, this is going to soak up every resource I have. Wouldn't our time be better spent working the cases and tracking the leads?"

"That's why I'm leaving Clint off the stakeout schedule. Look Charlie, it's a rare thing when a police agency can predict who might be a victim of a homicide, but that's where we are, aren't we?" She nodded begrudgingly. "Is there any doubt in your mind that the next victim is one of the offenders left from your cases in kiddy crimes?" She shook her head. "Then what are we arguing about?" he asked, handing her the stakeout schedule.

Charlie had closed thirty-eight cases as a detective. Twenty pedophiles were in jail. Two had committed suicide. One was a fugitive and on the run. Three had been killed by the serial. That left twelve offenders that had received relatively light sentences following plea bargains to protect the victims from testifying.

Wed, Thu, Fri 2100–0500 Cavanaugh/Adams—Daniel Silver residence.

"That work for you Charlie?" the captain asked, rhetorically.

"Sure, Captain. Do we have enough bodies to cover the other potential victims and still work other cases?"

"It's going to be tight but we can manage for about a week." The captain ran his hand through his thinning hair.

Charlie prepared for her first stakeout with Jake Adams, reminding herself over and over that this was an assignment, not a date. Her stomach was churning and her hands were shaking. *Focus, Charlie*, she admonished herself. The admonishment sent a shiver up her spine and across the back of her neck for reasons only she knew. It had to do with her "unconventional" introduction to sex and it made her smile. It always made her smile.

Charlotte Cavanaugh took her job very seriously and anyone who had ever worked with her thought nothing less. She was smart and tough. She skewed male more than female when it came to handling stress. Being overwhelmed by a man just was not in Charlie's DNA. She was very uncomfortable with the impact Jake Adams was having on her. He was making her think about everything but the job—and she needed to stay sharp. She had clawed her way back from her divorce. All the personal crap was over, long since committed to the tattered pages of the manuscript of her life.

Jake Adams was a game changer. The problem was she wasn't sure that was a good thing. He was making her dream about things she had given up dreaming about; passion, heat, companionship, laughter . . . love? It hurt to even think about the possibility, but it hurt more not to. Charlie had spent a lot of time convincing herself that she could do this life on her own, but even as she found a way to live this life sentence of loneliness and self-doubt, she knew in her heart it wasn't what she wanted—it was just resignation and fear and she hated herself for it.

"Fucking suits," Moses squawked.

"Moses, be nice," she reproached the obnoxious bird.

"Hi, Brown Eyes," he chirped.

"That's much nicer, Mo. Thank you." She grinned thinking of Thompson's special greeting for her and put her lips to the cage to receive a peck from Moses.

She smiled at her reflection in the mirror. Jake Adams was making her feel desirable. It had been a while since that happened. Charlie wanted to be wanted. Hell, everyone wants to be wanted. Everyone wants to be excited to see someone and to have that excitement reciprocated but for the abandoned—it is life-sustaining. She wondered if Jake Adams was as nervous as she was. *Probably not*, she thought. Then she stopped herself and forced herself not to go to that place of inevitable disappointment. Here she was spending extra time on her hair and make-up just to sit in the dark all night and stare at a house. She tried on three different outfits in the hopes of seeing desire in his eyes. *Damn it! Focus, Charlie!* And she snickered to herself again. Over her protest Jake had decided that they would use his fed SUV instead of her unmarked Caprice.

"Do you think that doesn't look a police car Charlie?" He had rolled his eyes at her.

"Do you think that doesn't look like a Fed Mobile?" She had rolled her eyes right back.

She was waiting for Jake outside in front of her apartment when he pulled up. He was right about one thing, the Fed Mobile was much more comfortable than her aging fleet cruiser. It had satellite radio and heated seats and heavily tinted windows. When she sat inside it, she felt like she was wrapped in a cozy little cocoon. She handed Jake a portable police radio and explained that he could keep it for as long as he was going to be working with them. "Really? Thanks." Local agencies weren't usually so accommodating but nothing about this assignment was usual.

An hour into the stakeout, it was like no other two people existed on the planet. They were both vigilant about keeping one eye on the house but they were locked in on each other. *He was feeling it too, wasn't he?*

Jake talked about what it was like losing his parents at such a young age and Charlie told him about her unconventional upbringing . . . not all the nitty-gritty details but most of it. We are all a product of our fucked-up parents.

March 1992, Sterling, Virginia

Charlotte Cavanaugh didn't exactly aspire to police work growing up. There were no police officers in her family, no police friends, but there were police. Police who chased her, who hunted her down trying to return her home when she ran away and tried to take her smokes and her weed. Life at home as a young teen was . . . unsatisfactory. Charlie's mother left when she was ten years old and Charlie's older brother was twelve. Her mother had said she didn't want to leave and that she loved Charlie and her older brother very much, but she was, in fact, leaving them. It was a theme that would carry on throughout Charlie's life . . . "I love you—Goodbye."

Her mother had told Charlie three months before she left of her intentions and asked her to keep quiet about it until her plan was set. "Okay Mom." That was all Charlie could manage to say. Young Charlie's head was swimming with questions, with confusion, with fear, and with anger—a lot of anger—but all she could say was "Okay Mom." Three months later, right on schedule, Charlie listened as her mother hummed a carefree tune while she packed up her dark green hatchback, hugged her children, told them she loved them, and drove away.

"Tom?" Charlie said to her big brother "What do we do now?"

"Enjoy the peace and quiet," he said, sounding very much like their father. "She'll be back. She'll be back," her brother assured her. But her brother was wrong.

A week turned into a month, and a month into six months before their mother finally called. "So, how's my little Bunny? You doing okay sweetie? I'm sorry I haven't called but I have been so busy. I've had job interviews, busy setting up my new apartment, and dating! Can you believe that Bunny? Your mother is dating!"

And after six long months the tears finally came, they came big and they came hard and Charlie was gasping for breath as she sobbed into the phone. "Mom, I've missed you. Daddy and Tom have missed you. Why haven't you called us or come to see us? I'm scared, Mom."

"Scared of what Charlie?" her mother asked in an icy tone that was all too familiar. It meant Charlie was feeling something she shouldn't feel, saying something she shouldn't say, or doing something she shouldn't do.

"I told you I would need some time to get settled, Charlie. Do you remember me telling you that? I told you that I would see you soon and I will. Okay?"

"Okay Mom."

Charlie's father fell into a deep depression. John Cavanaugh tried to take care of his young children but he was dealing with his own grief and his children were a daily reminder of everything that had gone wrong in his life. Two years passed and at age twelve, Charlie and her fourteen-year-old brother Tom started stealing their father's cigarettes. One night their father caught Tom with the cigarettes and he beat him while Charlie screamed and looked on in horror, finally physically attacking her father to get him to stop. The next morning there were two cartons of cigarettes on the kitchen table and a note from their father.

*These have to last each of you a month. If you run out don't come crying to me.*

Charlie was staring at the two cartons of cigarettes when her brother came upstairs from his basement bedroom. His eye was swollen shut and his lip was split. "Cool!" he said after reading the note. Charlie just looked at him, her mouth agape. *Cool?* Inside her head she was screaming. *This is not cool! Doesn't anybody care about us? Doesn't anyone give a shit if we do right? I'm twelve years old!* She turned away from her brother as her eyes pooled with tears and started making their lunches for school.

"What are you doing, dumb-ass? I can't go to school looking like this! They'll lock Dad up. Then where will we be?"

*Where indeed?* Life gets very scary when you're a child and you get down to one parent. *What if their father got sick? Died? Left like their mother?* Charlie was forever pushing these thoughts from her head. She decided that if her brother wasn't going to school she wouldn't go either—and so it began. These were the days of TV, smoking, and Pop Tarts. When you are a budding teen that actually sounds like a pretty good day and Charlie and her brother had no real grasp on just how bad things were. By age fourteen and sixteen, they saw even less of their father. He would come home most nights but it became later and later in the evening. His only stop, once inside the house, was to throw some processed food into the freezer for his children before heading to his bedroom. It didn't take long before the Cavanaugh house became the dark, scary, and foreboding house all neighborhoods dread. Teens hung out at all hours, the barely teen girl could be seen sitting on the front porch smoking a cigarette, surrounded by teenage boys without a parent in sight. The neighbors knew of the divorce but were too busy with their own dysfunctional lives to take on the burden of another family's dysfunction. It was weed, nicotine, music, and mayhem. The furniture got trashed pretty early on and their father refused to replace it since his children were "behaving like animals," so they went without.

Charlie was blossoming into a young woman and her brother's friends were noticing. A friend of Tom's once made the mistake of grabbing Charlie's butt when she walked through the living room and Tom beat him unconscious.

Tom Cavanaugh was one crazy son of bitch, especially when it came to protecting his younger sister. If anyone touched her, hurt her, or made her unhappy in any way, he would make sure that they were motivated to never do it again. Tom was prone to unprovoked flashes of anger and violence. He wasn't particularly large in stature but he was huge in crazy and his friends were resolute in their effort not to piss him off.

Teachers, neighbors, and old family friends wrote she and her brother off as those "dreadful Cavanaugh children" followed by, "poor things." Charlie and her brother attended just enough school to keep from being expelled.

One day Tom went to school and fourteen-year-old Charlie stayed home without her brother, which was unusual. Tom's friend Kip came by and walked right into the house through the unlocked door, as her brother's friends often did. Charlie was sitting on a tattered couch her brother had "tactically acquired" from an eviction in the neighborhood. She was in her underwear and a t-shirt and she quickly pulled her knees up to cover herself.

"Hey kid. Where's your brother?" Kip said with a look in his eye that made Charlie nervous.

"He went to school Kip. Now get out of here. I'm not dressed."

"You look okay to me," he smirked. "How about I just hang out until he gets home? I got some good shit."

"I don't want any weed you moron, and no you can't stay, get out. He'll be home at two-thirty." Charlie stood her ground.

"And if I don't?"

"If you don't then I'll tell my brother you attacked me and he'll kill you, you shithead," she said matter-of-factly. Kip moved toward the couch and Charlie's eyes widened. She tried to look aloof but there was fear in her large brown eyes and the predator easily sensed it, as all predators do.

"What if I did attack you, Charlie? It could end up being the greatest day of your life," he said as he stood in front of her, his crotch level with her face.

"Fuck you Kip. You're way too old for me and you stink. Now I mean it, get out," she said, setting her jaw and looking up at him defiantly. She flinched when he reached for her and hated herself for doing so. Then Kip did something unexpected—he started softly stroking her hair.

Charlie hesitated for a moment. *Touch.* She barely remembered what it felt like. Then she quickly shook her head clear and pulled away. Kip grabbed a handful of hair and drew her head back causing her to gasp.

"Easy little girl," he whispered. "I'm not going to hurt you. Everybody has to start some time. Don't you want to know what it feels like to be a woman? Maybe you should let an older guy show you how it's done," he leered.

She really did want to know, especially if it involved physical contact with another person, which she desperately needed, but as always Charlie was in defense mode. She was always on guard, always ready for a fight, and always masking whatever she was truly feeling. At age fourteen, Charlie had become a master of disguise. She didn't know how to respond to her feelings and desire was a new feeling she hadn't quite learned how to process. Charlie could feel her stomach tighten and she could hear the blood pounding in her ears. The sensation of Kip holding her by her hair and controlling her was exciting her. She just didn't know what to do about it. "You've got five seconds to let go and get out or I am telling Tom," she growled.

"Okay, little girl, but don't say I didn't offer," he said, turning her loose. Charlie was breathless and shaking when he left, relieved, but not as much as she should have been. *Maybe I should let Kip teach me,* she pondered. He was a burn-out from smoking too much weed, but he was cute, with long hair, a faint mustache, and a long lean body. He was older than her brother by two years, making him eighteen to her fourteen. *Was that even legal? Did she care?*

After Kip left, Charlie's thoughts drifted to the sex novels she and her friend Laura once found in Laura's parents' room. Stews Layover was their favorite. It was a very detailed book about the sexual escapades of a team of stewardesses and the passengers and crew they seduced. She knew a lot more than Kip thought she did. *Maybe she would teach him a few things. Humph!* Her friend Laura was also still a virgin but she was a master of oral sex. Laura loved oral sex and would explain to Charlie, in great detail, the power that came from controlling a man with her mouth. It used to sound gross, but more and more Charlie was intrigued by Laura's escapades.

Kip stayed away for almost two weeks following the hair-pulling encounter. She guessed he was probably worried that Charlie had told her brother on him. When Kip finally returned, he did so with a new girlfriend in tow; a burn-out like him. She had wild blond hair and was a good twenty pounds overweight. Charlie had been fantasizing about telling her friends about her eighteen-year-old boyfriend. When she realized he had given up after only one attempt and moved on, she was crushed. When Kip showed up with the chubby blond, Charlie's fourteen-year-old world came crashing down. Again.

Charlie couldn't believe how she was opening up to Jake. She never liked to talk about her childhood. Jake already knew more about her in four hours than her ex had ever known. *Was that her ex-husband's fault or hers?* She wondered.

Jake reached for Charlie's hand when she teared up talking about her mother leaving and Charlie didn't pull away. She knew she should, but she didn't.

"I think maybe yours was worse than mine," Jake said compassionately after a long period of silence between them. "I mean, my parents, when they left, they had no choice, but your mom, she had a choice and she chose to leave you. I think it's worse."

Charlie stared blankly and nodded in understanding, touched by his empathy. *He got it. Someone actually got it.* "I'm sorry Charlie," he said squeezing her small hand tightly. "I'm sorry she left you," he clarified and though the tears pooled in her eyes, she willed them not to fall. *I'm at work. This is work. You don't do this at work, Charlie.*

Charlie desperately wanted to tell Jake about her childhood neighbor and her strange introduction to sex—what had been done to her; but how could she? She barely knew Jake Adams and she had never told anyone about her neighbor, Mr. Daley, and the effect he had had on her and continued to have on her throughout her adult life. She was sure it played into the failure of her marriage though she wasn't sure how. She couldn't tell Jake. He would never understand. He would judge her. No one would ever understand the impact the thirty-two-year-old man had had on her when she was just fifteen years old, effectively ruining her for every man that would follow.

Jake saw Charlie on the verge and saved her. "Favorite movie?" he prompted, quickly changing the subject.

"You first," she said, as she gathered her emotions.

"Ewww," he winced. "I spend a lot of time with my movies," he said a little embarrassed, and she smacked his arm with each word as she said, "So. Do. I!"

Jake laughed, "Oh no my dear Sergeant Cavanaugh, I mean I spend a lot of time with my favorite movies. I watch them over and over and over. It drove my last girlfriend crazy."

Charlie looked at him with an impish grin. *Did he mean that that girlfriend was his last girlfriend and Charlie might be his new girlfriend? Jesus! What was it about this man that made her feel like a teenager? Of course that's not what he meant. He meant his last girlfriend you idiot,* she scolded herself. Jake found himself laughing at the ridiculous look on Charlie's face. "You okay Sarge?" he chuckled to mask his concern.

"Oh, yea yea, I just, yea me too. I mean I watch movies over and over too," she blushed.

"Okay, let me see, my top movies . . . My Cousin Vinny," Jake started.

"Of course." Charlie high-fived him.

"We have a full tank of gas, half a pack of cigarettes, it's dark, and we're wearing sunglasses."

"Blues Brothers."

"Yes!" Charlie approved.

"Hey Wang, it's a parking lot," Charlie said raising her eyebrow to him and Jake looked puzzled for a second before recognition came over him. "I'll bet if you buy a hat like that you get a free bowl of soup." Charlie thought she might jump into his arms.

"A Few Good Men," he countered and they both said in unison, "You want me on that wall. You need me on that wall!" Both of them laughing hysterically.

Jake launched into the full monologue as Charlie nearly melted into her seat.

"Otherwise, I suggest you pick up a weapon and stand a post. Either way, I don't give a damn what you think you are entitled to!"

"Shhhh," she admonished him, "We are supposed to be on a stakeout. Stealth! Stealth!" she said laughing and gasping for breath, completely impressed by his skill.

"Christ Charlie, it's four a.m. Who the hell is listening?" he laughed.

*How could the night be over so fast?* It was like the laws of time and space ceased to exist when she was with him. It felt like their shift had started only an hour ago.

"When Harry Met Sally?" Jake rolled his eyes. "Chick Flick!" he proclaimed, looking away.

"Holy shit Adams," she said accusingly. "Seriously?"

Jake shrugged.

"Busted. You are so busted. You homo!" Charlie doubled over in laughter.

Jake interrupted her laughter by grabbing her by the hair and pulling her close to his face. "I thought we were supposed to be stealth, Sarge?" Jake said breathing quietly and controlled as his eyes melted into hers. Forgetting where she was, who she was, and completely lost in the moment, she closed her eyes and leaned in to kiss him. Charlie could already taste his breath on her lips when she felt his grip tighten on her hair just before he jerked her head away from him and held her in place just inches from his face and whispered, "If and when we kiss Charlotte, it will be my decision, not yours. Do you understand?"

*Chapter 13*
**The Train**


"Do you understand?" Jake repeated, releasing her hair and pushing her back to her side of the vehicle. *Holy shit.* Charlie nodded and damn near climaxed. Jake reached for his coffee.

Charlie remained completely unnerved for the final hour of the stakeout while Jake appeared completely unaffected and rambled on about living like a penniless beach bum in Malibu with a bank account full of cash he kept as his deepest secret. *Well, almost his deepest secret, but he felt instinctively that she wasn't giving up everything so why should he?*

The sun started to glow in the morning sky, making them both sleepy and their position obvious as the commuters started to come out to start their cars. They packed it in and headed for her apartment. She didn't want it to end. She knew she would see him again in just fifteen more hours but now, that sounded like an eternity.

"Do you want to come up for some coffee?" she asked casually.

"I've had enough coffee and so have you, young lady. Bed. Now," he ordered.

She nodded nervously and climbed out of the SUV. "Eight forty-five?" she asked, realizing that the balance of power had completely shifted to him.

"Eight forty-five, Sarge. Sweet dreams, Charlotte," he grinned, as if he already had been given a peek into the dreams that lay waiting for her. *Anything but the train,* she hoped.

"Hey Moses," Charlie nodded to her parrot before

covering his cage.

"Hey Moses," the bird squawked. He started banging around inside his covered cage.

"I know, I know, Moses but when I sleep, you sleep, that's the deal. Otherwise you'll be in here running your bird beak all day."

"Hey Moses," the bird squawked again, loudly. "Can't pour piss out of a boot."

"Zip it, bird," she grouched at the agitated bird. She was too tired for pajamas so she peeled off her clothes and walked to the window to close up the curtains to her bedroom, pausing momentarily in the window to drink in the sun before closing them. She was unaware that Jake Adams had not yet left the parking lot and was watching her. Charlie crawled into bed exhausted, aroused, and swimming in an ocean of emotions and memories.

September 1996 Sterling, Virginia

"Where you going?" Charlie's brother Tom asked as fourteen-year-old Charlie put on her coat.

"I'm babysitting for the Daley's down the street."

Tom shook his head, amazed that anyone in their neighborhood would trust either one of them with anything, let alone a child, but he had learned early that girls were victims and boys were punks. Kip piped up, "Anything good over there we can steal?"

"You're an asshole, Kip," she said, ignoring Kip's girlfriend and turning on her heel and leaving. *I handled that well*, Charlie thought. She got the last word in, ignored the girlfriend, and made it very clear that she had no interest in him. *Fuck you and your offer to teach me, Kip. I don't need you. I don't need anybody*, she thought resolutely as she walked the ten houses to the Daley's.

Mr. Daley was a good-looking man for an old guy.

He had a Robert Redford rugged kind of face, but he was at least thirty. *Ancient.* He was actually thirty-two. Mr. Daley had to take Mrs. Daley to the airport so she could visit her "bitch of a mother," who was in a hospital in Boston, and they didn't want to drag their toddler along to the airport past his bedtime. Charlie had babysat a dozen times or so since Dillon was born. He used to be sweet but now he was a brat. It was going to be easy money however, as the brat was already asleep.

After the Daley's left, Charlie settled in on the couch with her best friend—the TV remote—and began looking for a movie to keep her company. She eventually got bored and took a stroll around the tastefully decorated home.

Charlie surveyed the furniture, the family pictures, and the well-stocked refrigerator, and started to get that feeling in her chest; that tightening that came whenever she was faced with the reality that she so often avoided. She didn't have a normal life or a good life. With the exception of her brother Tom, she was truly alone in this world. Nobody, especially her parents, gave a shit about her. This made her want a joint and she wished she had hit Kip up for some weed before she left, but she was worried Mr. Daley might smell it on her.

Mr. Daley was cool, but probably not that cool. He often told Charlie if she wanted to sneak a beer while she was babysitting she could, but to just make sure that she pushed the evidence down deep into the trashcan so that his "bitch of a wife" wouldn't see it.

Charlie opened the one can of Miller beer in the fridge and quickly drank it down. She didn't like the taste of beer but she liked that it was alcohol. It made her feel grown up. Then she looked around in the cupboard and found a bottle of rum. She hadn't tried rum before and didn't notice the 151 on the label as she poured it into a glass. If she had noticed, she wouldn't have known what 151 meant. Figuring that if vodka went with orange juice, rum must go with it too. She checked the fridge. The refrigerator was stocked with things that were never evident in Charlie's house—milk, fruit, vegetables, no OJ though.

*Not such a perfect little household after all*, she judged.

The brat's apple juice would have to do. After two glasses of apple juice and 151 she was really feeling it and that started her thinking about Kip. As the liquor warmed her from the inside, she thought about how he had grabbed her hair, how he had whispered to her, and how her stomach felt. She wanted to touch herself. The last thing Charlie needed was to be walked in on by Mr. Daley so she stumbled up the stairs. She listened at the brat's door . . . all quiet. *Thank God for small favors*. She shuffled through the hallway to the Daley's neatly made bed, leaving the lights off. She put her drink on the nightstand and slid her jeans down to her ankles. With her knees bent and off the end of the bed and her long shiny hair sprawled across the bedspread, she slid her hand inside her panties. Charlie's mind was fuzzy as she thought about Kip. She was apple juice/151 fuzzy and it felt good to slide her fingers in and out. That's when she heard him. He was standing in the barely lit door way.

"What the hell are you doing, Charlie?" he said in a low voice.

"Damn it Kip! How did he get in here? Charlie was certain she had locked the front door.

When her eyes focused, she realized it wasn't Kip at

all. *Oh shit. It was Mr. Daley.*

This wasn't like in the sex books where the older neighbor was turned on by catching the young girl masturbating. Mr. Daley was angry. Charlie struggled to sit up as he marched to the nightstand, turned on the bed lamp, and lifted the drink to smell it.

"Are you out of your mind? Jesus Christ, Charlie, what if Dillon had woken up?" He must have realized how loud he was getting because he quickly closed the bedroom door. Charlie was trapped, half naked and drunk.

"I, I'm really sorry Mr. Daley," she stammered. "You . . . you said I could have a beer. Remember?" she reminded him.

"This is not a beer," he said accusingly and pointed at the cup.

"I know. I screwed up. Please don't tell my Dad. He'll kill me," she pleaded.

"When would I tell him, Charlie? The man is never home. I'm not even sure he still lives there. You and your brother are out of control. No one is in charge of you!" Mr. Daley ranted on. "We trusted you with our child. Do you know what Carolyn would do if she knew about this?" *So Mrs. Daley had a name after all.* Before Charlie could answer his clearly rhetorical question, Mr. Daley sat down next to her on the bed and jerked her over his knee in one move. Her jeans were still around her knees. Her damp panties were the only thing separating her from the blows from his hand as he spanked her hard. "If your parents aren't going to take responsibility for punishing you, then I will!"

Charlie instinctively moved her hand behind her to protect herself but he wrestled it away and clamped harder down on the back of her neck with his free hand, using his legs to pin her legs in place. Charlie's stomach tightened as confusion set in. She should have been fighting, crying, or at least scared but she was none of these things. She was turned on.

She started to moan and it caught him off guard. It caught her off guard. *What the . . . ?*

He stopped spanking her. He was breathing hard. She was breathing hard. He held her in place and neither of them moved. Except for the panting, there was not a sound, not a move from either of them. The silence seemed to go on a long time before he finally spoke.

"Is this ever going to happen again?" he asked, his tone still stern, but much more hushed now.

"No. I promise," she whispered breathlessly.

"I may have hit you a little too hard here. Let me take a look." He slid her panties down just to the top of the back of her legs and let his hand rest on her bare and perfect flesh. Charlie whimpered, but it wasn't from pain. He slowly slid his hand over the curve of her red ass and she stayed completely still, not wanting it to end.

He finally snapped out of his trance and stood her up forcefully. "Pull your pants up Charlie. Is your brother home?" he asked, deliberately averting his eyes.

"Y-yes," she stammered. Charlie sat on the bed, her head hanging down, mostly so he couldn't see the bewildered smile she was suppressing. Mr. Daley called the Cavanaugh house and could hear the heavy metal music blaring as Tom answered the phone. "Get over here and pick up your sister, Tom. She's drunk," he said, slamming down the phone.

Mr. Daley helped Charlie down the stairs and into the kitchen and sat her down on the kitchen chair, hard.

He picked up the bottle of rum and pointed to the label, shoving it in front of her face. "This is 151, Charlie. That's the strongest rum there is. Do not ever touch this stuff again, do you understand me?"

"Yes," she blinked, still wide-eyed and tipsy, though more tipsy from the spanking than from the alcohol.

"Look," he said, looking and sounding embarrassed, "I'm sorry I spanked you. It's just a reflex, you know? When you have a toddler, you know? Are you okay?" He seemed to be genuinely concerned about her. Charlie nodded.

Tom showed up and walked Charlie home, telling her she was a dumbass for drinking at the Daley's. She could smell the weed on his clothes and she guessed Mr. Daley could smell it too. More proof of what he already knew, that the inmates were running the asylum. Once inside their own house, Tom pushed her toward the stairs, "Go to bed, Alky, and if you throw it up you clean it up."

Kip was on the ugly couch making cat call noises. "Ohhhhhhh the little good girl isn't so good after all, is she?" Tom shot Kip a warning glance that filled the room.

"Fuck you, Kip," Charlie shot back. "What's with skankapottimus?" Charlie motioned to the pile of blond hair and wide hips passed out on the floor.

"She's toast," Kip said rolling his eyes. "She always overdoes it. Dumb bitch."

"I'd say it's a match made in heaven," Charlie slurred before steadying herself with the railing and pulling herself up the stairs. *Good one*. Charlie grinned.

Once inside her room she pulled all of her clothes off and looked through the pile of washed and unwashed laundry for a nighty, settling on one from the unwashed pile. Her bed was unmade and her untouched books were thrown into the corner. *Must clean room,* she made a mental note as she fell into bed and turned off the light. Sleep should have come quickly with the help of the rum but Charlie was restless. She was embarrassed by what she had done and very aware that if Dillon had woken up, she would not have been able to take care of him.

She was disappointed in herself. She thought about the many bad decisions she had made that night. She began to think of all the things that could have gone wrong.

*Jesus, she was a loser. No wonder her mother left,* she thought.

Just because she had been shit on by the adults in her life, didn't mean she should shit on a defenseless little kid. She thought about the Daley's trusting her, even though no one else in the neighborhood would and how she had violated that trust with her selfishness. She went into their bedroom, where they slept together every night, like normal parents and she . . . she couldn't even finish the thought.

There was no one to teach ethics, or manners, or hygiene, or anything else to Charlotte Cavanaugh but somehow in the midst of a life of chaos she had found it. It mostly came from TV. From Norman Lear actually. Norman Lear had taught her what her parents did not. He taught her how to be a decent human being. He introduced her to compassion, inclusion, and the value of freedom and diversity. His humor and his sense of decency and dignity filled his programs and characters and touched Charlie's heart. It made her soul ache to be normal, trustworthy, and loved, though she had no right, nor any indication, that she was entitled to be any of these things, ever.

She thought once that her instincts might have been

a gift from God. *God? Fuck God. God had abandoned her at age ten. No. Wait. That was her mother.* She was always getting them mixed up. With the help of Mr. Lear and the characters and families he created, Charlie understood and embraced the idea of justice, equality, kindness, and compassion. There was so little of these things to be found in her life. Maybe we always want most in life what we don't have.

All of these thoughts were swirling in young Charlie's head as she tossed and turned and tried to keep from thinking about what she really wanted to think about . . . the spanking. Even in her half drunken state she felt her stomach tighten again. *Did it really happen?* She wondered. She ran a sleepy hand across her bottom. Still sore—*oh yea it happened. Why did it turn her on?* Charlie was fascinated.

*Was it the adrenaline of getting caught? The fact that she was drunk? The rugged good looks of Mr. Daley? Or saddest of all, was it just overwhelming gratitude for the simple sensation of touch and for someone caring enough to be angry with her?*

Charlie was too young to understand the impact of the abandonment of both her parents. No hugs or bedtime kisses, no talks at the kitchen table or moments of sweetness or guidance. No one to say "good job" when she did something well or "I'm proud of you." All Charlie knew was survival. It was all she knew how to do and she was barely succeeding at that. She had no idea why this connection with an adult, however screwed up, was affecting her in this way. Not even Dr. Laura would be able to help her with this one. Blow job Laura, not the radio chick.

As Charlie pondered her spanking, she heard the

door to her bedroom creak as it opened. *Oh my God*, she thought. *Mr. Daley? Shit! Did he leave Dillon by himself in his crib? Had Charlie's brother let him in? Maybe he just wanted to check to make sure she was okay. Maybe he wanted to finish what he started.*

Charlie decided to play possum. Maybe if he had come to just check on her he might touch her if she pretended to be asleep. Charlie lay quiet as the dead trying to control her breathing but there was nothing she could do about her heart beating out of her chest. She felt his hand stroke her silky hair and she felt a quiet moan escape her throat. *God, his touch felt good.* Now this was an experienced man. She felt him pull the covers down as he very lightly slid his hand under her nightgown and over her stomach and chest, barely touching, but definitely making contact with her breasts.

Inside her head, she was pleading, *please do it. Slide my nightgown up. Touch me.* And as if hearing her thoughts, he slid her nightgown up exposing her perfect little budding breasts. She groaned louder as he caressed her nipples and she slowly opened her eyes. "Yes, please," Charlie whispered through sleepy eyes as she looked up in search of Mr. Daley's rugged face. *Oh shit. Not Mr. Daley.*

*Chapter 14*
**Losing Your Virginity is Overrated**

"Kip!" *Jesus. She hadn't been right once tonight.*

Charlie yanked her nightgown down and sat up in protest. "Who the hell were you expecting, Charlie?" Kip said, sounding hurt.

"No one," she fumbled. "I—I thought I was dreaming. Get out of here asshole!" She demanded trying to mask her embarrassment.

"We're going to have to do something about that mouth of yours little girl," he admonished, running his fingers over her pursed lips.

Charlie suddenly realized that sitting up was not a good idea. The room was rocking. *How long had she been asleep?* Kip reached over and rubbed the tip of his finger across her hard nipple that was piercing the fabric of her nightgown.

"It doesn't really look to me like you want me go, Charlie." He moved in close to her face, reaching underneath her mane of hair and massaging her neck and head at the same time. "Let me teach you Charlie. I won't hurt you. I promise. If you want me to stop, I'll stop. I promise. I just want to make you feel good," he purred as he guided her onto her back with a handful of her hair.

Charlie didn't consent, but she didn't protest either. She wanted him to be Mr. Daley and he wasn't, but he was there and he wanted her. *Wanted her*. It was a powerful feeling. He was the wrong guy, at the wrong time, and in the wrong place. Tom would kill him, but it was too late to weigh all of that. It was out of her hands now. Kip peeled her nighty over her head, and immediately his hands and mouth were everywhere. Charlie had never felt anything like it. She couldn't have objected if she wanted to, her breath had left her. In a flash Kip was on top of her and after a little awkward fumbling and some intense pushing, he was inside her.

"Wait!" she pleaded. She was confused. *Where did the oral sex fit in to this chaotic scene? What about kissing?* She ached to feel his mouth on her nipples but as hard as she tried, she couldn't speak and she couldn't will him to do what she wanted. Then she felt it. The excruciating pain as he fully penetrated her and it was over. Kip collapsed on top of her. No condom, no whispering, no hair stroking, no kissing—nothing.

"That was hot," he grinned as he pulled on his jeans. "You're not going to tell Tom, right?" In a daze Charlie shook her head 'no.' Kip left her room and didn't even close the door.

*If he really liked me, he would have closed the door for me*, she thought.

In her bed, in her apartment Charlie tossed and turned as she dreamed. She was desperate for sleep as thoughts of Jake Adams, Mr. Daley, and Kip all mixed into an overcooked soup of regret, rejection, and longing. Longing for a way to forget the dismal circumstances of the loss of her virginity. Longing for the way Mr. Daley made her feel and hoping against hope that Jake Adams might finally be the man who could make her feel like that again.

She knew better than to think he could be that man. She had been disappointed so many times. It was too early to wake up. She tried to settle back into sleep but it was too noisy. The noise was distant but so persistent and getting louder. God she hated working midnight shifts. The baby was there and was staring at her.

"What? I have to sleep."

His sad little eyes pooled with tears, then suddenly Mary Jane was there too except she also had baby's eyes. Before Charlie knew it, the persistent noise was coming from behind her was upon her. She turned to see the train heading straight for her. Her feet were sunk deep into the earth making any movement impossible. "Mary Jane! The baby! Save the baby!" DING! DING! DING! DING! DING! DING! DING! DING! DING! DING! DING! DING! DING! Charlie shot up from her pillow screaming "Noooooooo!" She threw her arms up to protect herself from the oncoming locomotive.

Finally, she realized through her sobs that she was safe in her apartment. Safe in her bed. *No train.*

She was gasping for air as she reached over to turn off her alarm clock—ding, ding, ding. She cried quietly into her pillow trying to get the image of the train out of her head before heading to the kitchen and opening her laptop. AJ, she needed AJ.

VABlueAngel: Are you there AJ? Please be there.

**AJ101-789: I'm here Angel. How'd the stakeout go? Did you sleep well? Long time since you worked a midnight shift eh? Heh heh.**

VABlueAngel: I wish you could hold me AJ.

**AJ101-789: What's wrong? Charlie, tell me.**

Alarm filled AJ's gut. Charlie was tough, but that was only on the outside. Inside she was fragile as glass and broken, and it was killing him.

VABlueAngel: I just wish you could reach through this damn screen sometimes that's all.

**AJ101-789: The train again?**

He asked the question but already knew the answer. The train. AJ hated that fucking train as much as Charlie did. He dreaded it. It was so foreboding. Why did it have to be a train and why did it have to hit her?

VABlueAngel: Uh huh.

**AJ101-789: Oh sweetie, I'm so sorry. It's okay. You're safe. I'm right here.**

*But you're not here*, Charlie thought sadly. *You're not here and Jake is.*

VABlueAngel: I'm tired of being alone AJ. I'm tired of doing this alone.

**AJ101-789: I know you are Angel. I know. I would give anything to take you in my arms and make it go away. I would do anything for you, Charlie. You're not alone.**

*Anything?* she thought. *Then why aren't you here? I've been waiting for over a year. I am so alone. Why can't you come to me?* Instantly she felt guilty. He would be with her if he could be. She felt it in her bones.

VABlueAngel: I didn't log on to make you feel bad AJ. I just needed you.

**AJ101-789: What time does your stake-out start?**

VABlueAngel: In an hour. "I need to eat and get a shower," She said out loud as she typed.

"Get a shower scumbag," Moses screeched.

VABlueAngel: That bird is getting on my nerves.

**AJ101-789: Aww don't yell at Moses lol. Remember, everything he learned, he learned from Thompson. It's not his fault.**

She loved that AJ so frequently referred to her mentor as if he had known him.

VABlueAngel: Thanks for the smile AJ. Be safe buddy.

**AJ101-789: You too.**

*Buddy? I'm losing her to the Fed,* AJ thought.

*Chapter 15*
**Louise**


Charlie took a long hot shower to wash away the remnants of the freight train, then shared a grilled cheese sandwich with Thompson's loud-mouthed bird before dressing in her black BDUs, a black turtleneck sweater and combat boots. She was hoping against hope that a more on-duty look and feel might help her behave better than she did last night. She blushed as she remembered trying to kiss Jake Adams and him rejecting her. Charlie did a quick press check on her Glock 21, catching a glimpse of the gold colored round in the chamber of her gun to make sure she was ready to go. She slid it into her holster, savoring the clicking sound it made as it locked in. *Fucking poetry.*

Though she only had an hour to shower, eat, and dress she still found herself ready fifteen minutes early and was excited when she looked out the window and saw that Jake and the Fed Mobile had arrived early as well. She raced down the stairs and climbed into the car and tried not to grin when she saw his deep eyes and the smile he had waiting for her. He was wearing an open-collar polo shirt and a sports coat and looked completely huggable.

"Are we doing a SWAT raid tonight, Sarge?" Jake asked as Charlie climbed into the car.

"I gotta hunch we might see some action tonight," she smiled mischievously, both because she was thrilled to see him again and because she wanted to make sure he knew that he hadn't rattled her last night.

"Really?" he said confidently, "Well I am always up

for action."

"Hmm, funny, I wasn't left with that impression," she said looking away, referencing his refusal to kiss her last night which was not something she planned to bring up. She was shocked by what had come out of her mouth. Jake raised an eyebrow and shot her a sideways glance.

"As I said, I'm always ready," he said as he pulled an M4 assault rifle from under his seat and raised it between his legs. He racked the charging handle, sending a shiver through Charlie's body. *Damn it and holy shit.* He looked amazing holding the gun between his legs.

Charlie feigned boredom as Jake grinned at her, knowing full well the temperature in the SUV was rising. Ignoring him, Charlie looked out the window as Jake headed toward Daniel Silver's house. She could feel him glancing at her and she started to feel uncomfortable. She needed to find something to do with her hands and finally reached for the satellite radio, tuning it to the oldies channel.

"What are you, fifty years old?"

He turned the station back to the Lithium channel causing the SUV to fill with a haunting tune she remembered from her brother Tom's collection.

"Could you go a little easier on the Aqua Velva if we are going to be stuck in the same car all night?"

"I'm not wearing cologne. It's soap. If you want me not to shower, I can accommodate you," he said deadpan. They drove in silence to the target's house and picked their spot.

She wanted to continue to ignore him but she couldn't help looking at him. It was obvious he had dressed up a little for her. He was full of shit when he said he wasn't wearing cologne. She knew that was for her. She usually doubted herself on every front on the rare occasion she was attracted to a man, but not this time. *It was so sweet of him.* Charlie had to fight off the urge to climb into his lap and nuzzle her face against his chest.

"I'm sorry Jake," she said quietly. "I didn't sleep well."

"How come?" he asked with a look of concern that made her want to touch his face.

"Nightmare," but she offered no further explanation and he nodded in understanding, all irritation reduced to dust. He reached for her hand and gently brushed his finger across her knuckles but did not look over at her just yet.

"Favorite food?" he asked quietly, not taking his eyes off the house.

"Grilled, broiled, or blackened seafood of just about any kind. Unless you're talking takeout." He turned sideways in the seat to face her and she became lost in his eyes.

"And if we are talking takeout?"

"What?" she asked in a whisper, not quite able to both hear him and look at him at the same time.

"And if we are talking takeout, what is your favorite?"

"Oh. Easy" she smiled. "Orange crusted chicken from the Gay Dolphin."

"The Gay Dolphin?"

"You're going to love it. My treat."

They both relaxed and fell back into the comfortable rhythm that preceded the kiss that wasn't last night.

Jake took a long deep breath, drinking her in. *God she was beautiful.* She was even hotter in her SWAT clothes than she was in her girl clothes. She caught him gazing at her. He needed a distraction. He didn't really care, but he had to think fast.

"So, you never told me. How did you end up in Landon? Did you grow up here? What made you decide to become a police officer?"

"Oh that." Charlie grinned slowly and sweetly, the light coming up in her eyes. "Louise Brown."

1997 Landon, Virginia

Charlie's father had met a woman. Apparently, someone had fixed them up on a blind date and Charlie's father had been seeing the woman for over a year without introducing her to his children.

*So that's where her father had been*, Charlie fumed.

Louise Brown looked like a real estate agent complete with elegant suit, upswept hair, and tasteful jewelry. Carol Brady came to mind. *Gag me*, Charlie thought. *No wonder Dad made us dress up for the "surprise".* It took forever to get to Carol Brady's house in the upscale neighborhood of Westridge in Landon. That was at least forty miles from her scruffy neighborhood in Sterling. The rest was a blur. They would leave their home in Sterling, their school, their friends, Mr. Daley. They left their whole life, such as it was, and they moved into the Home Interiors tacky McMansion of Louise Brown and her twit twins. Their house would be clean, laundry would be done and put away, meals would include vegetables and friends would be—*gone*. Charlie didn't think it was possible to feel more alone in the world than she already felt, but she was wrong. The only life Charlie and her brother knew was over.

Tom immediately settled down. This new life was

doing wonders for him. He took to his new high school like a duck to water, made the football team and quit smoking both weed and cigarettes.

*Well fuck that!*

Charlie made a half-hearted effort to fit in but it wasn't working. She couldn't stay in her father's new world and she couldn't stay with her mother and she couldn't go back to her real home. At age sixteen Charlie had lost the little bit of baby fat she had and had transformed into a truly beautiful young woman. Petite with long straight brown hair, and massive brown eyes. She was stunning. Though she would die before admitting it, the butterfly transformation was entirely due to her step-mother Louise, who just wouldn't give up on her. Very subtly and with the stealth of a jungle cat and the patience of Job, Louise would stalk Charlie when she was dressing, doing her hair or putting on her make-up and would gently engage her. "I've never seen you wear this dear, have you thought about pairing it with these pants? Would you like to try this blush? I bought it for myself but it's too young a color for a woman my age, but I'll bet it would look lovely on you. I'm going to the salon today, would you mind driving me?" Then once inside the salon it would be cut, color, wax, paws and claws for both of them.

In the year she spent with Louise, Charlie had learned grooming, manners, how to dress, how accessorize, and even how to flirt, all without even knowing she was receiving the training her real mother had failed to give her. It wasn't enough.

At age sixteen, Charlie packed a backpack and hit the road. She hid out at Laura's at first, but that was too obvious. She thought about going to Mr. Daley's but she knew that showing up at his place would raise too many questions and just get him into trouble. Plus, he would be disappointed with the decision she had made to run away, though he couldn't possibly be more disappointed in her than Charlie was in herself. She stayed with friends, hidden in their basements or garages, fought off creeps, ran from cops, and generally gave up on her young life. After two long months she finally had to face the facts. It wasn't working out to be on her own either. She decided to return home to Landon. *Home to Landon.* She had nowhere else to go.

Charlie sat on the hill behind her stepmother's house for hours before mustering up the courage to go inside. She wondered; *what would her father and Louise say? Would they even let her stay? Maybe they would have the police come pick her up and take her to juvey—or worse, they would put her on a bus to her mother's.*

The front door was unlocked. It was 8:30 at night and it was Christmas break so the twits would be home. *Great—she would be berated in front of everyone for the trouble she had caused, for the worry she put them through.* Running away was the most selfish thing Charlie had ever done and she was filled with remorse and self-loathing. She prepared herself for what she knew she had coming. They would hate her for what she had done and she deserved it.

As Charlie stepped inside the house, she could hear the TV in the family room. She stood in the doorway to the room and looked around. The house was beautifully decorated for Christmas. She couldn't remember the last time she and her brother had Christmas decorations or even a tree. There was a warm fire crackling in the fireplace and Charlie's father and Louise were snuggled up on the sofa. Tessa was in the Lay-Z-Boy and Tom and Tina were sprawled out on the floor. She made eye contact with her father first, but it was Louise who spoke. "Charlie," she gasped putting a hand to her heart. "Oh, thank God. Welcome home sweetheart. Come here, don't we even get a hug?" Charlie dropped her backpack and ran to Louise and hugged her and never wanted to let go. Her father joined the hug. Tears streamed down his face followed by her brother who was not happy but who was clearly relieved as were her two step-sisters who were both holding back tears. *What the . . . ?* Charlie was floored by her family's reaction.

*Her family.*

In the weeks that followed, Charlie was placed in a catch-up program at school designed to spark an interest in trouble teens. The idea was to develop any interest that might divert them from their self-destructive behavior. Each week they had to choose a job site to attend in the afternoon following accelerated classes. At the end of the program they had to have completed seven of ten sites. Animal hospital, repair garage, emergency room, funeral home, retail store, elementary school aid, homeless shelter, hair salon, and police ride-along.

Charlie's counselor was a very sweet man; very Mr. Rogers in his little sweater, with his round glasses and his sweet soft voice. "Well there, Charlotte, let's see your worksheet. I see you have passed on the police ride-along?"

"It's Charlie and you bet your ass I pass," she quipped. "Sorry. I just spent two months running from those jerks. I do not want to be in a police car with them for ten hours."

"You know Charlie," he chided, "sometimes it is a

lack of understanding that causes us to make judgments and assumptions about people or this case, professions. I think this would be a good experience for you. I'm going to override your list and trade out one of the other selections for the police ride-along."

"You can't. It says I have to be seventeen. I'm only sixteen." she smirked.

"You'll be seventeen before the end of term, Charlie." She squared her jaw and stared at the floor. *Mr. Rogers is an asshole*, she decided.

*Chapter 16*
**The Ride-Along**


Charlie really enjoyed the experiences of the other sites, especially the emergency room and fire department. They were both a rush of adrenaline and she could see herself doing either of these jobs. *But now it was time to ride with the fucking police.* When the date arrived, Charlie read the instructions carefully and chose appropriate attire, had her parents sign the release form, and headed for the Eastern District station of the Landon PD.

Landon PD wasn't a large agency as police departments go, about eighty-five sworn officers, but the expansive area they covered outside of Virginia Beach necessitated two stations. She arrived at the Eastern District station promptly at 3:30 on Saturday afternoon and met with the station Captain, J. K. Sullivan, who would later become her chief. He showed her around the station and led her to the Roll Call room and left her there, where several officers were already sitting and doing paperwork. A ridiculously good-looking officer was snickering as he came into the Squad Room. He was pointing to a paper bag he held in his other hand.

*Whoa! Hottie McHot!*

The officers laughed at his paper bag and one officer admonished, "Don't do it Toomey! Sarge will shoot you with your own gun." More laughter.

Toomey pulled something out of the paper bag and taped it under the podium at the front of the room and scurried to his seat, casually noticing Charlie. "Ride-along?" he asked.

"Um yea, yes Sir," she sputtered.

"Oh, you picked a great day to be here, kid!" Officer Toomey laughed. "Officer Ross Toomey, ma'am. Single. I like fast cars, fast motorcycles, and fast women." Charlie sat there with her mouth half open and looked behind her. *Was he talking to her?*

An older leathery looking officer growled, "She's from the high school, you twit!" *Hey!* Charlie thought. *Twit? That's my word.*

"High school, huh?" Toomey winked. "So? I won't tell if she doesn't!" More laughter. Toomey ran back up to the podium and added another piece of tape to the underside of the podium and then ran back to his seat next to Charlie. He looked at her and held a finger to his lips. "Shhhhh."

*Were these guys drunk?* For the next ten minutes they insulted each other, called each other "homos, station rats, and skates" and threw wads of paper at each other. It was like being in study hall—in the Bronx. A total of eight officers were in place when an officer with stripes on his sleeves strode in and took the podium. Everyone immediately settled down except for Officer Toomey, who was still suppressing a giggle.

"Toomey, what the fuck are you up to?" the sergeant said, with no regard for the seventeen-year-old guest in the room.

"Me? Nothing, Sarge."

The sergeant was a nice-looking man, tall classic features, older but clearly handsome in his day. The lines that ran across his face were a reflection of age and stress but he was still handsome and it made Charlie think fondly of Mr. Daley. The sergeant began roll call.

"Okay, we got a complaint about speeders on Delray again. Goddammit, this is the third time this month!

Hoard, you're killing me. Deal with this would you? Goddammit, where's Hoard?" he barked as he looked around the room.

The old leathery officer spoke up. "She's off tonight, Sarge," said Officer D. M. Thompson. He had been pretty quiet up until now, except for chastising young Mr. Toomey for flirting with a high school student.

"What?" the sergeant raised his voice again.

"The leave slip's been in your box for a week and you signed it so don't start humping my leg," Officer D. M. Thompson said. He stuffed the unlit cigar back in his mouth.

"One damn split-tail on the squad and she's gonna take off the night we have a female ride-along? Well that's just great."

Toomey started to speak up to volunteer but Officer Thompson cut him off. "I'll take her," Thompson said without looking up.

*Oh shit. Not him. Not him! I want the hot guy!*

"Okay. Thanks, Thompson. Miss, you'll be riding with Officer Thompson tonight, you lucky, lucky girl." More laughter, from everyone except Charlie, who smiled uncomfortably. Officer Toomey stood up and walked to the podium. "Speaking of leave slips Sarge, you haven't signed my leave slip for that motorcycle race next week." As Toomey slid the leave slip in front of the sergeant, he held a lighter in the other hand and lit whatever he had hidden under the front of the podium. Toomey quickly grabbed the signed paper and scurried back to his seat.

"You're going to kill yourself in that damn race, Toomey. I don't know why you young bucks have to . . ."

POP! POP! POP! *What the . . . ?*

The sergeant stepped back and put his hand on his gun.

POP! POP! POP!

The room erupted in smoke and hysterical laughter as the string of firecrackers continued to pop under the podium. Once Charlie realized what was happening, she couldn't contain herself. She covered her mouth with her hand, not sure she should be laughing along.

"Goddamn it, Toomey!" The sergeant yelled as he waved the smoke away and without missing a beat, threw a set of keys at Toomey, hitting him in the head while he was doubled over with laughter. Toomey picked the keys up and looked at the tag that hung on the keychain.

"Not 455! Oh come on Sarge, it was just a joke. Please don't make me drive the widow- maker!" "Toomey! 455!" the sergeant repeated, "and B13 is your beat!"

"What?! Not the pit!! Please Sarge! Have mercy!! Don't assign me to the pit!"

Toomey pleaded while the other officers were laughing so hard there were tears rolling down their cheeks, except for Officer Thompson who chewed his unlit cigar and muttered under his breath, "Assholes."

The Sergeant continued with the car and police beat assignments and ran down the wanted list. *Yawn,* thought Charlie. Landon is boring. She couldn't wait for this night to be over. *The firecracker thing was funny and Officer Toomey was very cute, but then there was D. M. Thompson. Ten hours in a car with this cigar-smoking grouch. Maybe she would fake a stomachache and Officer Thompson would sign off on her paperwork.*

"Let's go, kid," he barked as he walked past her. She quickly followed and had to double time it to keep up with him.

"Where's the fire?" she joked as she caught up.

"I'm no station rat!" he grumbled, "and I'm damn sure no fucking fireman. Humph! All brawn, no brains! Fucking heroes."

Charlie chuckled thinking about the day she spent at the local fire department. Officer Thompson was so right. Not the brightest bulbs in the chandelier. He opened the police car doors front and back, pointed to the passenger side and directed her to sit.

"Woof!" she replied and she couldn't be sure, but she thought she could see him suppressing a grin. "And don't touch anything," he snapped, composing himself and putting his stern face back in place. She watched as he checked out the police cruiser, walking around it, turning on all the lights and checking them to make sure they all worked and then searching the back seat.

Curious, Charlie asked, "Do you have to drive a different police car every night?" Officer Thompson chose that exact moment to test the siren, causing Charlie to jump out of her skin.

"Jesus Christ!" she screamed when he cut the siren sequence off.

"Sorry, I guess I should have warned you," he grinned.

"We'll play twenty questions once we've hit the road. I'll get hives if I stay at the station too long. Too many goddamn white shirts and suits. Assholes."

Officer Thompson finally got in the driver's seat and said into the police radio mic,

"Unit 257 on duty."

"10-4 Unit 257 1626 hours," a sexy voice replied.

"Oh, thank God it's Jan," Thompson said, mostly to himself. "Okay Brown Eyes, what was your question?"

*Brown Eyes? Is this old leathery fart flirting with me?* Rattled but undeterred, she asked, "I was asking if . . ."

"Wait," he cut her off, "let's go over the rules first."

*Rules?*

Then a loud tone came over the radio. Beeeeeep. "Units 257, 282, 310, burglary in progress 1-1-2-8-2 Batton Place, 1-1-2-8-2 Batton Place; cross street Madison Lane," the sexy disembodied radio voice purred. Officer Thompson answered the radio, turned on the siren and yelled, "Buckle up Brown Eyes. Time to go to work."

*Holy shit!* The next eight minutes were like nothing Charlie had ever experienced. She was flying through Landon's intersections and really red traffic lights while her driver provided a steady running commentary of expletives. "Yield right you stupid sons of bitches! Don't stop in the middle of an intersection you twit! Who the hell gave you a license? If I weren't on a call I'd be stroking your ass in a heartbeat! Press hard! Five copies!"

This officer was clearly insane.

Charlie had her feet pressed into the floorboard as though she thought she might find a brake pedal there and had a death grip on the arm rest. Thompson halted his expletives for a few seconds to check on his ride-along.

"You okay, kid?"

Charlie turned to show him the smile plastered across her face.

He grinned and went back to berating the public.

"Stay in the car, Brown Eyes," he instructed as he climbed out of the cruiser. When Officer Thompson returned, he explained that the call was a misunderstanding, no burglar.

"Can I call you D.M.?" Charlie asked breathless.

"Not if you expect me to answer," he said through his cigar clenched teeth. "What movie is that line from, kid?" he asked as he looked at her with a sideways glance.

Charlie didn't need further explanation. She knew exactly what he was asking. "Pretty Woman," she replied proudly.

"You're okay kid," Thompson grinned through his cigar. Then he picked up where he left off, as though he hadn't just risked their lives and about a hundred other drivers along the way. "Rules," he continued.

Charlie's heart was beating out of her chest, her face was flushed and her ears were ringing. She wanted to look cool and unaffected but she had no chance of faking this. She could only compare this feeling to one other time in her life. She pushed Mr. Daley from her mind quickly and tried to focus on her insane police officer chauffeur.

"Rule number one," he barked, "know our location at all times. If I am fighting somebody and you don't get on this radio and call for help, the next ass I kick after I put somebody in the hospital will be yours. Got it?"

"Got it." Charlie grinned. *Fighting? There is going to be fighting? Awesome!*

"What's my unit number?" he quizzed.

"Unit 257," she replied before he finished the question. Thompson grinned. She had impressed him.

"Rule number two, you stay in the car unless I tell you otherwise. Vicarious responsibility."

*She would have to look that one up.*

"Rule number three, no stupid questions." She was glad she hadn't asked what vicarious meant.

"Rule number four, no whining."

"Rule number five, I don't care if you have to go to the bathroom—you'll go when I go."

*Damn.* Charlie wished he hadn't mentioned that. He continued.

"Rule number six, I decide when and where we eat and you buy your own dinner. This isn't a goddamn date."

"Rule number seven, anything you see on this ride-along is confidential in terms of people we talk to or crime victims so don't go running your mouth at school on Monday about people's private business."

"Rule number eight, I smoke cigars—deal with it. Got it?"

"Got it," she said, grinning.

"Rule number nine, I listen to Howard Stern. If that offends your delicate sensibilities that's tough shit. Howard's my guy."

"And Robin is my girl," Charlie replied referring to Howard Stern's sidekick. Which brought an approving nod from rugged officer.

"Ha! Dead inspection!" he yelled, causing Charlie to jump in her seat as a broken-down van passed in front of them at the intersection. Again, the emergency lights and siren were activated as Officer Thompson pulled over the mini-van. Charlie studied him as he got out of the car. Officer Thompson was actually a slight man; in both stature and weight. Actually, he wasn't much taller than Charlie, but that wasn't saying much given that she was only 5' 4". He seemed bigger though, taller, intimidating even. *It might have been the uniform. No*, Charlie assessed, *it was the attitude. He was all show. A Billy Badass.* She watched as Thompson strode up to the van and talked with the driver of the badly worn mini-van.

It was an older woman driving a carload full of kids. Charlie bet Officer Thompson was giving it to her good. *Press hard! Five copies!* He returned to the car, took his nightstick out of his gun belt and pushed it between the seats and picked up the radio.

"257 10-8 Warning."

*Warning? What happened to Billy Badass? Press hard, five copies?* He sensed her eyeing him.

"What? She can't afford to get the crack in her windshield fixed so she can get that POS inspected; you think she can afford a ticket?"

Charlie looked at him perplexed.

"P-O-S. Piece-of-shit," he barked. "Questions! Ask!"

Very few people surprised Charlie. She always expected the worse from them and she was almost never disappointed, but Officer Thompson was in a league all his own. She was instantly enchanted by this old leathery saddlebag of a man. For the next several hours the radio was virtually silent and she hit the poor trapped Officer with every non-stupid question she could think of. She listened intently as Officer Thompson explained beat assignments, crap cruiser assignments "for nitwits like Toomey who dig their own graves by pissing off the people who control their fate," and explained why he had to search the back seat at the beginning of every shift in case an arrestee picked up by the previous shift had stuffed a weapon or drugs into the seat.

Charlie was fascinated. She didn't even mind the cigar smoke. Actually, she kind of liked it. In the years that would follow, the smell of cigar smoke would always bring a smile to her lips and a hug to her aching heart.

"When are we going to get another call?" she asked

and Thompson raised a warning eye brow her way. *Oops—broke rule number four, no whining.* "Sorry," she said.

In spite of the lack of calls, the night was going by way too quickly, and there was never a moment of silence between them. Guarded and untrusting, Charlie had never taken to a stranger like this before and she had never had so much fun in her life. It was intense. It was exciting and she knew that Thompson was unlike any person she had ever known. She knew he would be in her life forever and he was.

The last call of the night was for a domestic assault that had occurred in the parking lot of a rundown apartment complex, Landon Gardens. "If it's got the name Gardens in it, it's guaranteed to be a shithole every time," Thompson told her. "You stay in the car, Brown Eyes. Eyes open—doors locked."

A woman had been badly beaten. Unit 310 caught the call and was first on the scene. Thompson explained that he was the back-up unit, just there for backup and assist. She watched as Thompson conferred with Unit 310 and then watched through the open-air stairwell as Thompson knocked on the door of every single apartment in eye view of the parking lot. It seemed to take forever. When he finally returned to the car Charlie promptly broke the no whining rule. "Whaaat took so looong?"

Thompson relit his cigar and shot her the look.

"Sorry," she said, dropping her eyes, "but I thought you said we were just the backup on this one."

"We?" he asked with an amused look on his face. Charlie's face flushed. "Somebody's been bitten by the bug," he grinned. "Good. You're smart. There is not enough smart on this job. As a whole, we're not as stupid as the fucking heroes . . ." *Heroes equal firemen*, she remembered, "but we could use more smart officers, even a split-tail." Charlie beamed, not knowing what a split-tail was but sure it was something special.

"The reason it took so long is because when you are the backup officer, you get the shit assignments. I never understood officers who complain about being the primary officer," he waxed. "When you catch a call, that's the best gig there is. That's the meat of it. The backup officers have to canvass, find witnesses, all the bullshit. Since this black and blue broad might not make it they will be calling the suits in on this one."

"Suits?" Charlie interrupted. "You said that earlier, white shirts and suits." Charlie chose to ignore the fact that Thompson just announced that the beaten woman might not survive.

"White shirts, command staff," he grumbled. "Suits, detectives. Both of them worthless as tits on a boar hog. Couldn't pour piss out of a boot if the instructions were written on the heel."

Charlie laughed. "Anyway," he continued, "whenever the suits get called out to royally fuck things up, the canvassing has to be taken up a notch. The suits are going to want everyone interviewed, anyone who might have seen anything, get it? The hooker, the handyman, and the goddamn parrot."

*Was that a movie line?* Charlie thought.

"It's not a movie line, kid," Thompson said as if reading her mind. "It's an investigative philosophy. Anything that's got eyes or ears and can communicate might have something to tell us. When you're investigating a crime you gotta get it all. Got it?"

"Got it," she said, resolutely. When they got back to

the station at 1:45 a.m., Thompson tried to drop Charlie off at her car in the parking lot. "It's only one forty-five," she protested. Thompson rolled his eyes but grinned as he was doing it.

"Rookies. That's zero one forty-five, kid," he sighed, and she beamed at the title he had bestowed on her. They fueled up the cruiser and he offloaded his gear at his personal car, a beat-up gray primer 1955 Chevrolet. "Incidentally," Charlie said, "talk about your POS!" she laughed.

"I've got big plans for this baby," he said with a wink. They walked back into the station, checked in the shotgun, returned the keys to the cruiser assignment board and she followed Thompson into the roll call room where he grabbed a marker and a blank piece of paper. OUT OF ORDER he wrote, then carried the paper to the elevator door in the hallway and taped it to the doors. Thompson smirked as he walked out with Charlie to the parking lot.

"Umm Officer Thompson?" she smiled and raised her eyebrows.

"That elevator leads to the second floor," Thompson explained. "It's the ivory tower that holds the white shirts and the suits." Officer Thompson raised his chin and grinned at Charlie. Charlie nodded and grinned back.

*Chapter 17*
**Daley Spanking**

Jake was so completely engrossed in Charlie's Thompson story he barely moved when a trash can being knocked over made a horrible racket right next to the SUV. Charlie had already cleared leather, her gun un-holstered and in her hand, and was crouching on the floorboard. Jake was impressed with her tactical speed and followed suit, hoping she hadn't noticed how slow he was to move into position. Charlie picked up the portable radio to call for backup.

"Not yet," Jake whispered. "Let's make sure we have something before we pull the others off their posts."

"I was going to call a patrol unit," Charlie whispered. Suddenly something sprang across the hood and over the windshield. Both officers leveled their weapons at the windshield, prepared to fire until they registered the beady eyes of the raccoon that had them both cowering under the dash.

"Jesus Christ!" Charlie yelled.

"Shhh!" Jake said, laughing hysterically.

"Jesus, Adams! I almost had to buy the government a new windshield," she sighed, grabbed her heart with one hand, and re-holstered her sidearm with the other.

"I would have had to split the cost with you!" Jake collapsed back into his seat. When he did, his mini-TASER fell out of his jacket and landed with a thump on the floorboard.

"I told you we were going to have some excitement tonight Agent!"

"It's right here, Ray. It's looking at me," Jake was

laughing so hard he barely got the Ghostbusters line out of his mouth. He discreetly slid the TASER back into his pocket.

"What the hell was that?" she asked, wiping away her tears.

"Mini-TASER," he flashed it at her before putting it back in his pocket.

She balked. "A TASER? Since when do Feds carry TASERs?"

"I'm more of a Boy Scout than a Fed. I like to be prepared. Fucking raccoon," he said and shook his head, and they both laughed again.

The adrenaline rush left them both giddy and jumpy for the next hour but the rising sun was a sure cure and they both started to fade. Charlie was fighting to keep her eyes open when Jake said, "When will I get to meet this guy anyway?"

"What guy?"

"The legend. The man. Your mentor. Thompson."

"Oh," she said softly and her eyes took on a pained look that ripped at Jake's heart.

"You can't," she whispered. "He died." Jake trained his intense eyes on hers and Charlie couldn't tell where her gaze stopped and his started. She had never known anyone who could give someone a hug with their eyes, but that's what Jake was doing.

"He had a heart attack two weeks before my academy graduation."

They were fell silent for a time.

"Does it ever feel to you like everyone is always leaving?" Charlie asked, sounding like a small child. This time she made no effort to hold her tears. She trusted him and because she did she let them fall. Her eyes stayed joined to his. Jake reached for her, caught a tear with his finger, and pulled her to his chest, hugging her hard and wishing he could hold her forever. He knew better than to wish that wish but wished it just the same.

"I really wish you could have met him."

His voice cracked when he said, "Time to break it down." He guided her back to her seat, reached over her to put her seatbelt on, and started the SUV.

When they reached her apartment and stopped, they sat in silence. Neither of them wanted to leave the other. "I guess I should go," he said. "You didn't sleep well yesterday. You need to get some rest. We have one more night to go."

Charlie nodded but didn't get out of the car.

"I think I'll hang out in the parking lot for a while though," he said, looking tentatively at her. Charlie looked at him, confused at first but then she understood. He didn't want to muddy the waters by coming inside, but he did want to be near her. It was a romantic gesture so gallant it caught in her throat and all she could do was nod, afraid that if she uttered one word, the dam would break. She reached up to touch his face. He tried to stop her hand, but she pulled her hand away from his and reached for his face again, this time making contact with his cheek and cradling it in her small hand. He closed his eyes and leaned into it, then brought her hand to his mouth, kissed her palm, and whispered, "Go."

"Hey Brown Eyes," Moses greeted her. Charlie reached into the cage and gently stroked Moses' head while he cooed. Then she covered the cage, went straight to her room, and slid on her Redskins jersey and footy socks. She washed her face, brushed her teeth, and tried to control her breathing. *Would he still be there? It had been almost ten minutes now. They were both exhausted. Did he like her enough to still be there?*

Charlie walked to the window like she was sneaking up on an indoor cat that had gotten outside. Slowly she peeked down into the parking lot. There he was, grinning up at her, waving like an idiot. She grinned back and used her thumbs to show off her Redskins jersey. He gave her a thumbs-up and she waved again, closing the curtains as her eyes filled with tears. *He did like her. He really liked her.* She peeked out again, still there. She grinned and climbed into bed, smiling like a fool.

Charlie was too excited to sleep, but knew she couldn't pull another midnight shift without eight-straight and there was only one way to ensure sleep. She needed to get herself off. She felt funny about longing for Jake while masturbating to Mr. Daley, but there was no alternative. When she needed to climax quickly, that was the memory that did it. Every time. She fished through her drawer for her favorite vibrator, Gus, as she immersed herself in the memory of her Robert Redford-looking-spanking-neighbor, Mr. Daley.

November 1984
Sterling, Virginia

Mr. Daley had clearly been avoiding Charlie since the 151-rum-spanking episode. Charlie would watch for him out the front window of her kitchen and would pretend to be passing by his house when he got home at night. However, whenever she tried to engage him in conversation he would make some excuse about being in a rush and brush past her.

She wondered if he was as turned on as she had

been, or was he truly repulsed and angry about catching her touching herself?

She desperately wanted to feel his hands on her again, controlling her body, but he wouldn't even make eye contact with her. Strike one.

Kip never returned for seconds. He still came to the house to see her brother Tom, sometimes with skanka-pottimus, sometimes without, but it was as if nothing had happened between them. Strike two.

"Maybe I wasn't very good. Maybe that's why Kip never asked me to do it again," Charlie confided to her sexpert friend Laura.

"Don't sweat it, Charlie. Some guys just get off on popping cherries. Once it's done it can't be redone, and they lose interest. That's why I stick to blowies. I'm still a challenge for them and they always come back thinking that maybe I'll give in." Laura laughed.

*Or maybe you are just prettier, more desirable, smarter, funnier—all the things I am not,* Charlie thought.

"Go for the old guy," Laura pushed. "You said yourself his wife works nights and he is there by himself with the sleeping kid every night. Seduce him."

"Seduce him? How? And hellooooooo. He's married."

"It's easy, just go over there and tell him you have a problem and need some advice. Dress sexy, he'll get the message." Laura winked and Charlie shook her head in disapproval.

Laura rolled her eyes then quoted a line from one of their favorite Katherine Hepburn movies, "Oh justice with her shining sword! Look, you're not trying to steal him. You just want to borrow him," Laura quipped.

*Oh, Dr. Laura what are you getting me into?*

It took weeks and Charlie's fifteenth birthday for her to get up enough nerve to knock on Mr. Daley's door. While she would never remember actually knocking on the door, she would forever remember the look of anger that engulfed his face when he answered the door and found her standing there in her tight jeans, her sexiest sheer black shirt, and her hot pink push-up bra.

"I-I need some advice Mr. Daley and I was hoping," she started but he cut her off mid-sentence, grabbed her arm, and dragged her to the living room where he pushed her down onto the couch.

He paced in front of her for a moment and she sensed that keeping her mouth shut was the best idea. Charlie was shaking.

"I know what you think you want little girl, and it is not going to happen," he scolded her. Charlie lowered her head and felt the tears starting to well up in her eyes. *Disappointment? Embarrassment? Maybe both.* He grabbed her by the back of her hair and lifted up her head. He was just inches from her face as confusion and excitement washed over her.

"Don't you dare cry young lady. I am thirty-four, married, and I have a child and you are not going to seduce me, do you understand?"

She nodded, dumbfounded. *Well then, what the hell is this?*

"This is what is going to happen, Charlotte. You will come here at eight o'clock every night on the nights my wife works, and you will bring your school books, do you understand?"

"My books? I . . ."

He interrupted her and demanded, "Yes Sir, is all I want to hear from you." His face was red and he penetrated her with his eyes. Charlie thought she might throw up. "I will tell my bitch-of-a-wife that I can no longer stand by and watch what is happening to you and that I am going to help you get back on track with your school work."

"But I don't," she started but he interrupted her again and narrowed his eyes. "Focus Charlotte. Do-you-under-stand?"

"Yes Sir," she nodded, which was a lie.

Mr. Daley nodded but didn't smile. He released her hair and took a step back and looked her over. "Stand up. Take off your shirt," he ordered. She stared at him wide-eyed but took it off without hesitation. The sheer-ness of the shirt wasn't covering much to begin with, but now she felt truly exposed . . . Exposed, confused, and aroused.

He sat down at the opposite end of the couch from her and stared at her. Charlie looked at the floor and used her arms to cover herself.

"Get me a beer."

Charlie turned to walk toward the kitchen.

"Do not cover yourself."

She lowered her arms and took a deep breath. She could do this. She brought back the beer and handed it to him. He accepted it without taking his eyes off her and told her to go into the kitchen and wash the dishes that were in the sink. Charlie had no idea what was happening but she did know, she asked for this, whatever this was. There certainly wasn't anything like this in Laura's sex books.

Charlie started the water running in the sink and then felt his gaze on her. He had come into the kitchen. She couldn't hear him over the water, the thundering of the blood in her ears and her own disturbed thoughts, but she felt him. She glanced over her shoulder as he sat at the kitchen table behind her to watch her. Self-consciously, she bent over to open the dishwasher.

"Are you deliberately trying to defy me?" he asked in a low growl.

"No. Um. No, Sir. You said to clean up the dishes and I . . ."

"I said to wash the dishes," he snapped. "Do you know what will happen if you do not do as you are told when you are here?"

*Oh my God.*

He got up and stood directly behind her. She could feel his hot breath on her hair and she started to visibly shake. He steadied her by grasping each of her shoulders from behind. He leaned down and whispered into her ear, "I am not going to fuck you little girl, but I will beat your ass if you don't do as you are told."

"Yes. Yes Sir."

Her voice quivered. She felt like her legs would go out from under her if he hadn't had her pinned against the sink. He left her in the kitchen and when she finished the dishes she splashed cold water on her face and collapsed onto a kitchen chair. She was shaking uncontrollably, from adrenaline, from fear, from excitement, and from extreme confusion. She thought she might cry but she didn't know why.

She finally mustered the courage to go into the living room, but she couldn't bring herself to make eye contact. "The dishes are done," she said quietly. She stared at the floor and kept her arms at her sides. When he didn't respond, she looked up to find him glaring at her.

"The dishes are done, Sir," she quickly corrected

herself and he nodded.

"Put your shirt back on, Charlotte, and take a seat." Charlie obeyed and sat down on the couch and stared at the floor. Mr. Daley knelt on the floor in front of her and took her trembling hands in his.

"Look at me, Charlie."

"I . . . I can't," she said breathless.

He gently tipped her chin up. "Yes, you can. Look at me." Charlie's eyes started to well up with tears. The anger in his eyes was gone.

"It's okay baby. Don't cry," he comforted her and stroked her hair. "Did you enjoy that? Do you want more of that baby girl?" he asked, his eyes dancing. Charlie couldn't speak. She had no idea why she enjoyed it, but she did and she definitely knew she wanted more. She quickly nodded 'yes.'

"I just don't . . ."

"Shhh," he said as he ran his finger across her soft and trembling lips. "I need you to listen to me baby." She loved the way he called her baby. "This is very important. You will go home tonight and you will go straight to bed. No smoking, no weed, no alcohol, and no sugar. You will not discuss this with anyone. In the morning you will get up on time and go to school and attend every class. You are not to speak to any boys, unless they are a teacher or your brother or father. If you obey me completely, you may come back here tomorrow night at eight o'clock with your books and the day's school assignments. Do you understand, Charlie?"

"Yes, Sir," she said in a choked whisper. "I want to come back."

"I know you do, but you must obey me," he said, his eyes serious. Charlie nodded. Mr. Daley took her hand

and led her to the door with his hand on the back of her neck. He gently guided her through the door and he quietly closed it. She could feel him watching her but she didn't turn back to look. He told her to go home and go straight to bed and that's what she was going to do.

*Chapter 18*
**Focus Charlie**


And so it began.

Monday through Thursday at precisely eight o'clock p.m. she would arrive with her books to the Daley's house. Every night would start with her standing in front of him in the foyer until he instructed her to go to the dining room and put down her books. She would put her books on the table and stand with her hands at her sides looking at the table until he gave the next instruction. Sometimes he would make her stand for thirty minutes before speaking to her and she wouldn't move a muscle. Then he would usually have her remove some article of clothing or arrange her hair in a certain way, or change into a pair of his wife's sexy shoes before sitting her down at the dining room table to begin her homework.

Their communication was very formal. Most nights he would stand behind her while she studied, shattering her concentration. He would lean down with his hands on her shoulders and whisper in her ear, "Focus, Charlie. You can do it." Sometimes he would brush her hair which drove her mad with desire. She had no idea why it affected her that way, but it would set her entire body quivering. "Focus, Baby," he would whisper, and she would have to push through and finish her homework while he gently pulled the brush through her long shiny hair. She had to push the thought of how the back of the hair brush would feel against flesh out of her mind.

Occasionally, there was talk of various punishments he might subject her to if she failed to obey him. It frightened her, but also excited her and moved her in a sexual way that drove her body wild. As a special treat when she was a "very good girl" he would give her permission to touch herself when she returned home and went to bed. She was never permitted to touch herself in front of him and she could only do it at home with his permission. Mr. Daley made it very clear that there would be no sex between them and Charlie believed him. She was completely infatuated. She loved obeying and pleasing him and being rewarded with his approval when she had done well. When she brought home a test with an "A" on it, his eyes would light up as he stroked her hair and told her what a good girl she was for studying so hard in spite of his distractions and how proud he was of her. Her favorite times, in addition to hair brushing and talk of punishments, was when he would make her wash the dishes. He would press his hardness against her back like he did that first surreal night, but she was not allowed to react.

When she did react, he would make her stand in the corner, put her over his knee and gently spank her through her jeans, or be made to walk on her hands and knees for the evening. Charlie ached for his touch and his control.

From Friday to Sunday she was lost without his commands, his soothing sexy voice and his confident but tentative touch. It was all so unnerving and raw and sexual. He didn't make physical contact every time but still managed to move her in places never actually touched. He not only aroused her sexually, he made her feel loved and protected. She would do anything to see the pride and sweetness in his eyes when he told her she was his good girl.

One Thursday evening as Mr. Daley was driving past her house on the way home from work, she was speaking with one of her brother's friends on the front porch. She was explaining to the boy that her brother was not home and that she was not permitted to have male visitors, which made her feel good and special to say. The boy had just told a joke and Charlie was laughing as Mr. Daley drove by. She caught his glare and knew instantly that she was in trouble. She hadn't done anything wrong but she knew she would not be given a chance to explain. Her stomach did somersaults for four hours until it was time to arrive at the Daley's. She knew better than to show up early. She knew better than to show up late. She knew the rules.

As she walked in, the color of his face told her what she already feared. She was in trouble. He slammed the front door closed and she reflexively looked up the stairs to listen for Dillon. Then he knocked the books out of her hands. Charlie froze, but held her tears. *Don't cry*, she reminded herself. He seethed at her but said nothing intelligible as she stood perfectly still, holding her breath. She looked at the floor and offered no explanation. "On your knees," he ordered. She immediately dropped to her knees and waited. Her mind was racing. What was going to happen now? After what seemed like an eternity with him towering over her, he finally spoke.

"Pick up your books and go to the dining table and do your homework and do-not-speak," he ordered through gritted teeth.

Maybe there wasn't going to be a punishment. This thought brought her both relief and disappointment. But she was wrong, there was a punishment. The worst punishment of all, deprivation.

Charlie sat at the dining room table doing her homework, trying desperately to focus while Mr. Daley sat one room away in the dark, not making a sound. She couldn't see him but she could feel him. She could feel his anger, his frustration, his disappointment and she wanted to die. It was worse than any physical punishment he had ever doled out or taunted her with. It was gut-wrenching. After an hour she started to choke up and she broke her ordered silence.

"Please, Sir," she sobbed, "I can't take this." From the next room came the barely audible order.

"Not. One. Fucking. Word. Charlotte."

The dam broke. The tears came and she couldn't stop them. She didn't cry this hard when her mother left. She was broken. *Why tonight?* Thursday night, the hardest night of all to leave him. At ten o'clock she put down her pencil and gathered her books and stood next to her chair awaiting his command as she did every night.

"Leave," he said, without getting up.

*No*, she thought. *No fucking way. I am not leaving like this. I can't. I won't survive the weekend. S*he sobbed.

"Leave now!" he screamed and she ran for the door. Charlie cried all the way home, she cried as she crawled into bed, and she cried most of the night and most of the next day at school. From Friday afternoon until Monday she was bedridden and practically catatonic. Not that anyone noticed. She had no idea what Monday night held. *Was it over? Was she expected at 8:00?* She had broken the rules and he said there would be punishment, and there was and she never wanted to feel that way ever again. *Would he give her another chance?* She would gladly take a hundred beatings than to ever go through that again.

After school she prepared herself and then paced in the kitchen like a circus cat, willing the clock to move faster. At seven fifty-five she walked to his house. He opened the door before she knocked and pulled her inside. He stared at her tear-filled eyes and again knocked her books to the floor.

Then, he pulled her into his arms and embraced her in a way he never had before. He let out an audible sigh as he pulled her in closer. "My poor baby. Are you okay?" he whispered, fully aware of the power he had over her. Charlie collapsed in his arms with relief and exhaustion. He picked her up and carried her to the rocking chair where he held her and rocked her while she gently wept in his arms. She wrapped her arms tightly around his neck and nuzzled her face into his neck while he soothed her.

"I hated doing that to you. I have been out of my mind since you left here Thursday, but you gave me no choice," he said gently stroked her hair. "You have to follow the rules. You have to obey me, Charlie. There is too much at stake and I have to trust that you will do what I tell you to do and I told you no boys."

Charlie nodded and tightened her grip on him. He could have been saying anything. Charlie didn't care. All she cared about was how this was making her feel; his protection, his compassion for her, and his concern. The connection she was feeling, she had with no other human being in her life.

"It's okay baby girl. I've got you. You will do what you are told now?"

"Yes, Sir."

At ten o'clock he woke her from her sleep, still draped over him, still rocking.

"It's time to go home Charlie."

He pushed the hair back from her face and she

smiled shyly at him. They were locked in a moment. His eyes were soft, hers were sleepy and they both felt it at the same time. Something had changed between them. Some line had been crossed. Charlie wanted his mouth on hers, but she sensed his panic and quickly jumped up and grabbed her books and headed for the door not wanting to give him any opportunity to examine it.

The next few weeks were strained. Mr. Daley was clearly losing his battle to remain unaffected. Several nights he sent her home early with no explanation, but she knew why. Charlie was painfully torn. All these months Mr. Daley's behavior towards her could be considered weird and even inappropriate, but what else could anyone say? They hadn't had sex. They had never even kissed. But now, there was a hunger in his eyes she hadn't seen before the deprivation night. She knew instinctively she could tip the scales, if she chose to. Her body wanted to, but her heart couldn't bear the thought of taking him someplace he said didn't want to go— couldn't go. Then, fate stepped in to solve the problem she couldn't solve on her own.

One night, Charlie was late arriving at Mr. Daley's house. Very late. She was never late. It was against the rules, but this was out of her control. Her brother Tom had gotten into another fight and was hurt and his friend had ditched him. Charlie had no car, but Laura did and she came to pick Charlie up so they could go and pick up Tom together. Laura refused to go get Tom alone. Like everyone else, she was afraid of him. After Laura dropped them off Charlie ran into the house to get her books and rushed to the Daley's house. It was nine-fifteen. She was nervous but had a good excuse and she was sure that Mr. Daley would be understanding. He was not the same man since he rocked her to sleep in his arms. He cared about her and he was helping her. It was weird, kinky, sexual-without-sex kind of help but Charlie was responding to it. She was eating well, sleeping well, and her grades were through the roof. He would understand.

There was no answer at his door when she knocked. She turned the door handle and it was unlocked. Perplexed, she opened the door a little and called to him. There was no answer, but she could hear the TV. She set her books on the kitchen table and spotted the 151 on the counter. *Uh oh.* She crept slowly into the living room and found him standing with a drink in one hand and his belt in the other. He cracked it against the leather couch and she jumped.

"I'm so sorry, Sir," she whispered and lowered her eyes. "My brother was . . ." she started but stopped mid-sentence. She could see from the fire in his eyes that there was no point. *Fight or flight? Which was it going to be?* Neither, she was frozen in her tracks.

"Don't say one fucking word," he barked. Okay this was not sexy. Not sexy. Again, he hit the couch with the belt and it made a loud popping noise followed by him emptying the contents of his glass into his mouth. Charlie glanced at the baby monitor. It hummed quietly. Mr. Daley was drunk and he was angry. This was new and it was scary.

He threw his empty glass on the carpet and she bent down to pick it up but he reached for her hair, grabbed a handful and pushed her onto her knees.

"Why am I angry?"

"Because I'm late. I, I broke the rules."

"Wrong!" He hit the couch again with the belt. It was even louder now that she was on the floor and she flinched instinctively.

Charlie's mind raced. "Because I, I . . ." Crack! The belt hit the couch again and she started to cry.          " I don't know what to say!"

He knelt next to her and got right in her face, "Because I was scared something had happened to you Charlotte! Do you have any idea what I have been through for the last seventy-eight minutes?"

Charlie looked up at him bewildered. "I'm so sorry. I should have called you to tell you I would be late. It was so thoughtless," she offered through her tears. His eyes flared again and his tightened jaw flexed.

"To ask you . . . to ask you if I could be late, Sir."

He let go of her hair and started to put his belt back through the loops in his jeans. *Oh thank God*, she sighed as she crumbled into a heap on the floor wiping her eyes.

"Do you think this is over?" he asked in a tone that made her shiver.

"Pull your jeans down. Now!" He sat on the couch and slapped his hand on his lap. "Now I said!"

She slid down her jeans and laid herself across his knee and he immediately began spanking her but this was different than before. This wasn't the gentle pretend spankings he had issued before. It was hard. This spanking was intended not to administer discipline, but to inflict pain. At first Charlie tightened herself against his blows but then she focused.

Focus Charlie.

She focused as he had taught her to do through all those nights of homework and distraction. The blows kept coming, each more forceful than the last, but somehow they stung less. Charlie felt her juices starting to flow. She felt a build-up coming from deep inside her.

She had no idea what was happening but she knew she didn't want it to stop. She could hear her own voice. She was both whimpering and moaning. A scream caught in her throat as he picked up the pace, pushing her over the edge. She felt her body disengage from itself as he wrapped both arms around her to keep her from falling to the floor.

"Let it go, baby." She could hear his voice in the distance as her body convulsed over and over. She couldn't see. She could hear. She wasn't even sure where she was. It felt like she was flying and then she collapsed.

He pulled her upright into his lap and held her tight.

"Sir, I don't know what…" she slurred.

"Shhhh. It's okay," he said, holding her tight. Her limbs were like Jell-O. She could not command them to respond. He held her, breathing heavily, and said nothing until she had almost nodded off in his arms.

She was startled when he started to speak.

"Do you know what that was? That was your first orgasm. You know what this means, don't you?" he asked stroking her hair.

She didn't answer and she didn't want to hear his answer. She clenched her eyes tightly willing him not to say it.

"It means our playtime is over, little girl."

Oh my God. No. Please no.

"If you come like that again in front of me, I am going to devour you and ruin my life in the process."

Charlie's eyes filled and her lower lip quivered.

"Don't baby. I have a family and this is getting out of hand. I was really scared something had happened to you tonight. I've allowed myself to get too close. You are a beautiful and amazing young woman. The guy who gets you is going to be so lucky." He hugged her tight. "You are doing so great and I am so proud of you. I want you to keep doing well, but we have to stop this. Do you understand?" She shook her head 'no' as the tears fell.

"Charlotte, all I can think about anymore is taking your virginity, and I can't do that. I won't do that." She didn't see any reason to tell him that Kip had beaten him to the punch.

"But, I think I love you Mr. Daley," she said quietly.

He laughed, not meaning to hurt her feelings but hurting them just the same.

"Oh my beautiful little girl, in a year you won't even remember my name. It will be okay," he promised. "Now, let's get you straightened up here," he said as he helped her get dressed. He lifted her chin and wiped her eyes. "Hey, no more crying." She pressed her lips together and made herself stop, for him. "That's my good girl," he said and she closed her eyes, savoring it.

"Will I see you anymore? Babysit sometime maybe?" she asked nervously.

"Charlie, why are you asking me a question you already know the answer to?"

She nodded and let a few more tears fall. He walked her to the door and gazed down at her with sadness in his eyes, kissed her on the forehead and it was over.

*Chapter 19*
## I Did It for You

Charlie lay in her bed in her apartment, right on the brink of orgasm. She used the memory of that last spanking from Mr. Daley as the fuel she would need to climax and sleep. She writhed at the thought of the pain as his hand crashed onto her bare flesh and she came hard; her body rocking in her bed as she let go. The sunlight fought to invade her room. The curtains could have been standing open and it wouldn't have stopped her from drifting off into a peaceful, satiated sleep. She awoke to a loud banging noise.

*Not again. Not the train.*

Bang. Bang. Bang.

She sat up in bed and looked for it. It wasn't the train. Someone was pounding on her front door. Charlie hurried to the door wrapped in her green terry cloth shorty robe and opened the door without checking to see who it was. She found Jake Adams staring at her, his mouth half open.

"What? What's the matter?"

Jake stumbled to find the words, caught off guard by her bare legs and her partially opened robe. "We . . . aren't we . . . Sarge, it's five 'til nine."

"What?! Holy crap!" She motioned him in. "Please sit. Oh my God I'm so sorry," she ran in a circle. "Do you want something to drink while I get dressed?" Jake started laughing and grabbed her by the shoulders.

"Why are you laughing? Are you screwing with me?" she asked as she strained to look past him at the clock. Eight fifty-eight. He was not screwing with her.

"Charlie, breathe. Go get ready. It's okay." She nodded and took a breath. "Charlie, breathe! Fucking suits!" Moses squawked. Jake jumped, causing her to laugh as she headed for her bedroom, pointing to the covered cage.

It was their last night together. The stakeout schedule had only been drawn out for a week and the three days that she and Jake would cover were just about over. The thought made her miserable. She had been so adamant that he not be included in the stakeout schedule and now she couldn't bear the thought that it was almost over. She had time for a quick rinse off in the shower but not enough time for hair and make-up. *Damn it*, she thought. She wanted to be perfect tonight. *It's not a date, Brown Eyes,* she could hear Thompson saying and she shook her head at her silliness.

She threw on a pair of dark jeans and a sweatshirt, no makeup, and pulled her hair back into a ponytail which she pulled through her Jimmy Buffett ball cap. She was ready to go in just ten minutes. Jake was profoundly impressed and completely swept off his feet. He loved a woman who could pull off a baseball cap.

"Wow," he said before he realized it was out of his mouth.

"Wow?"

"Um, yeah, well, you got ready so fast."

She raised an eyebrow at him.

"I like you like this. No make-up, the baseball hat. It works," he smiled wryly, and she thought her knees would buckle.

"Oh." She grinned at him and they stood there staring at each other, lost in the place they always found themselves in, not sure how to make their way back.

"Fucking suits!" Moses squawked, and they both started laughing.

"That is one damn annoying bird."

"I know," she giggled. "That's Moses. Come on, we're late!"

"Because of you!" he yelled after her, following her out the door and down the stairs.

They marked-up on the radio hoping that no one would notice that it was nine twenty-five and they still had another fifteen minutes to travel to their spot, but they failed to mention that to dispatch.

"10-4 Unit 57," Jan purred over the radio.

"Jesus, who is that?" Jake's ears perked up and Charlie felt a flash of jealousy.

"Jan," she said with no further explanation.

"Let me guess. Three hundred pounds and a face that would sink a thousand ships?" He asked with a chuckle.

"No and no."

"Really?" Jake said with a grin. Charlie pretended to ignore his comment but he could tell she was annoyed and found it completely adorable. They got to their spot by nine forty-five and settled in. "Thanks to you we have no coffee," he complained.

"I know. I really am sorry. I'm not a flake, I swear it. I just slept so damn good today," she said smiling, as she remembered her descent into slumber.

"Hmm."

"Hmm what?" she asked coyly, grateful that the darkness was masking her crimson cheeks.

"Oh, nothing."

The target's car was not in the driveway but pulled in at ten o'clock p.m. on the nose.

Daniel Silver was a mousy little creep. He looked at

least ten years older than his actual age.

He was a former postal carrier, a loser, and a pervert. Shortly after landing the first decent job he had ever held, he began befriending young boys on his new mail route and quickly learned about an eight-year-old whose single mother left him alone on Thursday afternoons when there was a conflict between the time the child returned home from school and her second job. Charlie knew that there were other victims. There had to be, molesting is almost never a singular crime. Silver had taunted her with the fact that he had been doing this for years, and all she had was one lousy charge. Charlie wanted to kill him. The Daniel Silvers of the world needed to die, she had told her online friend AJ and AJ had agreed. Charlie had worked around the clock on the Silver case but she had been unable to find any other victims. She spent weeks conducting knock-and-talks on Silver's mail route but came up empty. The hooker, the handyman, and the parrot weren't talking.

Charlie found that the parents of the young children had a hard time dealing with even the mention of molestation. It was a form of denial that was consistent and baffling. They didn't want the police to speak with their children about such a horrifying subject and they didn't want or have the training to broach the subject themselves without traumatizing their children. Some realities are just too difficult for parents to process.

The truth is that one out of five children in America is likely to be molested by age fourteen, mostly by people they know and probably by someone to whom they are related. One out of five. Those are pretty powerful odds to dodge.

Charlie believed there was no such thing as an over-protective parent. She vowed that if she ever had children, there would be a lot of childhood pastimes they would miss out on; youth groups, scouting, church, sleepovers, and camping. These were the hunting grounds of predators. As long as she was with her children, they could enjoy all these things, but until they were old enough to understand sexual molestation and how to defend against it she would remain vigilant. Charlie pledged to children not yet born that their eyes would never look like the eyes of the children she interviewed; eyes that haunted her dreams, asleep and awake.

Silver gained the boy's trust by bringing him small gifts when he delivered the mail. That progressed to asking if he could come inside the house to rest or use the bathroom. By the tenth visit into the house he started molesting the boy. The lonely boy cooperated with the initial requests of you-show-me-yours-and-I'll-show-you-mine, then to touching with the promise of more gifts. When Silver progressed to sodomy the boy started to resist, but Silver convinced him that when the police learned that his mother had left a little kid home alone, they would take her to jail forever.

Daniel Silver knew that the look on the faces of the boys he was raping was nothing compared to the look in their eyes when they processed that the one parent they had left would be taken away from them forever for letting this happen. It was powerful insurance against cooperation and prosecution and it crippled Charlie's case. The boy's mother put it together when she started finding traces of blood in the boy's underwear and remembered coming home one day as the creepy mailman was leaving, saying that her son was kind enough to let him use the bathroom. Throughout the investigation there was nothing Charlie could say to the boy to convince him that telling the police what had happened to him would not result in his mother getting into trouble. He would only nod when asked if Daniel Silver hurt him, then he would shut down. Charlie knew the case was shaky, but she made the charge anyway, hoping Silver would try to cut a deal. Her hopes were dashed when Silver remained defiant and arrogant to the bitter end.

Silver's statement to Charlie that he had done this for years was insufficient in the court's eyes to count as a confession. The case was thrown out, though he did lose his job. Now here she was, having to sit outside his house and protect his sorry ass. *Maybe she and Jake should go for coffee*, she thought . . . *in Florida.*

"Jesus, we almost missed logging this because of me" she shook her head.

"Let it go, Sarge. The important thing is we are here now, and now we can settle in and relax. Log it in."

"Yea, I guess," she said still disappointed in herself.

"You need coffee."

"No, you need coffee."

"Do we dare?" he asked.

"No," she said firmly. "Suck it up."

"Okay, you stay, I'll go. I can walk it, it's not that far."

"Jake it's at least a mile to Stop and Sip! Let me call a patrol unit."

"And blow our cover?" he said. "No way. I won't be long." Above her protest he was out of the car and jogging away.

"Crap!" she said out loud. "Fucking Feds."

Over an hour later she jumped out of her skin when he raised the back hatch of the SUV. He closed the hatch and appeared at the side of the door, a cigar clenched in his teeth.

"Jesus Christ Adams! That is not fucking funny. Where the hell have you been? It's been over an hour. Don't you answer your goddamn phone? I was just about to send a patrol unit to look for you! Put out that cigar. It smells good though. Jesus! Your hair is soaked! Where is my coffee?"

"You're rambling." He handed her the double cupped coffee. "You like cigars?" he asked with an impish grin.

"I do," Charlie said, her eyes softening as she composed herself. "Thompson smoked them, and the smell always takes me back, but you're not supposed to smoke on a stakeout Super Fed. Didn't they teach you anything at Quantico?" He raised an eyebrow at her and she lowered her eyes. Damn it, how did he get her to do that?

"Face it Sarge, this stakeout idea is a bust." He blew a waft of smoke out of the open window and dried his hair and neck with a napkin. Charlie breathed in what she could of the smoke, and of him, loving the two smells mixed together. If women were capable of a hard-on, she'd have had one.

"It was farther than I thought," he admitted sheepishly.

"No shit. I guess it is a bust, but let's not get complacent. When you think you are in the clear, that's when it happens," she cautioned. Jake shrugged and put out the cigar.

They talked all night, savoring their last stake-out hours together. They both knew that this precious one-on-one time was about to be over and they both wondered what they were going to do about it. At about five o'clock a.m. Jake started to nod off and she let him go. Once he was fully asleep, she got brave and reached over and stroked the little waves in his hair.

The sun was starting to rise and Charlie was starting to drift off herself. In her half-sleepy state and with her defenses down, it hit her hard. She was falling for him. She was sure of it. She really didn't know for sure what was happening on his end; he was so guarded, but she was definitely . . .

"AHHHHHHHHHHHHHHHHHHHHHHHHH!"    A blood curdling scream ripped through the morning fog.

Charlie's thoughts were shattered. Jake jolted awake and reached for his gun. Charlie had her gun in one hand and her radio in the other as they both bailed out of the SUV and headed toward the scream. Charlie brought the radio to her mouth.

"Wait until we see what we have," Jake said as they ran. Charlie ignored him and keyed the mic. "Unit 57 unknown trouble—Detail #4. Code 1."

Jake glared at her while they ran, angry that she called for backup. They rounded the corner to find a woman standing at the open back gate to Daniel Silver's backyard. Charlie ran to the woman holding up her badge out in front of her, so the woman would know she was a police officer.

"Ma'am we're police officers. What's wrong? What's happening?" All the woman could do was point and cry. Charlie and Jake turned to look into the backyard of Daniel Silver, through the open gate of a six-foot fence. The yard was mostly taken up by a swimming pool. They could barely make out the writing scrawled along the back of the fence. Written in a dark paint, it read I DID IT FOR YOU. Floating face down in the pool was Daniel Silver and a dog, both lifeless. The woman continued her hysteria.

"Ma'am please! It's okay, come with me," Charlie said and motioned for Jake to hold his position while she tried to drag the woman away from the scene.

"Dora!" the woman cried as a ratty little terrier be-bopped out of the back yard and into her arms.

Finally, a cruiser arrived and she handed the hysterical woman and rat-dog off to the officer and returned to Jake. He started for the back door, but Charlie grabbed his arm. "We have more backup units coming, wait." He glared at her, but waited. As the sun continued to rise, the scene became more and more horrifying. Daniel Silver's body floated in the red pool water. His head was wrapped in plastic wrap and a large gutted Doberman floated a few feet away with blood still oozing from its sliced abdomen. The writing on the fence . . . clearly not paint.

I DID IT FOR YOU.

Charlie felt the blood draining from her face as she sat crouched next to Jake and the patrol units set up at the front of the house. Jake kept his eye on the back door but reached behind him and reassuringly gave her hand a squeeze. She nodded to the patrol sergeant and she and Jake made entry through the unlocked rear sliding door while the patrol units covered the front.

The inside of the house was a horror show and reeked of blood and chemicals. Charlie's stomach objected, almost to the point of upheaval. Once the house had been cleared, Jake and Charlie returned to the SUV where Clint and the captain, who had arrived at the scene, were now waiting with looks of both concern and...*what? Something else*.

"You two okay?" the captain asked. Clint draped

a protective arm around Charlie's shoulder, drawing a glare from Jake.

"Is this where you two were set up?" the captain said as he stood next to the Fed Mobile.

"Yes, Sir," Charlie answered.

"It's a good spot," the captain said and nodded.

"How long do you think he's been dead?"

Charlie shook her head, "I don't know, Cap. It looked like he'd been there a while."

"Do you think it happened before you got here last night?" the captain pressed.

"No," Jake jumped in. "We were here when he got home last night. Our last log entry was at twenty-two-hundred, when he arrived home alone. Nothing after that."

The captain rolled this information over in his mind. "I don't know why you didn't hear anything though."

"You will know once you see the crime scene, Captain," Jake said quickly, trying to disrupt the captain's thought pattern. "It looks like everything happened inside the house before the bodies were disposed of in the pool."

"Bodies? As in more than one?" the captain asked with alarm.

"One is a dog," Clint said absent-mindedly. Jake shot him a look, which Clint ignored. Charlie shook off her fatigue and shock, and filled in the captain and Clint about the screaming woman and the message on the back of the fence. Clint became visibly uncomfortable as Charlie explained what was written there, and the blood that was used to write it. Clint knew the message was for Charlie. He knew that Charlie knew the message was for her, but he didn't want anyone to say it out loud. No one did.

"Any ideas, Charlie?" the captain asked.

"How the hell would she know what it means?" Clint snapped protectively. The captain fired a warning look at him, ignored his outburst and made a mental note to chew his ass out later.

"You worked the Daniel Silver case, Charlie. Can you connect any of the dots?"

"I can't, Cap," she said quietly.

"The Count has arrived," announced Clint, trying to change the subject and motioning toward the Crime Scene van. The captain gave Charlie a quick paternal hug and a pat on the back. "You two can call it a night. A day. You can write up your statements tomorrow. Clint will take primary." Clint nodded in agreement.

"You want me to drive you home Charlie?" Clint offered.

"What? No, Clint. You've got point on this."

Jake glared at Clint. The captain saw what was happening and stepped in. "Okay, okay, we're all a little stressed. You two get out of here. Come in tomorrow and get your reports done. Clint will call you if he has any questions that can't wait so keep your phones on, okay?" Charlie agreed and Jake nodded toward the SUV and started walking, hoping Charlie would follow. He needed to get her away from Clint.

*Chapter 20*
**Breathe, Sarge**

Clint couldn't help himself. "Hey Count. Better double up your booties. It's nasty inside."

Grecko ignored Clint as he walked past him. A good CSI prefers to not know the facts of a crime scene and let the evidence speak for itself. If he listened to what Clint had to say, he might be influenced despite his best efforts, so he kept walking to the front of the house and waved his hand acknowledging Clint's comment. He had been apprised by dispatch that the bodies were in the backyard pool. Meticulously, room by room, Grecko documented with photos. All of the rooms appeared undisturbed. That's always hard to tell in a house you are unfamiliar with but bad housekeeping helps. Dust is a great tool for investigators.

Watching his footing, Grecko turned the corner of the foyer hallway leading to the kitchen and family room. He swallowed hard. *Some things, you're not supposed to get used to.*

Getting closer to the end of the trail of blood he followed, his nose inhaled that familiar odor . . . bleach. A CSI's worst nightmare. He straddled the trail until he reached the master bedroom. In all his years of working crime scenes this was one of the worst scenes he had processed. The wall nearest the headboard and the headboard itself were covered in blood and smeared. *The bleach, he used the bleach to clean up,* thought Grecko. Thrown on the floor adjacent to the closet were sheets balled up, red and wet with bleach.

Once Grecko was finished with his cursory he knew

exactly what he needed to process this crime scene . . . time and lots of it. The interior of the house could wait. The priority needed to be placed on the backyard and pool. He knew that if the bodies stayed in the pool water much longer, there was a good chance evidence would be lost. The water in the pool would need to be drained. The sliding glass door was open with the blood trail going over the top of the threshold, across the concrete patio, and coming to an end at the pool.

Floating face down in the red pool water was a white male in his boxer shorts, no shirt, and plastic wrap surrounding his head. The dog, a Doberman Pincher, was floating next to the victim. "Jesus Christ, the dog too . . . what a sadist." The dog's head was wrapped in plastic just like its owner. The dog looked like he had been butchered. On the fence scrawled in blood was a message . . . I DID IT FOR YOU.

"Charlie," Grecko whispered, and felt himself getting unsteady.

Distracted as he was, Grecko carried on. He made the call himself since he was going to have to convince the M.E. to let him pull the body out of the water. Forensic evidence was disappearing in the water with every passing minute. Clint was standing outside of the gated fence when he heard a bellow from within the perimeter. "Hey Clint I need some muscle in here."

"Is the CSI asking for assistance from me? Well, well, well let me go grab my ice skates." Clint walked into the backyard. As he entered through the gate he could not help but to again notice I DID IT FOR YOU written in blood. Clint's mind was racing. Was the killer taunting Charlie or the police in general?

"So, just what do you need my help with?"

Grecko was laying out two body bags and lining each with clean white sheets. Clint's eyes shifted back and forth. "Oh no, if you think I'm going to help you get those floaters out of the water you're mistaken."

"Come on Clint. How about backing it up and getting over here. I'll do the icky part so you won't need to dirty your pretty little hands."

Clint walked over to the pool and looked at the floaters, wrinkling his nose in disdain. "We have to wait till the medical investigator gets here."

"We can't. Exigent circumstances. We're losing evidence every second they are left in the pool. Just put on a couple pairs of gloves. See Mr. Boxer Shorts?"

"Yeah, what about him?"

"I'm going to take the pool catcher and pull him closer to the edge. While I pull him on to the patio I want you to slide the sheet under him. Then we'll carry the sheet and him into the body bag. Got it?"

"Yeah, I'm not a moron." Grecko had a grin on his face thinking what he truly thought about Clint . . . *moron*.

The two men struggled with Boxer Shorts but managed to get him and his dog out and into separate body bags. Grecko could now see the dog's chest and belly had been sliced open but the organs were still there. Daniel Silver was the same. His chest was sliced open. His organs, intact.

Clint heard a 'hello' coming from the other side of the fence. It was the medical investigator. Grecko yelled, "Come on in. By the pool."

"Bagged and tagged?"

"Yep, and all yours. We'll be lucky to find any usable evidence thanks to the water."

"What do you think is with the plastic?"

Rogers shrugged and said, "Lots to talk about at the next medical examiners' conference."

"Autopsy today?" Grecko asked.

Rogers sighed.

Grecko pushed, "This is our fourth victim and there is a good chance more victims are in our forecast since we are dealing with a serial killer."

"I know. I'll see what I can do. I'm still working up and writing the report from our last guy."

Grecko decided it was time to focus on the interior crime scene. Evidence never lies; people do, evidence doesn't. Follow the evidence. He needed to stop this for Charlie. He wanted to be the one to put an end to it. For her. He would do it for her.

"Breathe, Sarge," Jake ordered when they settled into the SUV, leaving Clint and Grecko to their work.

"I'm okay. Just tired. Confused. Jesus Jake, it happened while we were sitting here."

"Yeah," he said quietly and then turned up the radio to end the conversation.

"I'm coming upstairs," Jake said as he pulled into a parking space in front of Charlie's apartment. She didn't even pretend to object.

Once they were inside the apartment, she asked him if he wanted a beer, which he refused. "You need some sleep, Charlie," he motioned to the couch. "I'll just hang out here."

"Hi Brown Eyes," Moses greeted them. They both ignored the happy bird.

"Do you think he knew we were out there?"

"Silver? I doubt it."

"No, not Silver," she said, irritated. "The suspect.

The killer!"

"We're not going to talk about this now, Charlotte. We're too punchy. Now go to bed."

Their eyes locked and she had to force herself to look away so she could make her feet move toward the bedroom. She quickly stripped off her clothes and took a hot shower. In minutes she was under the covers and fast asleep. Jake was out cold as soon as he knew she was asleep. He didn't know how he knew she was asleep, but he knew. He sensed it. His last thought before he drifted off was whether or not he had thrown the dead bolt on the door, but he found himself unable to fight his way back out to check it. Jake and Charlie slept the sleep of the entombed in separate rooms; unconscious in their exhaustion.

Hours later he arrived.  He crept through the apartment like a panther. Without making a sound, he quietly opened the door to Charlie's room. For a moment he thought she was gone. She was barely audible as she slept and barely visible in the mound of blankets. He shouldn't do this. He didn't want to do it but it was out of his control and the thought brought him to a shiver. *Out of his control.* He instinctively looked behind him. Watch your six. He took very slow deliberate steps as he moved toward her. His eyes finally adjusted in the dark room and he could finally make out her face. She looked like an angel and slept like a child but that was where the innocence ended. A burning feeling heated up inside his gut. Inside his balls. *No. This is what he did not want.* Everything he did, he did to avoid this feeling. Suddenly, desire turned to anger. She would not do this to him. He would not allow her to do it to him. He was in control, not her. He reached for her, pulled the covers up around her neck, and gently tucked them all around her and left.

Charlie sighed in her sleep and it melted him. Melted his heat, his anger, and his heart. He felt tears welling up in his eyes as he willed himself to walk away.

*How did he get here? Why did he stop? Why was he crying? Tears? He hadn't cried since he was sixteen years old.*

Hours later Charlie woke as she did every day, with a song in her head she couldn't place. It was a strange way to wake up and she attributed it to years of waking to her brother and his partying friends with their heavy metal music blaring into the wee hours. The room was bright and she knew she had slept a long time. She must have needed it, she thought, because she felt good, really good, until she remembered.

*Oh shit. Oh no.*

She could see the blood on the fence I DID IT FOR YOU and the body of Daniel Silver and the gutted dog floating in the red swimming pool. She started to get up but realized she couldn't move. She was restrained—mummified in a cocoon of blankets. She fought her way out as if someone were holding her against her will. Breathless, her eyes darted around the room looking for danger but there was only sunshine. She started to reach for her laptop and then remembered Jake and bolted out of the bedroom to look for him, startling him awake as the bedroom door flew open. He was curled up on the couch, no blanket, still dressed, shoes and all.

"Hey there," he said with a sleepy half-smile. "You okay, Sarge?" She stared at him wide eyed, unable to answer.

*Am I okay? No. I am not okay. I haven't been okay for a long time*, she quietly confessed, but only to herself, not to him. Jake quickly got to his feet and guided her by her shoulders to the couch.

"Sit down, Charlie," he instructed.

"Y-you didn't have to stay," she stammered. "I'm used to being on my own."

"I did it for you," he said.

*Shit!* The second the words were out of his mouth his stomach jumped into his throat. Charlie stared at him in shock. He knew he had screwed up and quickly changed the subject.

"It's a cruel trick the mind plays on you isn't it? Mornings?" he said trying to engage her. "Mornings?" she asked, confused.

"You know, when something bad happens and you wake up the next day and forget about it for the first few seconds after you wake up?" She nodded, understanding exactly what he meant. Charlie had felt it after her parent's death, after Thompson's death, and after her husband left. She knew exactly what he meant and wondered how many mornings Jake woke up like that after his parents died in the earthquake. She wondered if her ex endured the mornings she had endured for months. Many months. Did he wake up and think "How could I do this to her?" or did he just smile and think, "Thank God I am rid of her," or "I have a new life to think about it, she no longer exists." Charlie was forever running these scenarios through her head. *Why didn't he fight for her?* But she suspected she knew the answer. She wasn't good enough to fight for. It was easier just to accept this.

"Did you sleep?" he asked.

"I did. I don't know how but somehow I did. Actually Jake," she swallowed hard, "I think it really helped having you here. I felt . . . safe," she said quietly, opening herself to him.

"You were safe. Perfectly safe," he said resolutely, "and you always will be when I am around," he lied.

She smiled a small smile and he reached for her face and pushed her bangs out of her eyes. Her stomach flinched at his touch and she could feel the blood rushing to her head. Then just as quickly he pulled away.

"How about I run out and get us some coffee?" he said.

"Coffee you twit!" Moses squawked and Jake rolled his eyes. There was a long silence as they locked eyes and she wrestled with the fact that he had just pulled away from her—again. The rejection closed her throat. How much rejection was one person expected to endure in one life?

"No, Jake you should go home," she said, embarrassed.

"Charlie, I want to stay," he said with determination. "I think we should stick together."

Confused she innocently said, "Why?"

His heart melted all over again. *Damn this woman.*

"Because of the message?" she asked. She shook her head. "We don't know that that was for me. It could just as easily been meant for the molestation victim." She waved a hand and avoided Jake's eyes. "I did it for you—could have all kinds of implications. Jeez Adams, how long have you been doing this job, ten minutes?"

Jake tipped her chin up and forced her to look at him. "Charlie . . ." He started to speak but the sound of his voice was leaving her. Her blood was pounding in her ears making it impossible to hear what he was saying. Electricity pulsed from his fingers, through her chin and into her stomach. She looked at his lips trying to follow his words but that was making it worse. His perfect soft full lips. *If we kiss, it will be my decision, not yours. Do you understand?* His words echoed in her head making her body ache. She leaned into him. He drew her closer and then quickly pushed her face down into his chest.

"Damn it, Charlie!" he scolded her while he held her tightly to him. "I'm trying to keep you safe and you are trying to distract the hell out of me. Now quit it!" he said with annoyance.

"Nice to know I am having some effect on you." She pulled back and dropped her head into her hands. He stood up and faced her as she sat. She could see his shoes toe-to-toe with her bare feet and she knew he was both towering over her and glaring at her but she didn't want to look up. It shook her to her core that he could resist her so easily. *Why couldn't he feel the connection she was feeling? And who asked him to protect her anyway? Is that what this was? Pity? She was a cop for Christ's sake! Why didn't he . . .* But before she could finish her thought she felt him gather the hair from the base of her neck in his fist and yank her head up and back.

Eye contact would be made now because he decided it would be so.

Whoa, she hadn't seen these eyes before. He looked angry and a little . . . crazy and she could swear she caught an actual flash of light in his right eye. She started to speak, but his mouth was on hers trapping the gasp in her throat.

Her first instinct was to pull away. Perhaps because he surprised her or maybe it was just a pure primal self-defense reaction but it was pointless, she had no prayer of stopping him. He tasted salty and sweet and wet and his mouth devoured hers. She used her hands to hold him at a distance she could manage but he grabbed her wrists and locked them behind her back and used his body to lay her back on the couch crushing her underneath him. She shook and whimpered while he bore down on her. Slowly she surrendered to it, giving up the fight, she relaxed her arms and he turned loose of her wrists and he held either side of her head guiding her mouth into his, their tongues jousting. When she forced her head to one side to gasp for air he grabbed her again by the hair and pulled down causing her to arch her back. He glared into her eyes, inflamed, exhilarated, and breathless and asked, "Regular or decaf?"

When she didn't answer he got up and headed for the door and added, "Lock this dead bolt." She stared at him, woozy and disoriented. He slammed his giant hands together . . . CLAP! And she jumped. "Charlie! Dead-bolt! Now!" And he walked out of the door.

"What the fuck was that?" she yelled out loud after he had closed the door. As he listened at the other side of the door, he grinned then his brow furrowed and his face turned grave. *Fuck!* He thought as he bolted down the stairs.

*Chapter 21*
## Charlie Has Left the Building

Charlie sat on the couch rocking herself for twenty minutes before she could bring herself to stand on shaky legs following Jake's kiss. "It's okay," she said out loud to herself. "It's okay. He's a cop and that's not okay and we are working a case together and that's not okay, but this is what you have waited for. A man who knows how to make you feel like this. Taken. He's here. Don't freak out. Don't freak out," she mumbled as she made her way to the bathroom.

After a long hot shower she was on solid ground. She felt bad that she had locked the bedroom door, worried that she might hurt his feelings when he returned with the coffee but it was a chance she would have to take. This man was completely unpredictable, and she did not want to reenact the *Psycho* shower scene with him if he decided to pop his head into the shower to offer her a cup of joe. The thought of Jake sneaking into her bathroom made her wetter than the water that rained down on her. She jumped out soaking wet and ran to the bedroom door, unlocked the lock and ran back to the shower, and waited. She stayed so long her fingers were raisins and the hot water was running lukewarm. No Jake.

She dried off, tiptoed naked across the room and listened at the bedroom door, but heard nothing. She imagined him on the other side of the door listening too and giggled. She dried her hair and applied her make-up, mortified by the pre-shower mess she had seen in the mirror after he left. The thought of his kiss made the hair on her arms stand up and her pelvis ache. She put on her comfy jeans with the holes in the knees—her holy jeans because she knew how great her butt looked in them, pulled on an oversize white sweater with no bra so her attentive nipples would teasingly poke through the light fabric, and casually strolled into the kitchen in her bare feet. On the counter she found her coffee and a note;

Gone to the hotel to shower and change. Do not leave the apartment until I return. I'll be back later with dinner. Lock the damn deadbolt I said!

No mention of the kiss, its heat, or their connection. No attempt to view her in the shower or finish what he started. Charlie's face flushed with confusion and embarrassment. *There is no way he was not affected by that kiss.*

It was three o'clock in the afternoon, but it felt like morning. She paced for about an hour and then called his cell. No answer. *Goddammit. What the heck was with the hot and cold treatment?* She paced some more. Unsure of what to do next she ran for her laptop. She had been unable to reach AJ yesterday and she prayed he would be online now.

VABlueAngel: AJ?

**AJ101-789: Hey Beautiful! I was just getting ready to log off. I miss you Angel.**

VABlueAngel: I know AJ, I'm so sorry. This serial case has really gotten out of hand. I just haven't had much time.

*Or privacy*, she thought.

**AJ101-789: Not another homicide?**

VABlueAngel: Yes. Except this time, I was there when it happened.

**AJ101-789: What the fuck Charlie?**

VABlueAngel: Hey! Hey! Hey! Language lol

**AJ101-789: Fuck my language. Are you okay? What happened?**

Charlie went into detail about the murder. She would normally never release this information about a case but this was an unsaved live conversation, not an email, and AJ was thousands of miles and another continent away. The delicate nature of his assignment in the Middle East and his police background made her confident that he would respect the necessity for complete discretion. She had been sharing details of her most horrifying molestation cases with him for the last year and she trusted him implicitly.

**AJ101-789: I don't like the sound of this at all. If they haven't pulled you from this case already, they need to.**

She frowned but then realized that she liked that AJ was a former cop and knew that she was too close to this. She assembled a flimsy defense.

VABlueAngel: It's not my case AJ. It's Clint's case. I was just on the stakeout. It could have been anyone of the other four targets we were sitting on. It just happened to be mine.

She decided not to share the bloody message on the fence with him but felt bad about it.

**AJ101-789: Who were you partnered with?**
VABlueAngel: Why are you asking me a question

that doesn't matter?

No response.

VABlueAngel: AJ?

No response.

VABlueAngel: Yo!

This was very unlike her friend. Was he jealous?

**AJ101-789: I'm here. I'm glad that you are part-nered up with the Fed. Someone needs to have your back. Is this guy any good?**

Now there was a loaded question. *Is he any good? Yea, he's any good. He's any good at melting me with his eyes; he's any good at making me feel more protected than I have ever felt in my life; he's any good at taking control of my body and soul and reducing me to a quiver-ing mass of sexual frenzy and he's any good at complete-ly dismissing me!*

VABlueAngel: Yea, he's good.

**AJ101-789: Okay, are you back at it tonight?**

VABlueAngel: No. I'm off today.

**AJ101-789: Okay good, then MAYBE I'll be able to sleep. Please be careful Angel.**

VABlueAngel: I will AJ, I promise. Sleep.

She felt better after her talk with AJ. He made her feel loved and safe without the sexual tension and loss of control. Safe wasn't good though—that was a crock. That was exactly the relationship she had with her ex and it had buried her. She had spent three years crawling out of the hole he left her in and she still wasn't completely clear of it. Maybe she never would be. It's never safe when you hand someone your heart. Besides, she hated safe. She hated the lack of an edge in their sex life and she hated that she couldn't lose control and be her real self with him.

It worked at first. At first it was thrilling. She was in love, truly and completely in love. He was so attentive, so loving and so caring. Even the sex was good, and she had never really liked sex. She still cringed at the thought of her first sexual encounter with her brother's burn-out friend. Sex just never really did anything for her, but with her new husband sex was definitely different. It was so loving and gentle. Not really her cup of tea but sweet. He never did call her what she wanted . . . Baby. He called her Honey, Sweetie, Babe. But never Baby. She tried to get him to call her that but he always forgot and she didn't want it to be her idea, she wanted it to be his. She wanted him to be what she wanted, but he wasn't. A few times she tried to introduce her deeper desires into their lovemaking but found that he too was more turned on by submission.

*Well hells bells, they couldn't both be submissive. Somebody had to be in charge.*

She remembered enjoying being dominant over him once or twice because of how hot it made him, but it left her feeling empty and unfulfilled—envious even. When she tried to explain to him what she needed he had made her feel like a freak.

"Hey, the only reason I did this freaky shit at all is because you wanted to." He judged her. "Jesus, what the hell kind of men were you hooked up with before me?"

*Oh no, not this conversation again.*

He was so insecure and so fragile that no matter how

much she loved him, his insecurity was a complete turn off to her. She wanted a MAN. Could love and mutual interests really sustain her for a lifetime? After three years she had her answer; it could not. And when her husband took up with the Sasquatch, the dispatcher he left her for, Charlie had her way out and she took it. Since then she had mostly given up on dating and focused on her career. Men were always a disappointment in bed. *Always*, she sighed. If they had enough size and girth they could bring her to orgasm but it was like plain old vanilla frozen yogurt—no exciting flavors, no surprises, no sprinkles. It wasn't real ice cream. She knew there was more. There had to be. The only orgasm she ever had that came close to satisfying her was at the skilled hand of Mr. Daley and, oddly, that was an unconsummated relationship.

But at this moment, after Jake's kiss, she was so hopeful she thought she might explode. It was like a book about her had been written, and Jake Adams had read every page. *How in the world was she going to be able to maintain a professional relationship with him after that kiss?*

The phone rang, snapping her out of thoughts. *Finally!* To her dismay it wasn't Jake, but Clint checking on her to make sure she was okay after last night. "What's not to be okay about Clint?" she asked in a tone she borrowed from her mother. It didn't work on Clint and she chuckled at his lack of intimidation.

"I'm fine Night Rider," she said. He suggested they meet at Amy's later for a beer but she declined saying she hadn't slept well. The lie seemed to pacify him.

She didn't like lying to Clint. They were friends. She actually owed him a great deal, and he owed her. Clint was probably the person she was closest to in the whole world besides her brother Tom, but that was more about blood than contact. AJ, on the other hand, was in a completely different category. Charlie hung up and set the phone on the table and watched it, like a pot, willing it to boil. She waited and waited and waited. She called Jake twice but he didn't answer and he returned only one of her three texts; it read:

*I'll get there, when I get there. Stay put.*

"Is that right? Well fuck you, Mr. Arrogant." God, she hated feeling desperate. Looking desperate. Jesus she was acting like . . . a chick! *Unforgivable.*

By early evening Charlie had enough waiting. She slid on her white Keds and a light jacket, bid farewell to Moses who answered with "AMF." She walked across the street to Amy's Café choosing a seat where she could watch her apartment complex parking lot. Amy's Café was actually a bar. It was an old, red brick, two-story building from days of old. The red brick was exposed inside. The building had texture, history, and familiarity. It was a safe place where people looked different but they all belonged, and it was a favorite haunt of bikers and cops. Bikers meaning men in their forties with Harleys and leather club jackets. Charlie and Clint had spent many a night closing the bar down and Amy, whom Clint lusted after, never rushed them out. Tonight, she ended up being there much longer than she had intended and having three beers too many, which is to say . . . she had three beers. She couldn't hold her liquor. Thompson had always poked fun at her about her limited tolerance for "libations," as he called them. "PBR! Nectar of the gods," he would proclaim.

Finally, she saw the ostentatious SUV pull in and park. Jake stayed in the car for a few minutes and the inside cabin lit up from his phone as he was tapping on the keys. "Probably texting some waitress or nurse or stripper," Charlie growled. The police officers' three major food groups. *When was she ever going to learn? They were all alike. ALL of them. They would offer the slightest glimmer of hope only to be shown for the fragile, needy train wrecks that they all were*—at least the ones Charlie was attracted to. It was all such a bait and switch. *Fuckers.*

"Ding" her phone text chimed. It was from him.

*I'm here, unlock the door.*

"Joke's on you pal," she sneered. "There is nobody home. Charlie has left the building." She held up her beer in a mock toast to him. *See how you like waiting and waiting and not hearing from someone, you jerk.*

She watched as he climbed out of the black tank. He was carrying the tell-tale aqua colored plastic bag from the Gay Dolphin; hmmm, *well that was thoughtful that he remembered; and a duffle bag; hmmm he wants to stay over? And . . . flowers? Fuck! Charlie, you idiot.*

He had told her to stay in the apartment and she didn't and now she was half trashed. He was going to be furious, or worse—completely repulsed. She had ruined it. She decided that the best thing to do was just stay at the bar and by the time she sobered up and went back to apartment he'd be so glad she was okay that maybe he wouldn't be mad.

"That's a terrible idea. He'll leave." She smacked herself in the head and Amy scowled at her. "Hey, Sarge.

You okay?"

"Just peachy, Amy."

Her phone rang and it made her jump. She knew it was him. He was standing at her locked apartment door and no one was answering the door, so it had to be him. She picked the phone up and glanced at the screen as she brought it to her face. It was not Jake but her captain.

"Hey Cap, if you're trying to call me in you can forget it. I'm on my third PBR."

"Ahhh," he said without judgment. "After last night, you're entitled, kid, just checking on you." Then he waited for the tongue lashing he knew would come for having the audacity to suggest that she wasn't okay.

"Thanks, Cap. I'm okay," she said resigned.

*Damn*, the captain thought as he hung up, the tongue lashing would have made him feel better. He hoped she was with Jake. He could see what was happening and he was glad that he didn't have to worry about her being alone, at least until the killer was caught. He wished it could be him, but he knew she didn't look at him in that way. He further knew that if she ever did look at him in that light, his wife wouldn't appreciate it. She was always asking about Charlie. Somehow she knew her captain husband was carrying a bit of a torch for his favorite detective. He knew his wife's inquiries were actually veiled warnings and he heeded them. Smart man, the captain.

Charlie watched as Jake descended the stairs from her third-floor apartment door and walked back to the parking lot. *God he was hot.* Tall and square and built like a mountain. He walked with something just short of a swagger. Not like he was looking for a fight, but like he was ready for one. He marched to Charlie's parked unmarked cruiser and felt the hood and then did a visual scan of the immediate area. She hated to admit it, but the man was good. When his eyes reached the window at Amy's where she sat staring back, he stopped cold and everything about his posture changed.

*Shit. Busted.*

Charlie threw a five spot at Amy for the three beers, gotta love that cop discount, and hurried outside. Jake stood in the parking lot, not taking his eyes off her as she crossed the street and walked up to him trying to look casual.

"What?" she said indignantly as he glared at her.

"Upstairs," he growled. "Now." The hair on the back of her neck stood up and traveled . . . south.

*Chapter 22*
**Are You Drunk?**

Charlie fumbled with the keys and tripped over the threshold as Jake closed the door behind them, just short of a slam. He put everything down on the kitchen counter and returned to deadbolt the door.

"Are you drunk?" he asked, incredulously.

"Drunk scumbag," Moses squawked.

"Shut up Moses!" they both yelled in unison, but neither of them found it funny. The air was charged.

"Are you?" Jake again demanded. Charlie decided a best defense was a drunken offense and she tossed her jacket on the chair and put her hands on her hips.

"Are you my father?" she shot back. He closed the distance between them quickly and grabbed her arm.

"Is this some kind of a game to you, Charlie? There's a killer out there. A killer that left a message to you in blood. Have you forgotten that?"

"Why yes I have," she smarted off. "It's my night off so back the fuck up," she warned.

Jake's eyes darkened and his lips tightened. So did the grip on Charlie's arm.

*Okay, perhaps this was not a good plan,* she thought.

She tried to pull away and there it was again, the flash of light in his right eye. "I told you not to leave this apartment, Charlie," he said low in his throat and squared off with her.

Damn it. She might not have had a poker face but she had a PBR face and the alcohol was making her fearless and arrogant. "So what? You told me to stay and I didn't. What are you going to do? Lock me up? Spank me?" she mouthed off, with no thought or plan for what was spewing from her pie hole.

He pulled her up by the arm, so her face would be level with his.

"Both," he said through gritted teeth.

Jake saw the fire light in her eyes. It was instantaneous. He knew what she needed. He felt it and he wanted to make her whole. He glared down at her, nose to nose, while she stood frozen. Her mouth hung open, the faint smell of beer coming from her breath. She was driving him over the edge and it was time to do something about it. Every nerve ending in her body screamed as he locked his mouth on hers releasing her arm and pulling on his waistband.

*Whoa, was he taking off his pants?* Her empty stomach lurched from the beer. Then she heard that telltale metal sound. In a flash her hands were handcuffed behind her back.

"Hey Adams! What are you . . . ?"

"You want to act like a child. Fine!" he said sitting down on the chair and pulling her over his knee. His large hand crashed against her flesh through her jeans. *This is not happening. I'm dreaming*, she thought as she basked in every blow. He hit hard and fast and it was beginning to sting.

"Owwww, that hurts, you jerk!" she faked, not wanting him to think she was a freak. He let go with one final blow and she screamed. *Damn*. That one did hurt and she felt it deep inside her.

He was standing on the threshold—he had his hand on the door knob, all he had to do was turn it and she was his. Instead, he yanked her off his lap and pushed her back, so she was kneeling on the floor at his feet while he glared down at her. He seemed to lose focus for a moment and then shook his head, regaining his cold stare. She gazed at him breathless, helpless and completely turned on, her brown eyes turning to gold from adrenaline. He reached around her and brought her upright on her knees and effortlessly unlocked the cuffs without looking while saying, "Have I made myself clear?"

Charlie nodded, unable to speak, still trying to catch her breath as she reached up to kiss him, but he used her hands to simultaneously stand her up and push her away. "You need to eat," he said and he walked to the kitchen. She followed and sat down on one of the stools watching him in wonder and lust, her eyes dancing. In the harsh light of the kitchen he looked older, more worn. His face was still slightly red and the lines that were etched around his eyes were more noticeable. His lips were trembling as he prepared her plate, opened a bottled water, and set it down in front of her.

"Eat," he ordered. They ate in silence staring at each other. Him, dazed and aroused; her, just aroused.

"I'm sorry," she said in a whisper. "I thought you were blowing me off and I . . ."

"And what?" he snapped.

She swallowed hard. "I'm not good with men, Jake. My feelings get hurt so easily. It's like I am always waiting for the other shoe to drop. I thought you were unaffected by that kiss and it made me . . ."

"Unaffected?" he broke in. "Do I look unaffected to you? Damn it, Charlie!" He closed the distance between them again.

"I wish the hell I was unaffected by you. The timing is all wrong here. The circumstances are wrong. Everything is wrong!" He slammed his open hand on the marble kitchen island and she jumped in her seat and started to tear up. He closed his eyes and brought her head to his chest. "Baby don't," he said, his eyes softening as he caressed her face.

*Baby.*

And the tears came. Tears that had been building for a very, very long time and she made no effort to hold them back. Jake gathered her in his arms and carried her to the couch and nestled her in his arms. "I'm so sorry baby," he said, apologizing for losing his temper as she continued to cry softly in his arms.

Jake had no idea. He had no idea that her tears were tears of relief, of a journey's end, of a faith found. He had no idea.

"You don't need this right now," he said. "I am the last thing you need."

She looked up at him through tear-filled eyes and spoke with absolute conviction, "I have been waiting for you forever. I wanted it to be you. I wanted it to be you so badly," he smiled at the Meg Ryan line and hugged her tighter and stared up at the ceiling while Charlie nuzzled into his chest.

He closed his eyes as he held her, and he remembered his dream. Her hair was longer, lighter and she was younger but it was her. Jake didn't know if it was deja vu or outright madness, but the memory and their connection were undeniable. He had done some research on cellular memory in his own journey with recovery, but this was the first time he ever really believed it. The memory was real. Unexplainable, but real. He knew he had to acknowledge that in his own heart, even if he never said it to her. He knew it from the first day he walked into her office, probably earlier than that if he was being honest, but he chose not to be. *He needed her as much as she needed him, but how were they going to manage?*

If they were to be discovered, he could be pulled from the case. She could be pulled from the case or even disciplined. Disciplined for what, he wasn't sure; they were two single consenting adults but agencies do not take well to these professionally incestuous relationships, particularly when a supervisor is involved. It muddies the waters. It muddies the command structure. It compromises the decision-making and it hinders the work. Charlie seemed well thought of and respected, and the idea that his involvement with her could taint her reputation or her future made his chest hurt. Jake had no idea what was happening to him. *Since when did he give a shit about how anyone else was affected? Especially a woman?*

He had long since given up caring about anyone but himself. He spent five years fighting for every scrap of dignity and sanity he could maintain, all his life really, and had lost by many accounts, but he fought back and in doing so made himself first and foremost his own champion. *How had this girl he held in his arms knocked him off his post with one punch and what was he willing to do to stop it?* That's when he made a decision. He would not sleep with her—and he would not hurt her—that was final, he hoped. There was no way he could predict what would happen if he went to the next level with her, so he would make sure it didn't happen at all.

She woke up in his arms at around ten, surprised that he was still holding her. "Come on," he said. "Time for bed. Let's get your clock right." The anticipation of this moment had been building in her since their first stake-out. She couldn't believe it was finally happening. He walked her into the bedroom by her shoulders and she started to peel off her clothes.

"What are you doing?" he asked, alarmed.

"Well I'm not going to sleep in my clothes, Jake," Charlie said indignantly. *Jesus after the day they had, why was he picking at her?*

"I'll step out," he said paternally.

"Don't be silly," she scoffed until she saw his eyes darken. "I . . . I have a camisole on underneath my sweater. I was just going to sleep in that. Is that okay?" she asked, though she had no idea why she was asking his permission in her own bedroom.

He stared at her, his eyes dark, but said nothing. Suddenly she became very self-conscious. She assumed he meant they were going to bed together, but it was clear now that he didn't mean that at all. She was frustrated by her confusion but still too buzzed from the three PBRs and the spanking to mount a fight. She continued to undress but didn't look at him, as if he somehow couldn't see her if she weren't making eye contact. She couldn't read him at all. She was very aware that she was visibly trembling, and it seemed to be having no impact on him.

*Was he angry with her for being so familiar? Turned on? Repulsed? Jesus, she never had as much trouble reading a man as she did this man. Was it her or was it him?*

She quickly slid under the covers and finally turned to face him. "Will you stay with me until I fall asleep?" she said quietly, looking so small. "Please?" Jake was standing over her, not quite glaring anymore but clearly not happy with her. Still, he said nothing as he sat down in the chair beside her bed, his eyes locked on hers. Charlie tried to look relaxed but she was crawling out of her skin. Her body ached for him, her mouth was wet with the promise of his kiss, but he made no move toward her. She decided to roll over, close her eyes and try to control her breathing. The silence was deafening. She wanted to ask him to lay down with her, but she knew from her limited experience with him that taking the lead would provoke rather than arouse him, so she remained quiet and decided to try something else.

*Lay down with me Jake*, she thought quietly in her head . . . *Please, Jake, hold me. I need you to hold me. I need your arms around me Jake.*

After her fifth incantation she heard him get up from the chair and unfasten his belt. Her eyes widened and she was thankful she was turned away from him as she held her breath. She tried to remain calm as he pulled the covers back and she felt him crawl into the bed behind her and wrap his long muscular arms around her. She disappeared into the safety of his steel clutch and sighed involuntarily.

"Is this what you wanted?" he whispered in her ear. She nodded, suppressing the urge to cry in relief. "Go to sleep Charlie."

*Was he kidding?*

As she lay on her side, her back to his front, she snuggled against him, grateful to be in his arms, but disappointed that she was not having the effect on him she had hoped. Jake controlled himself as long as he could. It didn't take long before his body betrayed him and he found himself rock hard against her as she snuggled in. She drew a quick breath. Jake remained silent and still.

"Jake," she said her voice trembling.

"Go to sleep, Charlie," he repeated. Charlie let out a loud sigh of frustration and desire and his arms tightened around her. She didn't need to see his eyes to know they were dark.

"I . . . I'm not sure I can." she whispered. "I need . . ." she started but her request was silenced when from behind he placed a giant hand gently over her mouth and again whispered in her ear leaving her breathless.

"I am going to help you relax so you can sleep but you must do exactly as I say. Agreed?" She nodded and he loosened his hand from her mouth but did not remove it.

"Put your arms out in front of you," he instructed, and she complied. She looked as though she were lying on her side praying . . . she was. Praying he would have mercy and unleash the heat that had been building in her since the moment she first laid eyes on him, praying for release before she ran mad, praying most of all that he wanted her. With one hand still gently over her mouth, he used his other hand to roughly massage the back of her neck. She groaned and bent her head forward, causing his loose hand to slide from her mouth to her throat where he cradled her neck and head.

"Shhh," he whispered and her stomach tightened. He moved his hand from the back of her neck and slid it across her shoulder and down along the curve of her waist to her hips, sliding the camisole up so he could make direct contact with her skin, sending a shockwave through both of them.

"Easy," he said in a low growl when her body jerked in response to his touch. His voice was driving her crazy and she started to grind her hips against him.

"Stop," he ordered, halting the movement of his hand and resting it on her hip. "Be a good girl and lay still," he whispered into her ear, as goosebumps covered every surface of her body.

He smiled behind her. Pleased with her reaction and convinced he could bring her to her climax, he took even more control from her by remaining completely still until she complied. Charlie took a deep breath, closed her eyes, and forced herself to stop grinding her hips against his hardness, as Jake stroked her throat and jaw with his thumb and fingers.

"That's it, Baby. Good girl."

With those words she felt it starting to build inside her, building from a place she hadn't felt since she was fifteen years old. He slid his hand to her abdomen. Half of his large warm hand covered her pelvis, the other half, her stomach. He gently pressed down while gently tipping her head back against him. She felt her muscles tighten and her juices flowing.

Her body ached for his touch where she needed it most. She was unaware that further invasion was neither forthcoming nor necessary. She was hurtling like a freight train, closer and closer to the edge, barely moving, panting uncontrollably.

"That's it," he whispered with more excitement in his voice. He applied more pressure with both hands—pulling her head back and pushing her pelvis down and grinding his hardness against her back. She started to whimper. He knew she was fighting it, but he also knew how to get her there and he would . . . when he was damn good and ready.

"Let it go Charlie," he finally said. "It's okay. I've got you, Baby," he said breathless as he twisted her neck so he could devour her ear with his mouth as the final assault.

"Now Charlie. Come now," he ordered.

His mouth, his voice, his breath, and his complete control over her body pushed her over the edge. "Jake!" she screamed, her vision invaded by exploding light. He covered her mouth and locked his grip down on her body.

"That's it. Let it go," he breathed and locked his body to hers while she convulsed over and over and over. He wrapped both arms around her as she shuddered and finally went limp. She wanted to speak but she couldn't. Her mind moved in and out of consciousness as she felt him completely envelope her.

"Sleep, Baby," was the last thing she heard.

*Chapter 23*
**Cellular Memory**

Jake slept.

His dreams took him again back to a place and time he didn't know. The walls were gray, wet, and made of some kind of stone, as was the floor. There was a musty smell that enveloped the room. The smell was rank. Not rank like a dead body, more like rank of old, like a grand-mother's basement. It smelled of mold, stagnant water and burnt torches and spilled wine and urine—hopefully not in the same chalice. The room was vast with a high ceiling, and the torches that burned barely succeeded in their effort to illuminate the expansive room. Every sound echoed; footsteps, giggles, slurps, and voices. The room was filled with all of these.

It took a minute for Jake's eyes to adjust to the dark-ness and at first he wasn't sure if it was really her. She was younger but yes, it was definitely her. She was wear-ing a long dress of bone white and gold silk and her am-ple bosom was displayed by a bustier that presented her voluptuous breasts like a gift. Her hair was loose in the back and braided across the top and along the sides. A tiara of wildflowers encircled her head. She looked like a princess.

She caught him staring at her and cast a shy smile at him before looking away. Her eyes were bright and round and filled with the most beautiful shades of gold, green, and brown. He had seen these colors in her eyes before. She was standing with four other women who were chatting and giggling and flirting with the other men in the room, all soldiers. The women may have been beautiful, maybe even as beautiful as she, maybe more, but there would be no way for him to know, not with her in the room. With her in the room, no other woman existed, as it should be for any woman who is truly loved.

If a man had any idea of the adoration and respect that would befall him for this single act of chivalry he would never again notice another woman when in the company of his love for the rest of his days. *Was it the character of the man or the beauty of the woman he was with that made this true?* Jake believed it was the depth of the man's love and his awareness that this love was his to protect and cherish. Only then would a man truly know what it was like to be adored, revered and loved. It was the likes of a depth he had never known. Until her.

Jake was pretty sure he was dreaming but not positive. It felt very real. He could sense the weight of the reality even as he questioned it.

Very little intimidated Jake Adams, but he found these soldiers intimidating. Which was strange considering the soldiers were wearing skirts; green and black checkered with white lines and a hint of gold thread among the green. Men in skirts should have been funny, but Jake wasn't moved to laugh. These were serious men, dangerous men; soldiers who long ago had lost their sense of humor. Jake knew this instinctively and felt threatened, for himself and for her.

The soldiers wore freshly polished chest plates, still bearing the scars of battle. Their helmets were polished as well, with gold trim along the high ridges and along the edges. A few of the soldiers had red and black feather plumes sprouting from the tops of the helmets. The scabbards hanging from their thick belts held long deadly swords that hung below their skirts and banged against

their massive bare legs. Looking closely, he could dis-
cern a hint of stain on the hilts of the swords. The stain
was very faint on the high side of the scabbard, while
wide, dark and pronounced on the lower side. On their
feet, they wore sandals with wide straps, made of thick
leather, crisscrossing fore and back and clasped with a
buckle just below the knee. A few of the soldiers had
animal hide strapped to their calves.

It was a bizarre outfit for battle and Jake was completely lost in the scene that lay before him. Like a stripper at a convent, he couldn't have felt more conspicuous
or out of place and yet . . . no one was eyeballing him.
Somehow, he belonged here. Except for the stolen shy
glances from her he wouldn't have believed he could
even be seen. Everyone was keeping a wide berth. Jake
grew more uncomfortable, confused, and alarmed with
each passing minute. A massive-chested soldier began to
cross the room with a stony gaze. His target was clearly
Jake. Oh yea, Jake could be seen alright. *This was it.*
*Confrontation.* He could see the question in the soldier's
eyes. Who the hell are you and what is your business
here?

*Jake Adams and I have no fucking idea.*

The soldier had one hand on the handle of his
sheathed sword as he took long deliberate strides across
the crowded room. A panic rose up and caught in Jake's
throat but he allowed his face to reveal nothing as he
locked eyes with the approaching soldier and raised his
chin in challenge. Years of training would not fail him.

She watched, her eyes wide with wonder and curiosity. "Legatus," the soldier said, formally addressing Jake.

Suddenly he felt her move in his arms, startling him.
Jake reached for his hip trying to find his gun, instead

finding a sword as he vacillated between worlds. The sword banged against his leg as he was ripped from his dream. "Don't go!" she screamed and ran toward him. "Please!" she pleaded through tear filled eyes.

*Wait! Wait!* Jake tried to reach back and fought to remain in the confines of the stone and the darkness but the smells were slipping away. He felt his grasp tighten around her, his hands cradling her breast as he pulled her back against his chest. Charlie sighed and snuggled against him as the sunlight streamed into the bedroom through the apartment window.

"Jesus," Jake whispered, trying to capture his dream to his memory.

"Hmmm?" Charlie purred in his arms, starting to wake. She needed neither seconds nor minutes to process that she was wrapped in Jake's arms. She knew it. She felt it all night and she would have been content to never wake again.

"Good morning Agent Adams," she purred, rolling over to face him.

"Good morning, Beautiful." *God she was. Beautiful and glowing.* He smiled down at her and they became lost in that place. Charlie was first to break the spell, reaching up to caress his worried face.

"Everything is okay, Baby," Charlie whispered. She said it without even thinking; without analyzing it and over-analyzing it. Without wondering if it would freak him out or push him away. She said it as if she had said it a thousand times before. His eyes softened. He took a deep breath, completely caught off guard by the comfort her words brought him.

Jake had been alone for so long. He had been with women, lots of them, but still alone. Always alone. Alone by choice. His choice. He had truly never felt a connection to another human being like this. He felt as if he had known her for a hundred years. More. He drew her closer and she disappeared in his arms and tucked her head into his chest and hid there, protected and safe for as long as she could until she finally had to say it . . .

"We have statements to write, Adams." His grip tightened as he tensed and she felt a small twinge of panic for a moment. Though her face was still buried in his chest, she could feel his eyes darken. She knew he didn't like it when she took charge. There would be a consequence. She remained still. She knew it was coming but she was still surprised when he grabbed her hair and yanked her head back and kissed her hard on the mouth, robbing her of her breath. "Right you are, Sarge," he said, his dark eyes piercing her. With that he bounded out of bed and got dressed while directing her to meet him at the station in one hour.

"Oh. Oh okay," she said, trying hard not to surrender to tender feelings that were already starting in. It was clear he wasn't going to come back and pick her up.

Reading her thoughts he said, "I've gotta touch base with Captain Kerns at the beach later today and I don't want to leave you stranded at the station. I haven't made contact with them or the regional office in a week. They are going to think you have kidnapped me," he grinned. She threw a pillow at him and he rushed out, yelling, "Lock this deadbolt Charlie!"

"Lock this deadbolt!" squawked Moses. "Shut up Moses!" they yelled; her from the bedroom, him from the stairwell.

She knew she should get up and shower—he hadn't given her much time to get ready to meet him at the station, nor had he asked how much time she would need, but it had been quite a while since she had enjoyed a morning afterglow and she wasn't ready to give it up. She pulled the covers around her and snuggled in and began replaying the previous night in her mind starting with when she heard him undressing to climb into bed with her. *No.* Starting with when she asked him if he was going to "lock her up or spank her" and he had said . . . "Both."

Even twelve hours later it sent a shiver through her and made her body ache for him. She ran her hands across her engorged and warm breasts and down to her stomach where his large hand had held her still while she convulsed in orgasm. She found herself reaching for Gus before she had time to argue with herself about how little time she had.

An hour later Charlie arrived at the station. She looked a little rough and she knew it and was feeling self-conscious. She was definitely not her usual controlled and composed self. Like the night before, she had only had time to pull her hair into a ponytail and throw on a baseball cap, making it now two days since she had washed her hair. No time for makeup either.

*Hadn't he said he liked her this way? We'll see.*

The Fed Mobile was already in the parking lot when she arrived—*of course it was*. She could feel her blood pressure starting to rise. She smiled and waved to the desk officer as she passed through the lobby, then popped into the locker room to check her look in the full-length mirror before going upstairs to the second floor of the white shirts and suits.

"Train wreck" she concluded as she looked in the mirror but she fluffed her hair anyway and retied her ponytail in a futile effort to look presentable. She started for the elevator and smiled thinking about Thompson and his pestering 'Out of Service' note he used to place on the elevator doors so the detectives and supervisors would be forced to take their "fat useless asses up the stairs." For no particular reason, she headed for the stairwell instead. Her stomach started to knot knowing that she would be seeing him any minute. She took deep breaths to calm herself as she opened the stairwell door and started climbing to the second floor. She imagined him sitting in the chair in her office and . . .

"Jesus!" A scream caught in her throat when she saw him standing on the landing . . . waiting for her. "Christ Adams!" she screamed. He grinned down at her as he casually leaned against the stairwell wall.

"Hi!" he said, cheerfully. He looked gorgeous. Tall, hot, and gorgeous.

Charlie was completely perplexed. They had the same amount of time to get ready, her time diminished by Gus and his time diminished by his drive to his hotel and she looked like she had been hit by a bus, *twice*, while he looked like he just stepped out of a magazine. He was wearing tan Truspec BDUs, a black silk LA Police Gear polo, black leather Danner boots, and a charcoal gray Michael Kors windbreaker. Like the werewolf, his hair was perfect.

"You gotta little glow in your cheeks there, Sarge," he said. "I hope you're not running a fever."

"You are not to discuss my cheeks in this station, Adams," she said sternly. Then she realized what she had just said and blushed harder. *Damn him!* She burst through the CID door with an extremely self-satisfied looking Jake Adams on her heels, almost knocking Clint

McCallister on his ass.

"Whoa! Where's the fire Sarge?" Clint said, pretending to lose his balance and banging into the wall in dramatic fashion.

"Screw you Clint! I'm no hero!" she said, as she marched past him. Clint and Jake looked at each other confused and shrugged.

Jake strolled into the doorway of her office and stared at her while Charlie focused on her desk, trying to regain her composure. He loved seeing her like this, flustered and out of control, but he knew she didn't like to be that way at work, so he backed it down.

"Sarge? Do I do this statement on a standard IBR report or just plain paper?"

She glared up at him, then suppressing a grin said, "Ask Clint to get you set up, please. I'm buried." Jake nodded and headed for Clint's desk.

"She okay?" Clint asked nodding toward Charlie's office and handing Jake the report forms he needed.

"Yea, I think so. She's not convinced the message was for her," he said casually.

"Really?" Clint said staring him down and sizing him up, asking the question with his eyes that he didn't need to ask out loud. Jake felt the need to shift in his seat but didn't move a muscle.

"The fact is we don't really know for sure," Jake finally said.

"Don't we?" Clint asked raising an eyebrow. Jake was impressed with Clint. He had underestimated him.

"I've gotta get this statement done, Clint," Jake said, heading to his cubicle. Jake tried to focus but had a hard time staying put, knowing the questions that were bouncing around in Clint's head. He also knew that Charlie would be struggling while she reconstructed the night of Daniel Silver's murder. Jake thought of an excuse that would enable him to check on her without coddling her, which he knew she would hate. This was "Work Charlie" and he had to treat her differently.

He peeked into her office and found her with her head in her hands as she brooded over the blank report form. Jake knocked gently on the door jam. "What?" she snapped without looking up. Involuntarily, he took a step toward her, causing her to look up. She didn't back down and returned his penetrating gaze. Jake regained control and forced himself to stop, though his instinct was to grab her by the hair and bend her over her desk.

"I'm sorry to disturb you, Sarge," he said coolly. "I just needed some guidance about the preamble here. I mean, we arrived late, and I didn't know if we were planning on ratting ourselves out on that, so do we start with—we were on a stakeout—and go right to the scream, or what?"

She shook her head. "No, Agent, we deal with facts here, even when we screw up." His eyes darkened again but this time there was anger tinged with alarm. He started to speak but she cut him off.

"I'm sorry Jake. God. I'm being awful. You're trying to cover my ass and I'm being a bitch. I'm sorry." Jake said nothing.

They were both silent, her eyes pleading for understanding, his eyes revealing nothing. Charlie broke first. "I say we just go with the log. We arrived at 2145, the target returned home at 2200, and the scream came at 0500 *yada yada yada*." Jake instantly relaxed, relieved that she didn't intend to include his jog for coffee and he couldn't help but smile at the *yada yada*.

"Thanks Adams," she said and flashed a grateful smile at him in gratitude for pulling her from the dark place she was in.

As she gazed up at him, for a split second his dream flashed in his head. "What?" Charlie said, coyly reacting to the strange look on his face.

Jake shook his head clear. "Nothing. Okay. Got it. Log. Okay," he said disappearing from her doorway. Charlie registered Jake's reaction but had no time to analyze it. She dove into her statement with a clearer head. *God he was adorable . . . when he wasn't scaring the shit out of her or pissing her off.*

About halfway through her statement, Mary Jane Klasky derailed her concentration as she bounced through the door and plopped into the chair. Her blonde hair was wild and untamed, and even though the clock was ticking away the morning and Charlie had three days of work piled on her desk, she was grateful for the distraction.

"What's up kid?" Charlie prompted. Mary Jane launched into a detailed rant about everything teen that made Charlie so very grateful that the teen years only came once in a lifetime and were far behind her. Mary Jane clearly wasn't looking for advice. She just wanted to rant. She could have been talking to a mushroom— Charlie was as good a mushroom as anyone else. Charlie smiled and nodded and uh-huh'd and oh-really'd for fifteen minutes and finally said, "Mary Jane. Duty calls."

The teen took it in stride, grinned, and bounced out of the office the same way she came in. "Jesus that kid wears me out," Charlie said to herself as Clint walked in and sat down in the chair just vacated by Mary Jane.

"What kid is wearing you out?" Clint asked.

"Never mind," she said.

"What?"

"Really Clint?" Charlie sighed as Clint raised an eyebrow.

"What?" Clint threw his hands up and flashed his most angelic smile, his large dark eyes dancing. "I can't just come in and see how you are doing?" Charlie motioned to the half-finished report on her desk.

"Christ Sarge! You're still not done with that report? It's noon? What are you doing in here? Writing it with your feet?"

Charlie rolled her eyes. "It is not noon," she said. "Is it? Well it's a little difficult to concentrate with all these interruptions." She started tapping her fingers on the desk.

"Oh! Oh! I see," he said, "he can interrupt you, but I can't! Okay, I see how this works," his hand covering his wounded heart. Charlie laughed. She was defenseless against Clint's childlike charm.

"Whaaaat?" she whined. "Whaaaat dooo youuuu waaaaant McCallister!"

"Oh," Clint said angelically, "I just wanted to see if you wanted to get a bite? See? I care!"

"Oh. I can't, Clint. After I get this report done, I have to check off on all these other reports. I'll be here all night."

"Well that makes it easy then," he said grinning. "Take-out from the Gay Dolphin it is."

"Oh my God, I love you!" Charlie smiled, realizing the last time she had eaten was the two bites of Gay Dolphin take-out she had eaten last night.

"I don't blame you," Clint said, smiling, snapping her out of her thoughts.

"Hey!" she yelled after him. "Why don't you check with Adams and see if he wants anything."

Clint popped his head back in the door. "He's gone. He left over an hour ago. Okay, let me make copies of my report for Heather so she can do her crime prevention PR thing and then I'll run out. Yum! Yum!" he grinned, referring to Officer Heather Hinson, not the Gay Dolphin.

*Jake had gone without saying goodbye? No big deal*, she lied to herself. Charlie picked up her pen and finished her report on auto-pilot. She would never be able to remember or testify to the words that were written on the page before her, but at least the report was done.

"Okay I'm going now!" Clint yelled as he passed by her door.

"Clint wait," she said. "I'm coming with."

"Cool!" Clint lit up. She started for her cruiser but Clint dangled his keys at her and she got the message.

"I'm not that bad a driver," she pouted.

"I didn't say a word about your driving," Clint said with a grin.

*Get out of my head asshole,* she thought.

*Chapter 24*
**Robbery Code One**

Before their seatbelts were buckled the tone alert went off "Beeeeeeeeep."

"Units 354, 377, 389, armed robbery in progress Circle 7 Convenience Store 12764 Prince Andrew St. Code 1," Jan purred.

"God, I love her voice," Clint said.

*Doesn't that woman ever take a fucking day off?* Charlie wondered.

"Come on McCallister. Let's roll!" Charlie yelled, flipping on the grill and visor emergency lights and activating the siren. "Hey! Hey! Hey! My cruiser, my toys!" Clint laughed as he playfully slapped her hand away from the siren switch box, accelerated out of the police lot and launched onto the main drag. Charlie picked up the radio but Jan started providing additional details about the robbery before Charlie could mark up and say that she and Clint were responding to the call.

"Units responding to the Circle 7 robbery, citizen reports pulling into the lot and seeing a young white male with a black t-shirt and tan pants and a red baseball cap pointing a handgun at the clerk. All responding units acknowledge." Units marked up along with their location and ETA, "354 Jessup St.—five minutes; 377 Rt. 6 and Donnelly—eight, 389 Virginia Beach Line—ten."

"Hot damn!" Clint yelled, taking the turn on Prince Andrew Street at 70 mph, "We're going to be first ones on the scene!" Charlie grinned at him and felt the adrenaline rising in her chest as she reached down and turned off the siren but left the emergency lights on—*Always a risk* . . . the chief reminded her from his perch on her shoulder. They needed to get there as quickly as possible, and they didn't want to give the robber a heads-up on their arrival, but hauling ass with lights and no siren was a risk that all chiefs wanted to be managed very judiciously.

Charlie dropped a reassuring elbow on her gun, making sure it was where it was supposed to be and silently asked her plastic partner to come through for her. Well, not all plastic. The barrel and slide were made from hardened steel. The Glock 21's main frame, magazine, and body were made from a high-strength nylon-based polymer, the inventor, Gaston Glock named Polymer2. Glocks are sexy.

"Jesus Christ Clint!" Charlie yelled as Clint almost lost control on the winding road that was the eleven hundred block of Prince Andrew Street. Clint giggled and hovered over the wheel like a bad Gremlin run amok from Kingston Falls.

"Oh I got this!" he said, "I fucking got this!" Clint grinned, correcting the over-steer and straightening out the cruiser like it had been his plan all along. Charlie was suddenly glad Clint was driving instead of her, knowing she probably wouldn't have pulled that off, but also knowing she wouldn't be driving 70 mph either.

"Slow the hell down, you fucking lunatic. It's coming up on the right. Pick a good spot. Shit! There he is!" Charlie started to bail out of the car while Clint was on the radio trying to mark out on the scene. Since they never told dispatch they were responding to the robbery they had to mark out first lest one of them be mistaken by a uniformed officer as the perp. Clint tried to grab Charlie's arm while he clarified their location to dispatch but Charlie pulled away and gave chase. Neither of them had grabbed a portable radio when they left the station so Clint knew it was critical to mark out and give their location first before he raced off after his overzealous sergeant—he loved that about her. She was fearless and he was fearless when he was with her.

Jan confirmed their location and directed the first marked unit to the store to check on the clerk, who might be bleeding to death by this time. Jan knew that the heroes would be staging nearby but would not be going into the store until police said the scene was safe. She also knew Clint would be following Sergeant Cavanaugh in the foot chase. Everyone knew that.

Clint was only seconds behind Charlie but had already lost her in the thick underbrush. He stopped and listened and could hear her footsteps. Then he heard her yell, "Stop! Police!"

"Charlie!" Clint yelled as he continued to follow the sound. The robber was young, in shape, and motivated, and believed there was zero chance he would be caught today. He knew he was leaving the little female cop who was pursuing him in the dust but just for good measure, he cracked off a round from his pistol in her general direction to slow her down. Little did he know the shot just antagonized Charlie and made her run faster.

The muzzle flash gave her a better fix on his position. *Idiot*, she thought. She picked up the pace, her pistol in her outstretched hand as she ran. A panic welled up in Clint's chest when he heard the shot. "Charlie!" he yelled louder as he plowed through the underbrush.

The robber was winded but could hear the pursing officer losing ground. Another quarter of a mile and all he'd have left to worry about would be K9. He knew from experience he'd have a good 20-minute head start on them as well. He knew this underbrush well as if he had been born a rabbit and knew every opening that would allow him to pass without obstruction while his pursuers got bogged down in branches, stickers, and brush so thick you had to go around rather than through. He could barely even hear his pursuer's footsteps as he crossed the last creek bed. That would throw the impending K9 off and take him to the street where his pickup truck sat waiting. He jumped into the creek bed and sloshed twenty feet in the shallow water before climbing out and passing through the last patch of woods.

BAM! It was the kind of a punch you never saw coming; just one punch, close range, right across the bridge of the nose. A bright white light flashed and encircled the robber's vision as he hit the ground. In the final second as he passed from conscious to unconscious he saw a large black leather boot kicking the gun away from him.

Charlie stopped at the creek to catch her breath and to listen for footsteps before she left her position of cover in the brush, but heard nothing. She wanted to yell for Clint so he could catch up but the robber might be lying in wait and she couldn't give away her position without making herself a target. She tried to control her breathing so she could hear, but the adrenaline drums were beating hard in her ears. She would have to hold her position and wait for Clint to find her. She battled her disappointment by reminding herself they could use the spot she was at as starting point for the K9 track. She had lost the perp.

Charlie kneeled down, trying to stay small and quiet and that's when she caught a glimpse of the red baseball hat on the ground. She pointed her weapon at the hat across the creek bed, scanning back and forth, back and forth and slowly moving toward it, knowing she was messing up the K9 track but too keyed up to stop. She wanted this son-of-a-bitch and was anxious to return the shot he had so foolishly fired in her direction. She moved closer, her finger on the trigger. Up until now she had kept her finger outside the trigger guard so that if she fell, she wouldn't accidentally squeeze off a shot but now it was finger-on-the-trigger-time. She loved finger-on-the-trigger time. Truth be told. . . most cops did. It's not the rush of maybe having to kill someone, it's the rush of the fight; the adrenaline of survival; the smell of blood in the water. There was nothing like it.

Aware that she could be ambushed, Charlie moved very slowly—then she saw him lying flat on his back.

"Police, don't move!" she screamed at the unconscious man.

"Clint!" she yelled. "Over here!"

"Sarge!"

"Here! Here!" She rolled the robber over, secured his hands with her cuffs and made sure he was breathing. She continued to yell to Clint who finally arrived out of the brush, scratched up, covered in stickers, and panting like a dog.

"Damn it Sarge!" he said. "What the fuck? Oh, you got him. Cool. What did you do to him?" Clint wiped his face and reached for a cigarette.

"Nothing. Found him like this," she said in broken sentences, still trying to regain her normal rate of breathing and motioning for him to give her a cigarette, too.

"Gun?" Clint panted as he took a deep drag on the cigarette. Charlie lifted up her foot to reveal the weapon under her tiny Rockport shoe and took a deep drag herself.

Clint laughed and said, "Grecko will be so pleased you didn't fuck up his little fingerprint pattern! Seriously, what did you hit him with?"

"Nothing. I swear. I found him like this. Maybe the dumbass ran into a tree," she laughed and coughed, the foreign smoke tickling her throat.

They stood in silence for a moment, trying not to process the danger of what had just transpired. Thompson used to say, "The quiet that follows a near miss is the loudest silence you'll ever hear."

"Take your sunglasses off," Clint said out of the blue.

"What?" Charlie asked. "What for?"

Clint reached up and slid the glasses down her nose, nodded, smiled, and slid them back up. Charlie looked at him perplexed but was too curious about the robber to be distracted by Clint.

"Let's search him," she said.

Clint pulled out his cell phone and gave their location to Communications. Jan had already positioned officers on the street on the other side of the brush based on the information Clint had provided so back-up units were there in moments.

The heroes were called to the scene to check out the perp who was finally coming to and complaining of police brutality and a wicked headache. Detective Cramlin offered to take the arrest since he knew Charlie didn't want or need the stat and Clint was tied up with the serial. "Thanks Crammy," Charlie said.

"Oh yea, thanks Crammy! Big sacrifice. Way to take one for the team," Clint said rolling his eyes at the pointy nosed detective for poaching the easy robbery arrest stat.

Police agencies try to pretend that stats and quotas don't exist, but they do, only now they call them performance objectives. Jesus, no wonder Thompson hated white shirts.

Clint and Charlie caught a ride back to their cruiser with a marked unit. Clint reached for the front seat passenger door but a raised eyebrow from Charlie had him open the door and step back saying, "I was just getting the door for you, Sarge. Geez." Clint climbed into the cage in the back seat, his long legs pinned to his chest as he closed the door. He banged on the plexiglass that separated him from Charlie and the patrol unit, "Hey! The dipshits who make these cage inserts know we arrest other people besides midgets, right?" Charlie laughed and ignored him.

Once they were back at their unmarked cruiser, they pulled into the Circle 7 to check the scene before leaving. The clerk had not been shot, which was good. That makes the report and the crime scene a hell of a lot less complicated. *This job really screws up priorities,* she thought.

"Don't forget the tape," Charlie said to Cramlin as they were leaving the crime scene. Crammy picked up the video tape from the counter that the clerk had already pulled from the closed-circuit video camera and waved it at Charlie. "Got it."

They both released a perfectly timed sigh once back in the cruiser. "Okay, ready to try this again?" Clint grinned as they climbed back into their cruiser and headed for the Gay Dolphin.

"That'll teach me to leave the office," Charlie laughed as she pulled the hitch-hikers from her jacket and pants. "How about you drop me at the station so I can clean up and get this supplement report done while you pick up the food so we don't get into anymore crap? How about that?"

"You cleaned up? Look at me Sarge!"

"You look great Clint," she smiled.

"Yea, I do, don't I?" Clint grinned.

He dropped her off in front of the station. Once inside she ran into a pack of patrol officers who were all trying to high-five her. "Nice job Sarge!" "Way to outrun a twenty-two-year-old perp!"

"No, no, no—I caught UP to him. I didn't catch him. He was unconscious. We think he ran into a tree." They weren't listening to her. She knew by the time the day was done, she would have single handedly chased the perp fourteen miles through quicksand and fought him off with only her hands and teeth, barely surviving the encounter. *Drama queens.*

She sat down at her desk and tried not to think about Jake Adams. She tried really hard. She wanted to call him and tell him about the robbery. That was one of the things she missed most about having someone; being able to call them when something good happened, when something bad happened. Charlie just wasn't sure he wanted to hear from her. He hadn't said goodbye or reached out to her and he had been gone for hours. He acted like he was all worried and wanting to protect her and then . . . nothing. She pushed it to the back of her mind and tried to start on the robbery supplement report and shut everything else out, but it crept in, as it always did, and the darkness enveloped her. She closed the door to her office.

The demons had arrived and she would have to deal with them. Her constant companions, self-doubt and feelings of unworthiness; the unintended mantra of the abandoned. The deep ache in the pit of her stomach was familiar and unwelcome. Charlie had felt it so many times in her young life. It was the very reason she had been alone the last three years. It just wasn't worth it. The span between the exhilaration she felt with Jake this morning and the excruciating pain she was feeling at this moment was . . . cruel. It was devastating and it was worth avoiding at any cost. She tried hard not to think, but it was a futile fight. *Don't go there*, she pleaded with her demons. *Please don't make me go there.*

This feeling she had was the kind that made her remember every other time she ever felt it. She wanted someone but was not wanted back. She trusted, and was made a fool. She loved, but was not loved. This was her story line. The evidence added up quickly. The common denominator was her. *These were the facts and they were not in dispute.*

Charlie grabbed the stack of reports out of her desk as the captain opened her door and cocked his head sideways at her. "Hey kid," he said. "You look good. Good job on that robbery. I hear he gave you a hell of a fight."

"No Captain, he . . ." she started and then surrendered. "Thanks Captain," she said forcing a smile. "Statement's all done from the Silver homicide, now I'm doing the robbery supplement but Crammy is taking lead, then I'll try to get through this stack of reports." She motioned to her in-box.

"Damn it, I told Willever from Special Ops to take some of those," the captain said, exasperated.

Charlie held up the Post-it Note. "She did. She took half, but there's still a crapload left." She laughed half-heartedly. "It's okay Captain. I'm no skate." She grinned and the captain grinned back, catching the Thompson reference.

God, how Charlie wished her mentor were still alive. There was so much she wanted to talk to Thompson about. What would he say about Jake, she wondered. She knew what Thompson thought about cops getting involved with cops, but she was equally confident that Thompson would see that Jake was different. He was, wasn't he? Her demons were trying to convince her otherwise.

"Where's Adams?" the captain asked, breaking into her thoughts.

"Isn't he out there? I don't know." She lied and went back to checking her paperwork, signaling the captain that she was through chatting. He knew the drill.

God her head hurt.

"Orange crusted chicken from the Gay Dolphin," Clint announced. *Oh, thank God*, Charlie thought. *Save me from myself Clint*. "Conference room," he directed as he passed by her office.

"Hey thanks for seeing if anyone else wanted anything!" Detective Cramlin said walking in from the robbery scene.

"Oh, right Crammy, I fly—I buy! Right? Yea, I caught on to that after about the 50th time you mooched a free lunch from me. Forget it," Clint said pushing past him.

"Okay," Crammy continued in his nasal drone, "Well, let me know if you guys have any left . . ." SLAM!

Clint slammed the conference room door in Crammy's face. Charlie laughed. "You're mean, McCallister."

"I know," he grinned. "But not to you."

"No," she smiled. "Not to me." *Never to me*. She

thought. *Maybe sex really does ruin everything*, she pondered. The truth was, the best relationships in her life didn't involve sex; Clint, Thompson, Mr. Daley, AJ. Clint laid out the food and picked a few more hitch-hiker stickers off Charlie's jacket and she picked a few off his pants leg, grooming each other like two spider monkeys.

Then Charlie took a napkin, wet it with her water bottle and dabbed at the scratches on his face. Clint was undeniably attractive. He was tall and lean and had dark features that matched his tanned and weathered skin. His eyes were deep brown and full of mischief. He had a rugged sweetness about him that made him irresistible to most women; definitely Hollywood material.

Clint could feel his blood pressure rise with her touch. "I hope the studio doesn't find out about this," she joked with her Hollywood handsome detective, but Clint didn't laugh. He made eye contact with her in a way that held her eyes on his. She couldn't seem to pull her hand away from his face.

Through the silence and intense eye contact they transmitted an unspoken conversation:

*Good job today Sarge. I'm glad you're okay. You're important to me.*

*Thanks for backing me up today Clint. I'm glad you're okay. You're important to me too.*

The moment went on a few seconds too long and got uncomfortable. Charlie finally broke eye contact first. She blushed a little and started looking through the takeout boxes on the table while Clint continued to stare at her. That's when Charlie noticed the printed articles scattered out on the table. She picked one up. "What's this, Clint?"

"Oh!" Clint said shaking off the tension that had filled the room, "I started pulling every case I could find involving known murderers of child molesters."

He became animated and started to explain. Clint loved being a detective. "Yeah, I know what you're thinking Sarge, that we don't have a shot in hell that one of these perps is our perp but maybe if the M.O.s line up we'll get a clue into this guy's twisted psyche and catch a break."

She glanced briefly at the first three articles laid out.

### Molestation Victim Kills Tormentor

*. . . something would finally have to give. One night in February 2009, he downed beers and vodka, drove to a mobile home in Fort Bragg, CA and shot the man he said was his tormentor once in the chest. "You're not going to hurt anyone again," Vargus, thirty-two, allegedly said as the sixty-three-year-old Darrell McNeill lay dying . . .*

### Serial Child Rapist Allegedly Killed by Molestation Victim in the Same Cell

*. . . the sixty-four-year-old man had been locked up for much of the past four decades for sexually assaulting several teenagers in the South Hampton Roads. He tossed one boy in a ditch and abandoned another in a wooden box. Now, a man who himself was a childhood victim of sexual abuse is accused of killing Ausley.*

*Dewey K. "Frankie" Venable, twenty-four, had vowed in a letter to his grandmother that he would not let himself be raped in prison. He also had told family members that he had been disciplined for attacking in-*

*mates who were sex offenders . . .*

### Thirteen-Year-Old Boy Shoots Sexually Abusive Parents

*. . . police report the pedophile suspects as the deceased. Gerard and Gwendolyn Jacobson's, thirteen-year-old son shot his parents while they slept and then called police to turn himself in. Investigation into the scene and crime revealed a wealthy and kinky life at the lavish Jacobson estate, complete with a full BDSM sexual dungeon. Mark Jacobson, a business man and sole heir to the Case Hard Steel Empire, a multi-million dollar . . .*

"It's a good angle, Clint," she said. "Really good."

Clint beamed.

"I know," he said arrogantly and then unleashed a suppressed laugh spewing a mouth full of orange chicken all over the articles.

"Nice work, Detective," Charlie laughed.

The food was good. The company was good. Add a cold beer and she'd be feeling halfway human again, but the report pile awaited her. Charlie and Clint ate and chatted about the cases until almost 4:00. She suggested that it was probably time for a pattern analysis, which Clint said was his next move. She thanked him for the food and tried to give him some money but he refused, as he always did.

"This isn't a date, McCallister," Charlie said throwing a ten spot at him.

"I know it isn't a date, Cavanaugh," he said. "If it was, you'd be buying." It was a skit that had played out a hundred times but it always made her laugh.

"So, how's Mary Jane?" Clint asked as Charlie left the conference room, ignoring him.

*Chapter 25*
**Flash**

Charlie returned to her desk and started in on the paperwork. There were several visits from multiple detectives and 1st Sergeant Willever who stopped in to see if she could take any more off of Charlie's plate. Lyn Willever was a good egg. Professional, nice, competent, educated—everything a good supervisor should be, so of course it took the department 18 years to promote her. Landon wasn't exactly progressive regarding the gay lifestyle. Gay dolphins were one thing, but a gay supervisor? That was a turd in the promotion pool. *Idiots.*

After the reports she had 165 emails to go through, interspersed with calls from everyone from God to Grecko who called to update her on the state of the evidence, or lack thereof, on the Silver case. The chemical the killer had doused the crime scene with had made the search for DNA all but impossible just like the last three, but the medical examiner did mention two very small puncture wounds in the victim's scalp that were still unexplained. Maybe they were related to the homicide. *Damn it, this killer knew his shit.* She could tell that Grecko was devastated. She didn't know if he was sorry that he couldn't help stop a killer, or sorry that he had let her down. Yea, she knew which it was. Oh well, at least there were some men she could count on.

No sex. That was the key.

*Crap.* It just occurred to her. She hadn't actually had sex with Jake Adams. Well, she had, but he hadn't so did that count? *Not legally it didn't. Did it count as sex at all? God, her head hurt. Why the fuck hadn't she heard from him?* She felt like she was slowly dying with each passing minute.

The next time she looked up, it was after nine. She had been at it for over twelve hours. Any other week, that was business as usual, but today it was kicking her ass. Her phone rang again. She figured it must be one of her detectives to be calling her desk this late, so she answered it, wondering why they didn't call her cell and she scanned the desk for her cell phone.

"Damn it, Charlie! Is it your mission in life to give me a goddamn heart attack?" It was Jake. He was angry and she was confused.

"What? I don't understand. Jake, what's wrong?"

"I said 2100! I said I would be back at your apartment at 9:00. I actually gave you a time. I checked Amy's Café. I even called Clint."

"What?" she asked, completely lost. "When did you say 9:00? Jake, you left here without saying a word."

"I sent you a text, Charlie. In fact, I sent several. At first, I thought you were just busy. Then I thought you were trying to get even with me for not answering you yesterday. Is that what this is, because—"

She cut him off. "Jake, Jake I-I don't think I have my cell phone. I can't believe it. I have been surgically attached to that phone since I made detective, but it's not here. I've used my desk phone all day. I think I must have left my cell at home this morning."

"Home. Now," he said. She hung up the phone without saying goodbye, gathered her things and ran for the parking lot. Inside her car she found her phone, lying face down on the passenger side floor board, she quickly checked it.

*11:00 a.m.*

*I'm going to head to the field office to Norfolk and then to Va. Beach HQ so I can get back in time to tuck you in Baby. I will be there at 2100. I'm sure you're tired but I'd like you to stay at the station until then. I am worried about you being out here alone. I know you are capable but I want to protect you, please let me. It has been a long time since I felt this way about anyone.*

*4:00 p.m.*

*I know you are trying to get through a lot today, but I need you to confirm for me that you are going to stay at the station until I get back and not go home to an empty apartment without me.*

*6:00 p.m.*

*You better have a good explanation for why you haven't returned my texts or answered my calls. Make that a great explanation. Apparently, that spanking last night did not convey the intended message that I do not put up with this shit. I can fix that Charlie.*

*8:00 p.m.*

*I am leaving the beach at 2030. I will see you at your house at 2100. Do you understand me?*

The last text was from Clint.

*9:00 p.m.*

*Hey Sarge, Adams is looking for you. You still at the station?*

She texted Clint back, then Jake.

*9:15 p.m. I spoke to him, thanks Clint.*

*9:16 p.m. Jake. I just found my phone in the car. I'm so sorry. On my way.*

Charlie felt nauseous as the blood raced to her face. Like a teenager who had been caught skipping school or watching a porn tape, she was sick to her stomach and her mind was searching for a way to explain things to

Jake in a way that would minimize the awaiting explosion.

What did he mean "I don't put up with this shit"? *It was an accident*. Not like last night when she was being a brat. *Did that mean he wasn't going to meet her at her apartment?*

Charlie struggled all the way home vacillating between anger with him for being so controlling and unreasonable and being upset with herself for worrying and upsetting him two nights in a row. She had no idea which Jake awaited her at her apartment but she feared the worst, the one whose right eye flashed light when he was losing it. She pulled in next to the SUV deciding that it was better that the initial encounter take place in the parking lot—a strategically safer location, but the SUV was empty. She looked up into the open stairwell but didn't see him waiting there. Panic began to well up in her.

*Where was he? Was he waiting on the landing like he did at the station? Was he going to try to scare her to punish her? Did someone else get to him first?*

Her heart was racing. She was coming unglued and it was pissing her off. She chased an armed robber through the woods today, was shot at and felt not one ounce of fear or trepidation. Now, she was standing in a parking lot shaking because a romantic interest from an unconsummated relationship was angry with her for forgetting her cell phone, causing her to imagine all kinds of ridiculous scenarios. *Enough.*

Charlie found her steel and marched up the stairs to her apartment. *Maybe she was falling in love with him, but so what? She didn't put up with shit either.* She unlocked the deadbolt and stormed through the door, coming face to face with a man inside.

The room was dark. But he was there. *Shit! She was in trouble.* The only other light in the room came from a small candle in the middle of her coffee table. The stereo was playing a song she knew by Judas Priest. *Angel.*

She was wrong to assume it was Jake in the dark room. It could have been anyone. It could have been the killer, but it wasn't. She didn't need to see him.  She could feel him.

First things first. Her Irish was up. She turned on the light.

"How did you get in here, Jake?"

Not taking his eyes off her, he picked up the remote and muted the stereo but said nothing.

"Look, you are welcome here, you know that and I appreciate how you've been looking out for me, but this door was locked when I left here this morning and I would like to know how you got in here."

He remained passive, his eyes fixed on hers, and she became nervous.

"I mean if you can get in, maybe the killer can too, and I wonder if maybe I need to upgrade the lock or something," she fumbled her words.

No reaction.

"Jake" she said, finding her backbone again. "I am not going to feel bad for forgetting my phone in the car. I'm sorry I worried you. I really am, but an awful lot has happened in the last few days. I didn't even tell you what happened to me today. I'm not making excuses but I'm not going to apologize for being frazzled right now."

He stood up and moved toward her. She was shaking on the inside but she refused to allow herself to shake on the outside.

"Now, you're a little intense, I get that and maybe even a control freak," she continued. "Well, that sounded worse than I meant for it to sound. But I don't think you're being very fair not to consider . . ." he took her face in his hands, kissed her gently, and took her by the hand.

"I have a bath ready for you," he said quietly.

*What?*

She followed him wordlessly. Her Susan McKeown Irish Love songs CD was playing on her nightstand, her bathroom was lit with candles, and the scent of fragrant bubbles filled the room. He removed her clothes gently while she stared at him, unable to speak and on the verge of tears.

She had been in this place before, rattled by a bad day. It had happened many times. She would hold it together at work like it was no big deal and sometimes she even made it all the way home before she dealt with the reality of whatever frightening or inhumane horror she had dealt with on the job. Once or twice she lost it in the car on the way home, but usually she made it inside her apartment where she would take that first real breath. After that, she would let it go, alone. Always alone when she took that breath. Even when she was married, she bore her burden alone, then the tears would come along with whatever emotions she had been holding hostage. Like a dam breaking loose, there was no containing it once it began.

Tonight, she was not alone. Tonight, she didn't have to take that breath alone. She didn't have to hurt alone. She didn't have to protect herself. Jake Adams would protect her tonight.

He pulled the ponytail band from her unwashed hair

and ran his hands through it, making her groan. Charlie was unable to keep up with the rollercoaster ride that was Jake Adams. Lusting after him one minute, scared to death of him the next, frustrated as hell by him somewhere in the middle . . . and then there was the suspicion she hadn't quite allowed herself to acknowledge, though she feared Clint had. Charlie kept her eyes closed as he ran his hands along the outside of her breasts and along her waist, pulling her in to kiss her again. Jake guided her into the bath and she lay back and sighed while he sat on the floor next to her sliding a washcloth across her bare breast and neck.

"Breathe, Baby," he instructed. When she did, her eyes filled with tears. Not sad tears, but tears of another kind. *Relief maybe? Or maybe it was someone caring for her so tenderly.* Someone who broke into her apartment to care for her—but still.

"Clint told me what happened today. I just . . . I wanted to have all of this ready by the time you got here so I let myself in." She nodded and closed her eyes again and sunk deeper into the tub as quiet tears rolled down her cheeks. Her hand covered his while he caressed her with the washcloth. She no longer cared how he got in. She needed him and he was here. It was something that happened so rarely in Charlie's life, someone, anyone, being there for her when she needed it the most. Jake reached between her legs to open the drain and re-start the warm water sending a quiver through her body.

Using a plastic pitcher she recognized from her kitchen, he tipped her chin back, wetting her hair. Then he stood up and slowly removed his clothes, never taking his eyes off of her. She watched in wonder as she was finally able to see what so far she had only felt. She gazed at his broad square shoulders, his wide chest, and his ample manhood, already more than half erect. He stood before her without an ounce of apprehension. Charlie found his confidence incredibly sexy. She slid forward, silently inviting him into the tub and he slid in behind her filling the tub to its limits. He wrapped his arms and legs around her. She let out an audible sigh and melted into him. He filled his massive hands with shampoo and began washing her hair. The sensation was like nothing she had ever felt and she let herself get lost in it, getting more and more excited by his full erection against her back.

When he was finished, he held her quietly against his chest. When the water cooled, he gently moved her forward, stepped out of the tub, and dried himself first before filling the pitcher with warm water and pouring it over her. He guided her out of the tub, wrapped her in a towel, and hugged her while he dried her the way she imagined a father would lovingly dry a small child. He started to slide her Redskins jersey on over her head but she shook her head no.

Jake was thrilled that she wanted to stay naked with him, completely exposed and vulnerable. It was a sign of trust and it further empowered him. She sat down at her dressing table to brush out her hair but he took the brush from her. He brushed it for much longer than he needed to and loved the response she was giving him. Her eyes were closed, her head was tipped back, and she groaned quietly. His eyes were fixed on her hard and perfect nipples.

Charlie let herself drift back to Mr. Daley brushing her hair. No one, until now, had done this to her. It was so intimate, so erotic. *Why couldn't her husband have done these things for her, to her?* Maybe things would have turned out differently for them if he could only have found a way to reach her, but he never had. No man ever really had, until now. As a girl, Mr. Daley brushing her hair aroused her but she didn't understand it. Now she understood it and she understood Jake Adams. He was as broken as she was, as alone as she was, and as frightened as she was. Someone had hurt him badly and whoever it was, she hated them.

Charlie abandoned her thoughts and kept her eyes closed as each stroke of the brush gently pulled her head back. Every stroke both sent a shiver through her and radiated warmth through her body. She wished it would go on for hours. She wanted him, needed him. She finally stood up, took the brush from him and led him to her bed. Their eyes stayed locked until he looked down at the bed and his expression changed.

Charlie followed his eyes and what she saw there horrified her.

*Chapter 26*
**Gus**

Gus.

Gus was laying there in the middle of the sheets where she had left him. Jake raised an eyebrow and gave her a wicked grin. She blushed and finally found her first words since she entered the apartment and confronted him.

"Oh, that," her voice cracked. "That's umm. Well, that's Gus."

"Gus?" he asked, his eyes dancing.

"Yea, Gus. You know, the fat mouse from Cinderella," she said matter-of-factly and shrugged her shoulders, hiding Gus behind her back. With that he burst into laughter, and tackled her onto the bed.

"Give me that!" he laughed, trying to wrestle Gus from her grasp.

"No, no, no. Oh no you don't! Nooooo!" she screamed and giggled.

Jake pinned her underneath him face down, her breath and pulse quickening as he ripped the vibrator from her grasp and turned it to full power with one hand. He stayed on top of her, his naked manhood fully erect now and lodged in between her full smooth thighs. He moved his vibrating hand underneath her while she struggled to get free, moving it fractions of an inch until he found the spot. Then she was paralyzed. She was his prisoner.

"Jake. Please," she begged, her body stiffening.

"Such a well-mannered young lady," he whispered into her ear. "Such a good girl," he panted, her paralysis driving him out of his mind.

It didn't take long. He could feel her getting close.

"Not yet, Charlie," he whispered.

*What?* Her mind was almost gone. *Did he say not yet?*

"Not until I give you permission to come, Baby," he said grinding against her.

"Jake," she begged. "I can't. I can't stop it. Please."

"Yes, you can, Charlotte. You will not come until I tell you to come."

She squeezed her eyes shut and started to whimper in frustration and ecstasy. He pressed the vibrator harder against her.

"Jake!"

"I said not yet."

"Please!"

"Okay, my good girl," he said. "Now Baby. Come now." He trapped her in his grasp like a vice.

"Now!" he commanded as his large hand crashed down fully against her flesh. The pain was ecstasy, the restraint was all-consuming, and the control he had over her ignited her and she lost it. Jake moved his hand to her mouth to muffle her screams. She bucked hard and finally won the physical battle, managing to roll him off of her and slap away the vibrator. She continued to spasm and scream, while he held her tight maintaining control of her body, gently muffling her whimpers until she started to come down from her orgasms. He counted three. She ripped his hand from her mouth and gasped for air, liquid coming from her eyes, her nose, and her mouth while she struggled to regain some kind of composure.

"Oh my God," she whispered, breathless. "Oh my God."

Jake rocked her in his arms and soothed her and said, "It's okay. It's okay. I've got you. Shhhh." He continued to rock her until she returned from where she had gone.

He handed her a tissue and she wiped her face before rolling to face him and wrapping her arms tightly around his neck. She couldn't have pressed herself any deeper into him. She lay in his arms trembling until her breathing started to normalize. Jake was almost asleep when she finally pulled away to look at him.

"What the fuck, Adams!"

Jake grinned, "You needed it."

"I've never lost control like that. I felt like I was possessed or something! Jesus that was intense," she confessed without a hint of reservation.

"You were possessed. By me."

He smiled warmly. "I had a dream about you last night. It felt more like a memory than a dream." he said. "It's hard to explain. I just feel like I have known you a lot longer than just a few weeks. A lot longer," he said sleepily, closing his eyes. "Why did you name your vibrator?"

"I don't know," she said shyly. "If you're going to take someone to bed shouldn't you know their name?" She shrugged, embarrassed.

He laughed, kissed the top of her head, and drew her head to his chest. She whispered, "I want you to make love to me, Jake."

"I just did," he said, his eyes still closed and his face nuzzling into her chest as he took her nipple into his mouth and gently sucked.

"No," she said becoming breathless again at the wetness of his tongue. "I mean . . ."

"Go to sleep, Angel," he said rolling her over forcefully and pulling her into his chest. Jake surrendered to sleep quickly and she lay still, listening to him sleep. Listening in love and lust and wonder and just before she fell off to exhausted sleep it hit her. *Angel?*

When she woke during the night Jake was still in a deep sleep beside her. She wrestled herself from his massive arms and ran to the bathroom to brush her teeth hoping to stave off morning breath. The bathroom floor started to vibrate and she looked around confused about where it was coming from. The vibration was subtle at first but then it became more violent. Charlie found herself hanging onto the bathroom sink to steady herself and that's when she heard it. The train whistle grew louder, then the bell started DING! DING! DING!

*Jake! She had to warn him!* She tried to make it back to the bed but the floor was shaking so hard she couldn't move forward. She could see the light from the locomotive bearing down on the room, coming right for them. "Jake!" she screamed.

"Noooooooo!"

"Charlie! Charlie!" he said, "Baby, it's okay. It's okay," he said as he shook her awake. She was sobbing hysterically and he had to continue to shake her to make her open her eyes.

"It's okay. I'm here. It's okay," he repeated pulling her close. "Charlie. What the hell were you dreaming about? Daniel Silver?"

"No," she sobbed. "No. Not that. The train. It was coming for you. It always comes for me, but it was headed right for you," she said, trying to catch her breath.

"What?" Jake asked, confused. He sat her up and pulled her close. "There's no train. No train," he said rattled by her terror.

He held her for a long time while she shook and whispered about trains in her nightmares and how she had no idea where they came from or why they terrified her. When he could no longer feel her heart pounding against his chest as he held her, he laid her down and stroked her hair until she fell back to sleep, but there would be no more sleep for Jake that night. His reaction to her nightmare terrified him beyond comprehension. He felt it was an omen of things to come. Bad things, and Jake Adams knew a thing or two about bad things.

In the morning he suggested they spend the weekend together. Jake worried about his SUV being parked in front her apartment complex all weekend and wanted her to come to his hotel but she argued that was just as obvious and that maybe leaving Landon all together would be a better idea. They finally decided that he would go to his hotel and pack for the weekend, then come back for her and they would head for the beach. Charlie took a quick shower and jumped at the opportunity to grab her laptop and catch up with AJ. She wasn't looking forward to telling him that she had fallen in love, but she had to tell him. They were friends. They were close. So close that she suspected that he probably already knew.

VABlueAngel: AJ?

She waited for his response, but there was none. It wasn't their usual time. She usually chatted with him at night. *Maybe he wasn't as tuned in to her as she had fantasized that he was?* she thought, already trying to minimize the significance he played in her life.

VABlueAngel: AJ?

**AJ101-789: I'm here.**

*Oh yea, he knew.*

VABlueAngel: You're upset with me. I'm so sorry AJ. You have been there for me for over a year and now I've disappeared on you. I'm so sorry. So much has happened.

**AJ101-789: Are you in love with him Angel?**

Damn it. He knew. She knew he would know.

VABlueAngel: Yes.

**AJ101-789: You are loved back?**

VABlueAngel: Yes.

**AJ101-789: I knew it. He's not good enough for you Angel.**

His words stung, and anger flashed in her eyes as she typed.

VABlueAngel: What a thing to say AJ! How could you possibly know that?

**AJ101-789: Because he's a cop. Because no one is good enough for you. Because you told me yourself you know almost nothing about him. Shall I go on?**

VABlueAngel: No. I understand that you are worried about me but please don't be AJ. I've never felt like this about anyone. I know that I don't know much about him but I know how I feel. It's been such a long time since I have let myself trust someone with my heart and only you truly know how lonely my life has been. You're my friend, please be happy for me.

**AJ101-789: Has he told you that he loves you Angel?**

Her blood pressure started to rise again. Why was AJ being so awful? But she knew why.

VABlueAngel: No. I just feel it.

**AJ101-789: I want you happy Angel—you know I do. I just don't want you to get hurt. I don't want to talk about him anymore. Tell me what's going on with the homicides. Are you off the case?**

VABlueAngel: No, but like I said it's not my case. It's never been my case. It's just my shop. I did however get into a foot pursuit yesterday. It was awesome! I didn't catch him but I chased the shit out of him! LOL

**AJ101-789: Another scumbag off the street. Good work Angel. ☺**

VABlueAngel: How do you know we got him off the street? I said I didn't catch him.

**AJ101-789: Which implies someone else did right? Damn girl, our mojo is off. See what happens when we don't talk every day?**

VABlueAngel: Oh. Yes. Well, not exactly. The perp was unconscious by the time I caught up to him. We think he ran into a tree or a low branch or something. He was out cold as a mackerel.

**AJ101-789: LOL are you sure he wasn't playing possum? If you were chasing me, I'd find a way to get caught. Was he with you?**

VABlueAngel: Clint was with me.

**AJ101-789: Ahhhh. And yet another admirer. You are surrounded Angel. I don't blame them. If I were there, I'd never leave your side.**

VABlueAngel: Clint's not an admirer. He's a subordinate. Enough about me. How are you doing over there?

**AJ101-789: It's been interesting. A roller coaster.**

Charlie could relate.

VABlueAngel: Just tell me you're safe.

**AJ101-789: For the moment. Yes. I miss you, Charlie.**

VABlueAngel: I miss you, too, AJ. I'll try to do better about checking in okay?

**AJ101-789: No Angel. We knew this relationship had a shelf life. It was just a matter of time before someone would steal your heart. I just didn't think it would be the Fed.**

VABlueAngel: Neither did I AJ. I never saw it coming.

**AJ101-789: I know. Time for me to crash.**

Charlie was unsettled by her discussion with AJ. *Did he just break off their friendship?* She was glad he finally knew what was happening with her but sad that she had hurt him. Maybe he was right. Maybe their friendship did have a shelf life. For the last year or so, AJ had been more of a surrogate boyfriend than just an internet buddy, but she had never really admitted that to herself until now. She often fantasized about him showing up at her office, carrying a bouquet of flowers, and wearing a military dress uniform and a big smile. He would be tall and handsome and perfect. "Hello Angel," he would say to her and she would know instantly that it was him and run to his arms.

It was a fantasy that sustained her through many lonely nights but the truth was she no longer needed a fantasy life. She had Jake now. She wasn't alone anymore.

*"Has he told you he loves you?"*

AJ's question was like a cold splash of water in her face. She pushed it from her head and started to pack. Jake would be back soon to pick her up and she still wasn't packed. She started going through her closet unsure how they would be spending their two days together. She hoped it would be two days of who-the-hell-needs-clothes but on second thought, they might have to eat at some point. Only a few of the hotels on the strip had room service and she had only stayed in one once on her honeymoon. She smiled at the thought of her ex. She was still mad at him, but she cherished many of the memories they had made together, especially at the beach. He had once written her a love note in the sand and then took her to the balcony in their room to read it. It was a happy time. Even if she had to give him up she did not want to give up the memories of the good times, of which there were many.

*Sweatshirts. She would need sweatshirts*, it was still pretty chilly, especially at night, even more so at the beach. She packed a bathing suit but decided that was stupid in the middle of March so she took it out. She dug to the bottom of her lingerie drawer for her sexiest nightgowns, her Redskins shirt notwithstanding, but her heart fell as she looked at the skimpy night gowns in the bottom of her drawer and realized that the last time she had tried on or purchased lingerie was twenty pounds ago.

"Fucking Gay Dolphin," she muttered.

She did however find some sexy underwear and a camisole. That would have to do. She put on her holey jeans, a red sweater, and white tennis shoes. She always liked the color red on her and was hoping Jake would too. Then she straightened her shiny brown hair with a flat iron. She rarely wore it straightened because it took too much time, but this weekend was special. Charlie hoped it would be very special. She also packed a few oversized t-shirts to lounge in and made a mental note that it was time to hit Victoria's Secret immediately following this trip. She looked at Gus and considered him for a moment, replaying last night's wrestling match in her head, but decided he would stay.

"Sorry buddy," she said, shaking her head and putting Gus back in her nightstand drawer. "Not this trip." She imagined him in the dark drawer with a boo-boo lip jutting out in disappointment.

Jake arrived looking very relaxed in tan khakis and off-white linen shirt with a London Fog windbreaker and deck shoes. "Wow, Charlie," he said, startled when she opened the door. "You look amazing."

"Really?" she squeaked. He reached out and touched her straightened hair, stroking it gently.

"I like your hair like this, Baby," he growled, and his eyes got that look. Charlie was anxious to get to the beach but she was frozen in place. When that look came over him, she was powerless to move, to object or to suggest. She was lost in his penetrating gaze.

"I-I guess we should go. I-did you get a reservation? Because even this time of year Saturdays can be . . ." He ran a thumb across her lips and she stopped midsentence and closed her eyes.

"Let's go," he said quietly. "Now Charlie," he said louder, snapping her out of her trance.

They drove in relative silence the thirty minutes to the strip on the beach. There was an undercurrent of electricity charging the Fed Mobile and she began to fantasize about Jake finally making love to her. For real this time. He seemed lost in his thoughts as well. *Was he nervous?* She certainly was. She couldn't believe how nervous she was, but him? *Calm cool Mr. Fed? Mr. Alpha Male?* Her thoughts were broken as Jake pulled into the Ocean Club Beach Resort. She looked at him and then looked up at the seventeen-story hotel-da-shit.

"Jake?" she asked, but he ignored her as he handed his keys to the valet.

By noon they were checked into their suite. The Ocean Beach Club was the most exclusive hotel on the strip. Even though Charlie had been in Landon for over a decade she never expected she would ever spend a night in a room in this hotel, not on a cop's salary, let alone a suite. The sitting room was magnificent, expansive, and exquisitely decorated in light turquoise and beach gold with a 60-inch flat screen TV. In the bedroom was a California king bed with a velvet chaise lounge and another giant flat screen. Charlie almost gasped when she saw the size of the Jacuzzi platform tub in the bathroom.

"Now this is a bathtub," Jake said in a low voice behind her, massaging the back of her neck as she stared at the tub. Charlie tried not to appear overly excited about the suite, worried that she would seem unsophisticated, but she was blown away and Jake was grinning at the look on her face.

"Jake, this is the most amazing room I've ever seen," she said, with wonder, "but I don't need this. Really. There are much more affordable hotels on the strip. Did Captain Kerns get you a discount or something?"

"No discount," Jake said flatly, sounding a little offended. "Don't you know I want to take care of you?"

Charlie was unable to process the weight of what he

had just said. Her heart desperately wanted to believe, but her mind put up a fight. "Why isn't it on the top floor?" she questioned. "I thought suites and penthouses were on the top floor?" She realized she had just let the cat out of the bag. Oh well, she was unsophisticated! Jake would have to be okay with that.

"Because the best views are not always from the top floor, Angel." She looked at him and narrowed her eyes. That was twice now he had called her Angel.

"What?" he asked perplexed.

"Nothing," she lied.

"Come on," he said as he guided her to the balcony with his hand on the small of her back. He opened the door and the roar of the ocean, the ocean breeze, and the smell of salt water assaulted her senses. The view was magnificent and it took her breath away. God, she loved the ocean and she said a quiet thank you to God for being lucky enough to be born close to one. She closed her eyes and breathed it in. When she opened her eyes, she saw him doing the same thing and she covered his giant hand with her tiny fingers and squeezed. He led her back inside and into the bedroom, where her pulse started to quicken as he kissed her, slowly . . . seducing her mouth with his, but her anticipation was short lived.

"Boardwalk! Come on, let's go!" he chirped, in a higher than usual voice, sounding like a little boy and melting her heart. She grabbed her sunglasses and her Dive Bahamas baseball hat and raced him to the door.

They lunched at the Beachside Diner and she ordered a mimosa, but Jake passed.

"You don't drink?"

"Very rarely," he said, offering no further explanation. She stared at him demanding an answer. "I like to be in control."

She felt her face flush and her pulse quicken.

"I've noticed," she said avoiding his stare. "Maybe, we could try it together. I don't drink very often myself but after the week we've had, maybe a little buzz before we take a swim in that tub would be . . . I don't know . . . fun." She grinned, hoping he would let his guard down enough to fully take her.

"We'll see," his eyes twinkled, knowing full well what she was up to.

They walked along the boardwalk for hours, talking about the case, about Landon PD and about Thompson. AJ was right—she knew very little about Jake Adams and two hours of walking hadn't gotten her any closer. Whenever she would ask him a question to learn more about him, he would pretend to answer by starting to talk about himself but then he turned it into a question for her to answer and the ensuing hours were spent talking about her instead of him.

"Why don't you talk about yourself?"

"I do. Tell me about the hat. You a scuba diver, or you just liked the hat?"

"I'm a diver," she said, proudly. "Ten years now." He had done it again.

"For fun or are you a police diver?"

She looked sheepishly at him. "I was going to be a police diver. But, I didn't make the team. There was an . . . incident. An accident." He motioned the gimme more sign with his hand. Charlie sighed. Oh well, if he hung around Landon PD long enough, he was bound to hear the story. He might as well hear it from her.

"I learned to dive in my early twenties in the Keys— you know, warm water, pretty fish, no wetsuit needed yada yada."

"Mhmm."

"Well, a few years ago I thought I might try out for the SWAT Team but my ex freaked out," she said, rolling her eyes.

Even the mention of another man invoked a reaction in him that he had difficulty hiding. A man who had been with her. A man who had hurt her and left her, but mostly a man who had been with her. Jake was no longer able to hear what she was saying so he took a deep breath and tried to focus.

"So I said 'that's ridiculous, just because you didn't make the team doesn't mean I won't.' I was in a little better shape back then," she qualified, looking down at herself briefly.

"Your shape is perfect," he said placing his hand on her ass in full view of the boardwalk foot traffic, and she grinned at him and at her butterflies.

"So anyway, when he dumped me, I put my letter in for the Dive Team because that was the opening that came available first. It didn't go so well. I kind of drowned during the testing."

"What?" Jake said, stopping on the boardwalk and facing her.

"Well, I mean, I didn't, obviously, but technically I did. It turned out okay but I was kind of unconscious at the bottom of Lake Ewing and they had to pull me out, resuscitate me and stuff." She delivered the information like it was no big deal. Jake pulled her into a tight hug as if it had just happened and she could feel his body trembling.

"It was just one of those freak things." She couldn't help loving him for his reaction. "Come on," she said, and started walking again but he grabbed her hand and pulled her back to the rail.

"You drained your tank?" Jake asked.

"You dive, Adams?" she asked surprised.

"I do," he said, and she grinned in spite of telling the story she hated to relive.

"Cool," she said. "Where have you been diving? How many hours have you logged?"

He glared impatiently at her and she shifted uncomfortably.

"Tell me the rest," he instructed. She glanced up at him, his eyes were dark. "Tell me."

Charlie took a deep breath. "Jake. I don't see the point . . ."

"Tell me," he ordered.

"I . . . well I spent the first thirty seconds convincing myself it was psychological and the second thirty seconds trying to get the emergency floats to activate," she looked up tentatively and his eyes were transfixed on her. "By the time I knew I was in real trouble, it was too late. I was in full panic mode. I was trying to drop my weight belt but I couldn't get my glove under the release latch. Finally, I just ripped off the mask and started clawing at the water . . . I was . . ."

"Stop. Okay. Stop," he said grabbing her hand, pulling her to him and hugging her so tightly she could barely breathe.

"It's okay, Jake. It wasn't that big a deal." But even as she said it her eyes started to fill. There was no one there to have this reaction when the diving accident happened. She went home to an empty apartment. Nothing about it felt right. Someone should have been with her. *That was a really close call*, she thought as she sat alone on her couch. . . . *and there is no one here*. The person who promised to protect her and be there for her was gone and she was alone. The feeling of loneliness that enveloped her that day, while her husband was off making a new life, was one of the worst feelings she had ever known, and there were a shitload of those feelings to pick from.

"It was kind of funny actually. The guys put an empty fish tank on my desk with a Barbie doll at the bottom . . ." He interrupted her. "It's not okay, Charlie." She struggled to keep from losing it.

*How did this man always find a way to reach parts of her she had purposely rendered un-reachable?* They leaned against the rail embracing each other for what felt like hours. Not talking, just hugging. Jake finally spoke first. He grabbed her by the shoulders and looked into her sad eyes, his face serious and dark.

"I wish I could make you understand what it does to me to think of you hurt, or scared, or sad," he said removing her hat and stroking her hair. "You almost drown, you get shot at, you have a killer writing you messages in blood. I just want to take you and disappear. What do you think of that idea, Sergeant Cavanaugh?"

She looked at him stunned and confused. "What do you mean? Leave Landon? I . . . I can't Jake. You know I can't. My job, my guys I . . ."

"Fine," he said, cutting her off coldly. "We'll do it your way." He stared her down for a moment, and then walked away leaving her standing at the railing by herself, sending her into a momentary panic. Her normal M.O. would be to stand there and let him walk away; *You don't want me? Fine, I don't want you either.* Not this time. This was a man she would risk everything for, a man she would finally have the courage to fight for. She ran after him and grabbed his hand, spinning him around.

"What?" he said, startled as she pulled him in the opposite direction. "Where are we going?"

"We're getting a drink," she said, marching him down the boardwalk. "Several, in fact."

They sat on the balcony patio at the Sunset Tower restaurant. Though the five-star restaurant had a dress code, it didn't usually kick in until after seven and it was only five. The mood was still heavy from the diving story, though his reaction was making her fall harder by the second. "Have a drink with me, Jake. Come on, we've had a hell of a week."

"No, thank you," he said flatly.

"Please, Daddy," she said batting her eyelashes, hoping the shift in tactics would seduce his dominant side. "Let me have some fun tonight."

Jake grinned, both aroused and amused. "Brat." He was angry with her for not letting him stay angry with her. "I'll have a scotch. Lagavulin if you have it," Jake said to the waiter.

"No, he won't.  He'll have what I'm having," she said confidently but then looked nervously at Jake. "Two Long Island iced teas." The waiter looked at Jake, but Jake was too busy piercing Charlie with his eyes to deal with him, so he walked away.

"Don't look at me like that, please," she said, sheepishly. "This is my party. I want you to drink with me."

Two lobsters, two more Long Island ice teas, and a magnificent sunset sky later, they were headed back down the boardwalk to their hotel. Charlie was fuzzy, but Jake seemed largely unaffected—except for his eyes and the tone of his voice.

They held hands as they walked. The sun had already set in the late March sky as they passed a tattoo shop. Jake pulled on Charlie's hand until they were looking into the shop window. He stood behind her, bent over with his arms around her waist and his head nestled against hers so he could whisper into her ear.

"Do you know what I want?" he asked in a hushed voice.

She shook her head, horrified at the idea of matching tattoos but said nothing, not wanting to disappoint him.

"I want to mark you," he growled.

"Mark me?" she swallowed. "You mean like . . . property of?"

"Not a tattoo. I want to mark you in a way that reminds you every minute of every day that you belong to me. An act of submission that forms a permanent bond of trust between us. A salacious secret that only we know."

Charlie's head was swimming, from the teas, from the smell of the alcohol on his breath, and from the site of the nipple piercing jewelry he was pointing at.

"What? Oh, no Adams. No fucking way," she started to move from the window, but he held her in place and moved his hand to her neck.

"Way," he said flatly. Her pulse quickened at his control over her body and her legs started to feel weak. "Jake. Jake. I need . . ."

"I know what you need, Charlotte," he said, breathing heavily into her ear and finally releasing his grip.

She sighed and took his hand and said, "Come on, you lunatic. We need to lie down." He grinned an evil grin and lost his footing as they stepped away from the window.

Back at the suite they both collapsed on to the bed. She on her back, him propped up on his elbow, looking at her like she was dessert. He slid up her shirt and bra and started teasing her nipples with his fingers.

"Right here," he growled. "Two beautiful little gold rings to remind you that you are mine. That you trust me and that you are all mine."

"Oh my God, Jake, you are drunk. Hell, I'm drunk too but I'll never be drunk enough to pierce my nipples, you freak." She laughed nervously, not sure if he was kidding, and confused by the fact the whole idea was turning her on.

Well, she had wanted him to drop his guard and dropped it was. *Be careful what you wish for*, she thought.

Jake smiled a sad smile of resignation at her and traced her full lips with his fingers. "You might . . . if you were in love with me," he said, his eyes closing, as if imagining it. Charlie looked into his sad and handsome chiseled face.

*If?* she thought. There was no if about it, but the words wouldn't come. He kissed her deeply and gently rolled her over and pulled her into him and they both drifted off to sleep.

At two a.m. Charlie awoke to a pounding headache and the realization that she had lost a night with him. *Damn it!* She slid out from under his arms. This was supposed to be a night of drunken revelations, a long luxurious bath, and out-of-control love-making.

She changed out of her clothes and into a t-shirt and panties pausing to look sadly at the oversized Jacuzzi before crawling back into bed and into Jake's arms. He didn't wake up but immediately re-enveloped her with his body. It felt like they had been sharing a bed for a hundred years.

"I do love you, Jake," she whispered, before drifting off into a peaceful sleep.

Jake awoke at seven, realized he was still in his clothes and gave his partner an annoyed shove. "We lost the whole night Cavanaugh. Good plan genius! Oww, my head hurts."

She groaned and rolled over to face him. "You can't hold your liquor Adams," she grinned mischievously.

"Oh and you can?"

"Well at least I changed out of my clothes," she retorted.

"I'll get you out of your clothes," he said, his eyes dancing. She squealed as she pretended to try to escape him. He caught her by the t-shirt tail and pulled her back, wrestling the shirt off and fighting for her panties.

"Jake!" she screamed, as he flattened her on her back, ripped her panties off and slid off the bed between her knees. His breath made contact with her wetness. His tongue barely made contact, causing her to arch her back and push herself toward him.

"Lay still," he ordered, his tongue slowly probing her. She floated in ecstasy while he played, teased, and tormented her before he finally plunged his tongue deep inside her. A scream caught in her throat as she let go, but he showed no mercy, opening his mouth to completely cover her mound. Then he started to suck, his teeth cutting into her flesh while he devoured her. She screamed again and begged him to stop all the while grinding into his face, wanting more, wanting so much more. She finally lay limp and semi-conscious while he gently licked her, letting her come down slowly. She didn't know if she had fallen asleep or entered another dimension but as she was coming back from wherever she had been she realized he was still licking her. Gently and rhythmically. The realization of what she awoke to almost triggered another orgasm, but he denied her by stopping just before she climaxed. He climbed on top of her, rock hard through his wrinkled khakis and kissed her with lips that were covered in her scent. To his delight, she devoured his mouth.

"Please Jake. Please," she begged. "I need you."

"Shhhh," he said quietly. "Easy Baby."

This time it was Charlie's turn to flash and the anger in her eyes caught him off guard.

"FUCK EASY!" she screamed.

*Chapter 27*
## I Confuse You? Don't I?


"hat did you say?"

"I said *fuck* easy!" She tried not to react as his entire body transformed.

"What the fuck is going on? Why am I not good enough for you?" she demanded, un-intimidated by his clenched fists.

Jake glared.

"I mean, Jesus Christ, Adams," she slapped the sheets in frustration. "Last night you want to mark me by piercing you know . . . my nipples and you practically told me that you're, you know, that you might be, you know, in love with me and this morning you want me to take it easy?"

His cold eyes pierced her and she knew she had gone too far but she was too frustrated to calculate how far, which might have silenced her, and she was not ready to be silenced.

"It's not fair, Jake. I want you like I have never wanted anybody in my life. My body is aching for you and you just won't, and I don't know why. I don't know what's wrong because I know you are feeling it too. Am I not thin enough? Not attractive enough? What? Just tell me. I tell you everything and you tell me nothing!"

"Are you finished?" he asked coolly.

Charlie laid flat on her back and stared at the ceiling, her arms folded and her jaw squared.

"Go make a bath for us. I'm going to order up some breakfast." He said in reply to her silence.

Charlie didn't move.

"Now, Charlotte," he said, but she didn't budge. He moved his face closer to hers. "I'm not playing this game, little girl," he said, willing her eyes to meet his. She looked up at him and her stomach flipped.

"Get up now and draw us a bath," he ordered again, "or I will beat your ass."

She hesitated for a second. The threat of a spanking sent a sexually charged shiver through her, but she decided it would be better not to push him given the look in his eyes. A spanking she could handle, a beating she could not and this Jake might not know the difference. She stomped her feet like a petulant teenager as she crossed the massive suite to the bathroom. Jake slowly followed her in step like a cat stalking a mouse. As Charlie pouted naked with her arms folded in protest and watched the water fill the bath, Jake moved in behind her undetected. In a split second he had his arms across the front and back of her neck in a chokehold.

"I don't like to be pushed, Charlotte," he hissed through gritted teeth, his grip on her neck tighter than he intended. Charlie stood on her tiptoes to keep from losing her breath all together. "Do you hear me?" She nodded her head as much as she could.

"I . . . I just want to make you feel as good as you make me feel," she said weakly.

His grip held fast while his erection throbbed against her back. She could feel the wheels turning in his head. She knew his eyes were going cold and as she tried to control her panic, he began to laugh. It was not a playful laugh, it was an evil, maniacal chuckle that Jake was clearly trying to suppress and it made the hair on her arms stand up. He could feel her starting to shake, a combination of fear and arousal he had provoked on many occasions with many women.

"I confuse you, don't I?" he said in a voice she barely recognized. She nodded. She didn't recognize the voice but she recognized the movie line—Spencer Tracy from *Dr. Jekyll & Mr. Hyde*. She prayed it was a coincidence rather than an indication of what was to come.

Jake could feel himself starting to lose control. It was a magnificent rush and he didn't want to control it but he knew if he didn't move quickly, it was going to get away from him. He didn't want to hurt her and he didn't want to leave, but if he didn't reel it in, he might have to choose one or the other and he feared his choice. With one arm still locked around her neck he started to stroke her hair.

"Tell me about the ocean, Charlie."

"What? I . . . I don't know what you mean?" she said as she felt her consciousness waning.

"Yes, you do."

She took as much of a breath as she could manage with a compressed windpipe.

"Tell me. Bring me down, Baby," he pleaded.

Somehow, she knew what he wanted. "I . . . I love the ocean but not the beach," she started tentatively. "I mean, I love looking at the beach, but it's the ocean that gets me."

"More," he said, sounding calmer as the tub continued to fill.

"I love being under the water. Inside the belly of the ocean. I love looking up at the sun through the water's glass ceiling, the gentle rocking of the current while the warm water envelopes my body. The silence of the ocean in a state of neutral buoyancy is like a symphony to me. It drowns out all the noise in my head."

"Yes," he growled, not yet having decided which way this was going to go.

"It shuts out everything. Doubt, loneliness, not being good enough. It makes all that go away." Her toes started to weaken as she struggled to keep her breath from being hijacked.

"Yesss," he hissed, nodding his head in understanding.

"It's not all bodies of water. Just the ocean. Only the ocean has the power that I want to surrender to. I love the feeling that I belong there, that I've always belonged there. I've never felt like I belonged anywhere. I feel safe under the water, in spite of what happened, it feels and has always felt like the safest place I could ever be, like no one can hurt me there."

"Until I met you, Jake. And now I . . ." her voice cracked as he made his decision.

*Chapter 28*
**The Accusation**

Jake's arm relaxed around Charlie's neck and the chokehold turned into a hug. A deep, desperate, hanging on for dear life, hug. Jake let a breath out as Charlie drew a breath in, relieved her neck hadn't been snapped.

"I'm fucked up, Charlie, really fucked up."

*Ya think?* she thought, but didn't say. She turned toward him and caressed his face with a shaking hand while still eyeing the door. Her love for him overrode her apprehension, though not entirely.

"Jake, I don't know anyone on this job who isn't fucked up. Talk to me please."

Jake remained silent, still trying to recover his senses, while Charlie's eyes, wide from fear, pleaded with him to trust her. Her instincts told her not to push. She started to undress him. She should have been planning her exit strategy but she couldn't do it. He needed her. It was her turn to comfort him. She got in the tub first then motioned for him to sit in front of her. The tub was huge and when she hit the button for the jets, they both let out a sigh. She wrapped her arms and legs around him and ran the washcloth across his chest. It was in her nature to push but she knew he was wrestling with some serious demons. In truth, part of her didn't want to know. She liked thinking of him as in control and stoic but she also desperately wanted to know the real Jake. The glimpse she just got was as real as it gets.

"I have some issues in my past, Charlie. These issues make relationships with women . . . challenging. That's why I've never been married. Between my temper and my sexual dysfunction, I just . . ." Charlie keyed on the words "temper" and "dysfunction" but she stayed silent, wanting him to give up as much information as he was willing to offer.

*The longer you are quiet, the more information you'll get, kid*, she heard Thompson say in her head.

"My parents explained once . . ." he started, then stopped, his body tensing. "It's just that it's hard for me to trust people, well . . . women, no, people. It's hard for me to trust anyone and that causes a mental block that causes me problems in the bedroom, if you know what I mean. Jesus, I can't believe I'm telling you this." He shook his head in disbelief and smacked his hand on the water, causing her to jump.

Charlie kept her composure and chose her words carefully. Part of her wanted him to unload his burden, but the experienced side of her worried that she was being played. She had been played many times before. It was a reflex to jump to suspicion, but to what end? He sure as hell wasn't interested in bedding her.

"I'm not sure I understand completely. I mean, you're incredibly sexy and very . . . umm . . . responsive and quite ummm blessed in that area."

"Oh no, I don't have *that* problem," he said, sounding offended.

"Well, what is it then?" The question came off as judgmental, which wasn't her intent. He stayed quiet and though she didn't want to push him, she couldn't help herself.

"What is it, Jake? You have to tell me. I need to understand what's going on here. I mean, you just had me in a chokehold and I . . ."

"I have trouble . . . finishing," he interrupted, then

turned to look at her to gauge her reaction.

Charlie was confused. "You mean it takes you a long time to come?"

"Yea."

"Jeez, Jake. I don't think that's so unusual is it?" she asked innocently. "Hell, being quick on the trigger would be a much bigger problem don't you think? No wait—let me answer that for you! Yes. Yes, it would." She was smiling, but stopped when he didn't smile back.

"It's more like I can't come," he admitted, still studying her face.

"At all?"

"It's happened, but it's very rare. I've been checked by a doctor and he said it's not physiological. You see, it's a trust thing. I got some therapy for it for a couple of years. It didn't really help the problem but it helped me understand it, you know what I mean?"

Charlie nodded. *A couple of years of therapy? Oh boy.* It took everything she had not to react.

"It's just that, women seem to take it personal. You know, that they can't get me there and it becomes this whole big issue and it's just not worth it to go through all that, so I basically just avoid it. Sex. I avoid sex."

"Oh," Charlie said, feeling the weight of what he had just told her.

"So, when is the last time you had sex?" she asked. "I'm sorry, am I being awful?"

"No, you are the farthest thing from awful I have ever known, Ms. Cavanaugh," he smiled, and her heart melted. "It's been about two years."

As much as she tried to conceal it, she was obviously sporting a are-you-fucking-kidding-me face.

"I know, right?"

Charlie looked him in the eyes and said with resolve, "Well, I don't think it would bother me the way it's bothered other women in your life, Jake. Maybe we should test that theory," she flirted.

He immediately relaxed and leaned his head back to accept a long hard kiss. His erection breached the water like a humpback whale.

"Hmm, look at that," she said, "All three of us agree."

The bath was growing cold and the room was heating up so they dried each other off and moved naked to the bed.

"My turn," she whispered. She laid him back on the bed while she explored every part of his large, long, and magnificent body. She listened intently for his groans to determine what he liked and gave him more of everything that moved him. He responded more when she slowed her strokes and laid her tongue flat against the shaft . . . so that's what she gave him, long, slow, wet strokes. One hand reached up to his chest and the other gently massaged his balls while her mouth drove him to madness. It didn't take long for him to seize control from her. He grabbed her by the hair, flipped her onto her back, and climbed between her legs. He teased her with the tip of the rock-hard rod while her body bucked trying to grab ahold of him.

"No more teasing, Jake," she panted. "Now."

"Do I need to remind you who's in charge?" he warned, their noses touching.

"Fuck you, Adams," she growled, sounding way too much like Linda Blair. She was frustrated out of her mind and it just came out—as it often did. Control was not an option. She was raw, she was hungry, and she was non-compliant.

She was fighting him for control and he was having none of it. He flipped her onto her stomach and crashed his giant hand on her soft, perfectly round flesh. Her ass stung with every blow. Charlie was possessed. She couldn't talk, she couldn't resist, and she couldn't breathe or think. All she could do was feel.

*She could feel.*

Jake landed one more blow before he forced himself between her legs and pulled her hips up toward him. He rammed his entire length into her without pause. Charlie screamed in agony and release, bucking him with every spasm. She lurched forward, instinctively trying to move away from the pain but she was helpless and unable to regain complete awareness. Jake pulled her back into position and mounted her again from behind. This time more slowly, taking time to feel every ripple, every ridge, every quivering bit of her inner flesh. He flattened her out and laid on top of her, her full round ass pressing against his stomach. He was holding her wrists down while he rode her rhythmically. Charlie groaned in ecstasy, completely unaffected by his full weight on her petite body.

"Take it all. Relax your body and take it all," he said, sending her into the stratosphere for the third time in the hour since they started.

When he had turned her on her back and was taking her for a fourth time she teetered on losing consciousness and drifted into a semi-dream state. She was aware that Jake was inside her and holding her wrist down, but she wasn't sure where they were. Her senses were playing tricks on her. She heard echoes indicative of a larger space. There were strange smells and she was unable to bring his face into focus, even though it was only inches away from hers. It was surreal and intense and she loved every single second of it.

Eventually Jake rolled on his side, pulling her into him and entering her again from behind. Rocking her, whispering to her, losing himself in her. An hour and a half and untold orgasms later Charlie finally waved the white flag.

"Uncle! Jesus Christ, Uncle!" she said laughing and rolling away from him and holding up her hands in defense.

"I never said there weren't advantages to this umm . . . disorder," he smiled.

Charlie was asleep before Jake finished his sentence. He covered her up, kissed her forehead, and ordered breakfast. She slept through breakfast and Jake tried to let her rest, knowing what he had in store for her. She looked so enticing lying there naked and satiated he was unable to resist. She awoke to him biting and sucking her nipples and it instantly brought her to the ready line.

"Are you hungry? Do you want to eat first?" he asked with genuine concern.

"Yes," she said with a sleepy smile. She slid under the covers to take him into her mouth again. Two hours later she again called it again, slapping her hand three times on the bed like a wrestler and begging him to get her some ice.

"Rookie," he quipped as he got up to grab the ice bucket and she threw a pillow at him.

After round three, they laid in each other arms in perfect contentment.

"You know, we're missing a beautiful day."

"No, we're enjoying a beautiful day," she countered.

She purred and reached to silence her vibrating phone. It was Clint calling for at least the fifth time since they arrived yesterday.

Jake glanced at her phone as she picked it up. "Doesn't Clint know that the captain is covering this weekend?" he asked casually. She nodded. "He calls you a lot." She nodded again and shrugged. He wrapped her up in the sheet and hugged her to him, careful not to disturb the ice pack between her legs. They talked until the sun began to hide from the sky. Jake tried to keep from starting up again, knowing she was hurting, but his hands always went for her ample and engorged breasts and before he knew it he had her whimpering.

"No, no, no. Jake, stop. You have to stop. Seriously, I'm not going to be able to walk."

At Jake's insistence they ordered a huge meal and an expensive bottle of wine from room service. They ate it picnic style on the bed while they watched *The Bird Cage*, quoting almost every line before it was uttered.

"Agador Spartacus! He insists on being called by his full name."

Before turning in, they returned to the giant soaking tub for one more bath, this one far less serious. They laughed, splashed, and flirted. Jake washed her hair and she washed his, all memory of nearly having her neck broken dispelled from Charlie's mind.

"I don't want to go back. I want more of this Jake."

He looked very seriously at her and took her face into his giant hands. "Charlotte, I can do that for you. We can leave here. I have enough money to last us the rest of our lives if we're careful."

Her smile vanished. "Jake. That sounds amazing. It really does. I just can't. My job. My guys. I can't."

A cloud settled over them for the remainder of the night. They held each other, but there was no more love-making and they drove in silence back to Landon on Sunday morning. Jake focused on the road while Charlie returned a dozen texts and emails. Jake said he would sleep at his hotel so she could recover and he could catch up on his paperwork for the taskforce. He insisted on clearing her apartment first to make sure it was safe.

Monday morning after a night of bizarre and erotic dreams, she arrived at her office where Clint sat waiting for her.

"Wow," he said, flatly.

"What?"

"I don't know. You just look different. Where you been all weekend? With Adams? You're falling for him, aren't you? Is that why you didn't return any of my calls?"

She looked at him coolly. "Do you have that pattern analysis for me, McCallister?"

Clint stared at her, got up from the chair without answering, and left her office. She felt bad about calling him McCallister, but it was the only way to reel him in when he was crossing the line. Jake was a no-show but sent her a text saying he would be in touch with her later. Even his text made her aching nether region start to throb again. She tried desperately to ignore that something was not right between them after she had refused his second offer to go away with him.

Four hours of weekend paperwork and no lunch later, Clint appeared in her office doorway and motioned her to the conference room.

"Let's see what you've got, Night Rider," she said trying to lighten the mood between them. Ignoring her attempt, he motioned to the chair in front of the paper-work he had spread out in the conference room. He sat down beside her. His face was serious. There was no trace of the playful Clint in sight.

Clint glanced at the open door and then at his ser-geant. She nodded and he got up and closed the door. Charlie watched him with concern and curiosity, but mostly with concern. Clint separated the papers he held and laid out his pattern analysis on the conference table. He was all business.

"I've really looked hard at this, Sarge. I spent the whole weekend on it. I've studied these case files ev-ery which way I can. There are a lot of consistencies but it's not amounting to anything. Here is what we have in terms of a pattern . . .

#1 All of the murder victims were child molesters that either beat the rap or got less of a sentence than they deserved to get for one reason or another.

#2 They all lived within the Landon city limits.

#3 They were all suspects from your molestation cases.

#4 They were all killed in their homes, except for Dumpster Doe, Alex Jordan. We don't know where he was killed before he was dumped behind Landon Mall, but we do know plastic wrap was used just like the oth-ers."

Charlie nodded in agreement.

#5 None of them had defense wounds. It was like they just lay there and let themselves be smothered to death.

#6 There was no forced entry in any of the cases. I think they all just let him in, which makes me think that all of the doors were unlocked, which is unlikely. More likely would be that the perp posed as a phone repair person or someone like that.

#7 There were no witnesses in any of the cases.

#8 All of the bodies were doused with either bleach or hydrofluoric acid following the murders.

#9 There was no collectable DNA, probably due to the bleach or the acid, and very little physical evidence. That's it. There is no pattern in terms of time or day of the week . . ." Clint paused.

"What?"

Clint shifted in his seat.

"Look, Clint I'm sorry. I know you want to know what's going on with me but I'm just not ready to talk about Adams yet okay? Yes, there is something, but I really don't know what . . ."

Clint interrupted her, "Sarge, this has nothing to do with Adams," he had a grave look on his face that Charlie had never seen. It sent a shiver down her spine.

"Oh. Then you have figured something out about the murders. Great. Let's have it then," she asked, not really sure she wanted the answer.

"Well, the first thing that is kind of strange . . ." Clint hesitated.

"What, Clint?"

"Well, one of the anomalies is that these are all cases from your second year in Crimes Against Children. None of them are from your first year of cases."

"Really?" Charlie was surprised she hadn't realized that.

"Yea," he said with a perplexed frown. "Given that you handled more kiddy cases in 2011, many of them more heinous, it just doesn't square that all the targets so far are from your 2012 caseload. So that means there are probably only two targets left."

"Hmm," Charlie said thoughtfully.

"Can you think of anything that changed from 2011 to 2012, Sarge? Maybe a different prosecutor, evidence tech, or polygrapher? Maybe someone assisted you on these cases in 2012 that didn't assist you in 2011?" he asked, but couldn't look her in the eye.

"Not that I can think of," she shook her head. "Assisted? Clint, you're not thinking the suspect could be an officer?"

"No," Clint said "but . . ."

"But, what?" she snapped, irritated by the weight of the thought.

"Well, you know Sarge, it's like you are always telling us, don't let the wish be the father of the thought, keep all possibilities open, don't decide on a suspect and then let the evidence prove your own theory, let the evidence be the lead detective yadda yada yada," he said defensively.

"I have no recollection of teaching you yada yada yada," she said, forcing a grin, but Clint's face remained grave as he looked down at the papers on the conference table. She locked her stare on him. He didn't have to engage her stare to feel its weight. He had felt it before.

"What is the second thing Clint?"

"What second thing?"

"Clint, you said the first thing that is kind of strange . . . that means there's a second thing. What's the second thing?"

Clint looked up and locked his eyes with hers and said without blinking, "The only case you have an alibi for is the Daniel Silver case and you and Jake were the team staked out on his house when he was killed."

Charlie took a deep breath and slowly stood up. Clint stood up in response, holding his breath. The room was starting to spin. She couldn't let Clint see what was happening to her.

Clint caught her shooting a glance toward the door. Not what he wanted to see. That's what perps do.

Charlie tried to ignore the sound of the train in her ears but it was deafening.

Clint could see the hurt in her eyes and it was ripping him in two. "Sarge, look, I know that you're not involved, but these are your cases, your suspects. It would have been careless of me not to at least consider it and look into it so I could eliminate it as a possibility, right?"

*Eliminate it? You mean me*, she thought. *Eliminate me as a suspect.* Charlie grabbed the edge of the table to see if that would help with the spinning room and the train that was growing louder and louder.

"Sarge, please . . . sit down. Please!" He forced her back down into the chair. "Listen to me." He spoke quietly and slowly. "You said yourself weeks ago that the killer had inside experience of some kind. No forced entry. Frying the crime scene with two different chemicals to destroy evidence, remember?" He ran his hand through his hair. "I had to eliminate the possibility that maybe your cheese slipped off the cracker and you iced these fuckers." He spun her chair toward him so they were knees to knees and grabbed her shoulders, his eyes desperately searching for forgiveness.

"Look at me Charlie," Clint ordered, trying to get control of the situation.

"But you haven't eliminated me," she said quietly. "How is it that I am still on the case? Still on the job?"

"Because I haven't said anything to anyone," he

said softly, taking her hand and dropping to one knee in front of her.

Charlie let out a long sigh and slumped back in the chair.

"Well, no one on the department," he clarified. Charlie immediately sat back up and pulled her hand away, her eyes demanding an answer from him.

"I talked to Jake." Clint recoiled when he saw Charlie's eyes catch fire.

"I had to talk to somebody, Sarge! You are the somebody I always talk to. I couldn't talk to you. I couldn't say anything to the guys, so I figured Jake would be my best bet because he's an outsider. Plus . . ."

"Plus what?" she asked, daggers shooting from her eyes.

"Plus I had to talk to him. I had to make sure he was with you the whole time the night of the Daniel Silver homicide."

Charlie said nothing and for once, she kept a poker face.

"And he was. Jake said you and he were together from start to finish so that cleared it up for me. So, see? I have eliminated you." Clint slid back into the chair exhausted and again took her hand. She tried to resist but he refused to let go.

"This has been killing me Charlie. You know how I feel about you. You do, right?"

Charlie nodded, staring through him, her anger subsiding and panic starting to set in.

"How did you establish my lack of alibi for the other murders?" she asked mechanically, putting her detective hat back on.

"I checked the time sheets. And your day planner."

He sighed. Again he ran his hand through his hair. "The usual stuff," he shrugged uncomfortably.

Charlie pursed her lips and nodded.

Clint had investigated her behind her back and Jake knew and had said nothing. The betrayal from both of them was like a punch in the face.

"Do you want a statement?" she said, flatly.

"Oh my God, Sarge, quit it! I had to tell you because I felt like a shit going behind your back. I should have just come to you, but that didn't feel right either. Jake convinced me the best thing to do once I knew that you and he were together every minute of the stakeout was to just keep it to myself, but it's been killing me. The bottom line is I'm satisfied. It's done and as long as I am satisfied, I don't see any reason to put this in the case log." She raised an eyebrow at him, the police supervisor in her returning.

"Yes. I know I am supposed to but I-am-not-going-to-sergeant. Now, can we please go get a drink? Jesus Christ, I need a drink!" He said laying his head on the table. "I mean a beer, not a drink. I need a beer." Charlie laughed in spite of herself. Poor Clint looked so pathetic.

"Okay, but I'm buying."

"Oh, hell yes, you are," he laughed. "You just took ten years off my life."

Clint and Charlie met at Amy's Café and enjoyed as good a visit as they had had in months. The investigation and Jake's constant presence had made it very difficult for them to connect. Charlie missed her friend. Supervising him at work and having a beer with him was not the same thing. Clint and Charlie had seen each other through a lot of personal drama—her divorce, his divorce, losing her parents, dealing with his drinking problem, and missing Thompson.

They had been there for each other, any time, day or night. Neither of them had any ulterior motive. He never made a move on her. She never made a move on him. They had consumed tequila together until they passed out, had seen each other half dressed and even slept in the same bed once when Charlie had awoken on his couch screaming from one of her train nightmares. It rattled Clint so badly he made her share his bed with him for the remainder of the night.

In another time and another place, who knows, but in this time and this place they were friends. That was all.

The only other person Charlie had connected with during this time was online AJ. Somehow, over miles of distance and the complete absence of sight, touch and sound, they too had managed to connect.

Clint and Charlie took seats at the bar and Clint slapped the counter saying, "Five Red- Headed Sluts, Amy!" Amy and Charlie both raised an eyebrow at him.

"What? I'm drinking beer. I just want five red-headed sluts. Bwahahaha." Charlie and Amy rolled their eyes at each other.

Sitting at the bar at Amy's Café with Clint, Charlie was distracted. Something was nagging at her. She shook her head in disbelief at how long she had been corresponding with AJ and she couldn't help comparing her feelings for AJ and her feelings for Clint. Clint, now relaxed and playfully trashed, recounted a story of his latest sexual escapade, "Now this chick was off the charts hot! So, then she says to me . . ." Clint said, getting animated, "'I like the taste of blood, does that freak you out?' Does that freak me out I said? Oh, hell no, I'm a cop! I'm around blood all the time."

"Wait. What did you just say?" Charlie asked in shock.

"I was losing you. I wanted to make sure you were paying attention." He laughed uncontrollably banging his fist on the bar.

"You asshole."

"Where'd you go?" Clint laughed trying to catch his breath.

"I'm sorry. I was thinking about this guy I have been talking to online for the last year or so and how much he reminds me of you."

Then Charlie froze.

"What?" Clint said reading the panic on her face.

"Charlie? What?" he asked again.

"I . . . umm . . . I . . ." she stammered. Clint turned his bar stool to face her and grabbed her by the shoulders. Her face had gone ashen.

"Sarge, tell me."

She looked around the crowded bar, grabbed Clint's hand and headed toward an isolated table in the corner.

"Hey! My beer!"

Charlie released his hand so he could get his beer and motioned for him to follow her by pretending to cast a fishing pole and reeling it in. Clint giggled. He sat down at the table. The look in her eyes quickly cured his giggles. Clint was all ears and goose bumps.

"Clint," she whispered. "I know what changed from 2011 to 2012." He looked at her in anticipation but said nothing, letting her open the flood gate on her own—a technique he had learned from her.

"Okay, maybe it's nothing," she said cryptically, now a little drunk herself, "but maybe it's not nothing.

Okay, in late 2011 this guy befriended me on the internet. He's a soldier stationed in the Middle East and, well, you know, we just started talking."

"Talking?" Clint asked accusingly. "About what, Sarge? Not your cases?" Charlie pursed her lips looking guilty. "Charlie? What the fuck?" Clint's tone was incredulous. "You talked to him about your cases?" he asked again, needing clarification.

"Not at first," she said, trying to defend herself, "but I dealt with some pretty heavy-duty shit with those cases Clint. You were going through your on again off again she-fucks-me-she-fucks-me-not cycle with Sandy, Mandy whatever the hell her name was and I needed someone to talk to!"

Clint looked hurt. "You didn't think you could talk to me?"

"Hello! McFly!" She made a fist and knocked on his head. "You're missing the big picture here. The point is I did talk to him about these very cases. The 2012 cases. I was devastated by what had been done to those kids and I was fucking furious with how little time they got and fucking Silver got off completely! I told him once that I wish they could be put to death. I actually said that. Well, typed it. This online guy, he kind of, you know, has a thing for me. What if there is a connection?" she asked, eyes widening as her revelation continued to settle in.

"Oh, come on, Charlie, you think that this Ranger Ramjet came back from the Middle East to kill these fuckers because you were upset that they didn't get enough time in jail?" He scoffed, unconvinced.

"Clint, you're assuming that this guy actually is in the Middle East."

"Holy shit," Clint said, the light bulb over his head

blinding Charlie.

"Fuckin-A right, holy shit."

*Was now the right time for her to tell Clint that she and Jake were not together the entire night for the Daniel Silver stakeout and homicide? That Jake was gone for over an hour while she sat on the house alone. No. Not yet,* she decided. She had to talk to Jake first and find out why he had lied to Clint.

*Chapter 29*
**Pull the Trigger**

Charlie and Clint staggered across the road to Charlie's apartment. She was nervous that Jake might be there waiting for her but she couldn't let Clint get behind the wheel and she was too drunk to drive him home. Clint had spent a lot of nights on her couch and Jake would have to deal with that.

Charlie was both relieved and disappointed when she found her apartment empty. "My bed!" Clint giggled as he stumbled to the couch. "I've missed you!"

"You're drunk, McCallister," Charlie slurred her words.

"Drunk and stupid!" Moses squawked, making Charlie giggle.

Clint was asleep before Charlie returned from her bedroom with a blanket to cover him. She watched him sleep and realized how lucky she was that Clint had her back and then pushed the thought from her head that she didn't deserve his protection or devotion. She peeled off her clothes and left them on the floor and crawled into her bed in her camisole and panties, checking her phone one more time to see if Jake had texted her. He hadn't. She sighed and fell into a drunken and fitful sleep.

Clint was awakened by the front door handle being jiggled from the hallway. At first, he wasn't sure where he was, but as he took in the room he realized he was on the couch in his sergeant's apartment. He reached for his gun as he heard a thump against the deadbolt and the door creaked open. Clint crouched low and aimed for the shadow and found himself staring down the business end of a government issued Glock 30.

"Clint?" Jake asked, without lowering his gun.

A fleeting thought crossed both their minds simultaneously. *If I want to get rid of this guy, there will never be a better chance.*

"Jesus Christ Adams!" Clint yelled. "Just come on in why don't you!" Clint re-holstered and walked toward the door, inspecting the unbroken lock. "Charlie gave you a key?"

"What are you doing here, Clint?"

"Sleeping it off. What are you doing here?"

The two men stood toe-to-toe, neither willing to yield. "Sorry Adams, but the guest room is taken," Clint said motioning to the couch, "So how about you just head back to your fancy pants hotel tonight. How 'bout that? Because I got your spot tonight."

Jake allowed a disturbing grin to cross his lips. "That's not my spot, Detective."

With that Jake pushed past him, walked into Charlie's bedroom and closed the door. Clint stormed toward the door and put his hand on the door knob ready to burst in and level Preppy McFed the second Charlie voiced her objection, but that's not what he heard; what he heard ripped his heart to shreds. He stormed out of the apartment and back to Amy's and ordered a double scotch.

Charlotte awoke to a ringing phone that Jake promptly picked up and attempted to throw across the room. "Adams!" she sternly whispered, like the person on the phone could hear her. She grabbed the phone from him. "Does your phone ever fucking stop ringing?" he groaned, not entirely awake.

"Cavanaugh," she answered, trying to sound awake. "Which one?" She asked looking wide-eyed at Jake.

"Okay. On my way."

"Fuck. It's Deborg. Damn it Adams, how did you get in here? Clint let you in?"

"You weren't very worried about it last night?" he grinned sleepily.

The phone rang again. "Cavanaugh," she said while she made apology eyes at Jake. "What? Where is he?" she asked, her face again turning grave. "Okay, I'm on my way there right now."

"What?"

"Number five is down."

"And?"

"And Clint was found passed out in his unmarked unit a half a block from the crime scene."

Charlie rushed to the living room as if she thought she would find Clint still lying there on the couch. She looked at Jake asking the question with her eyes.

"He was still here when I came in last night at around midnight." *More*, her eyes demanded.

"What?"

"Did something happen between you and Clint last night, Jake?"

"Not as much as what happened between you two. At least when you were finished with me I got to stay in the bed. Lapdog Clint got kicked to the couch."

"I have no idea what you are talking about Adams but you're pissing me off. He only passes out when he drinks the hard stuff and he only drinks the hard stuff when he is in a really bad place, so what the hell happened last night because he was fine when I left him on the couch last night," she said, accusingly as she got dressed.

"Where's the hom-i-icide?" he asked, ignoring her

accusation.

"It's Deborg, at his apartment on Clayton. I've got this," she said as she stormed out of the bedroom.

Charlie first went to the location she was given for Clint but one of his patrol officer buddies had already gotten him out of there as quickly and quietly as possible. Less seen, less said. She continued to the crime scene where she sought out Captain Grisolm who was shaking his head at her as she approached. "This is not your fault, Cap," she said, reading his mind.

"The hell it's not," he said running his hand through what hair he had left. "I should have kept up the surveillance."

"For how long? Forever? No agency has that kind of resources," she attempted to comfort him.

"For one more week," he said, grimly. "Clint?" he raised an eyebrow.

"A uniform took him home," she replied.

"Deal with your man, Sergeant," he ordered.

"Yes, Sir."

Charlie asked Crammy to take the initial report, promising him a free lunch afterwards, and headed for Clint's apartment. She let herself in the unlocked door of his apartment and found him drinking coffee at his kitchen counter. He held his hands up in defense. "I know, I know. Fuck!"

"What happened, Clint?"

He remained silent.

"Clint?"

"You! You fucking happened, Charlie!"

"What?"

"Fuck. I don't know what I'm saying, Sarge," he apologized. "It's just that . . . how can you end up with him? You don't know anything about him. He's a fucking fed and a pretty boy and something is off. I know you feel it too!"

She recovered her footing, took a step toward him, and put her hand on his face, "And what's wrong with falling for a pretty boy?" she smiled. He started to relax and smiled a small smile just before he felt her hand connect with his face. WHACK!

"Jesus Christ, Sarge!"

"Don't you fucking Jesus Christ me! Are you trying to lose your job? Because you are this fucking close. We had a deal! You feel the need to hit anything but a beer bottle, you fucking call me."

"You were busy hitting something else," he said caustically.

She glared at him, then relaxed in agreement, sighed, and sat down on the stool next to him, angry at herself for losing control. "Clint," she said. "I know this is tough on you. We've been in the same boat for a while and we both liked the company but spending my life alone isn't what I want and I don't think you want it for me either. I'm in love with him."

He rubbed his eyes. "I know."

"You're suspended, McCallister."

"I know. Who took the lead on Deborg?"

"How did you know it was Deborg?" she asked, her hackles rising up on the back of her neck.

"Uniform told me," he lied.

"Crammy took the lead."

"Well, that's the fucking cherry on the cake of my day," he said sarcastically. "I'm sorry, Sarge. I know I let you down. I'm really sorry."

"I know."

Back at the station Charlie read over Cramlin's report.

*On the above date and time I was called out to the above location in reference to a homicide. Officer Mansfield advised that patrol units received an anonymous call from a male caller at a payphone indicating that the resident in apartment 3A had been murdered. Officer Mansfield said the door to the apartment was cracked open but undamaged and reported that she and Officer Hoback performed a cursory safety search of the apartment when they found the victim, Jason Deborg, deceased in his bed. The victim's head had been wrapped in plastic wrap and his stomach had been sliced open and his organs removed. There were no signs of a struggle at the scene.*

Sitting at her desk, Charlie rolled it over again and again in her mind. No forced entry. No forced entry. The suspect could be a burglar, or a locksmith, or perhaps the killer befriended the victims and earned their trust before taking their lives. She put her hand on the phone and then took her hand off, shaking her head. Then she picked up the phone again and quickly dialed.

"Clint?"

"You at the scene, Sarge?" he asked without saying hello.

"I'm at the office. Clint, he gutted this guy like he gutted the dog except he removed the organs. He's getting worse Clint. It's building."

"Building to what, Sarge?"

"Clint. What were you doing a half a block from the crime scene?"

Silence.

"Clint, I need to know what's happening."

"I thought it was him."

"You thought who, was him?"

"Jake."

"What? What about Jake?"

"Look, Sarge, I know I slipped last night. I can't drink the hard stuff. I know that, but I only had one—honest. You can ask Amy. I was going to sleep it off in my car but I didn't want to stay in Amy's lot so I was going to just drive across the street to your parking lot and that's when I saw him coming down the stairs."

"Saw who? Jake?"

"Yea. He got into his SUV and headed west. It was weird because it was two fucking a.m., so I followed him. I know I shouldn't have driven, but I had to know. He was heading toward the Radisson so I backed off and lost him."

"Clint. I know that you are not okay with Jake but he was here all night. You saw him when he came in last night and he was here when I woke up this morning," she defended.

Ignoring her, he went on. "I went to the hotel parking lot and couldn't find his vehicle. There are two targets left from your 2012 cases so I decided to do a drive by. First I drove to Hanican's house and sat on it for a while and when I didn't see anything I drove to Deborg's apartment complex."

"Why Clint? I don't understand what one has to do with the other." she said, refusing to connect the dots.

"I couldn't find his vehicle there either, but I did see a man who matched Jake's build enter Deborg's building. I followed him."

"It's going to sound like I'm hanging up on you, McCallister!" she said angrily, before slamming down the phone. Charlie's head was swimming. She didn't know what to process first, the fact that her best friend and subordinate just admitted to being at a crime scene or the fact that he just accused her boyfriend of being a murderer.

She was sure Jake had been there all night. *Wasn't she?* She remembered a particularly rough lovemaking session with him but that was about it, she was trashed. *Ethics. There were professional ethics in play here. If Clint was at the crime scene he would need to be interviewed by Crammy. But what if he told Crammy what he just told her?* Before she could shit or wind her watch, which were about her only options, Mary Jane Klasky peered around the corner. Charlie tried to force a smile but failed miserably.

"Geez Louise, Officer Cavanaugh. What's wrong? This case is really fucking with your head huh?"

"Don't say fuck Mary Jane, it's not ladylike," Charlie admonished.

Outside Charlie's office the captain stood listening, his face grave, as Jake approached. Captain Grisolm held up a hand directing Jake to wait. When Jake started to ask what was happening, the captain held up a shush finger and pointed toward his office. A concerned Jake walked to the captain's office and became even more concerned when the captain closed the door.

"What's going on Captain?" Jake asked. "Who is Charlie talking to? Do we have a suspect?"

The captain ran his hand through his thinning hair. "Agent Adams. I'm going to share something with you about someone I think we are both very fond of, but I am going to have to insist on your discretion." Jake nodded, his face serious and his gut anxious.

"When Charlie was a rookie patrol officer, she worked her first molestation case. The Mary Jane Klasky case."

Jake listened intently. Charlie had already told him of the Klasky case but Jake said nothing.

"It was a rough case. The kind of case that stays with you forever," he sighed. "I should have been there for her, but I had just gotten promoted and my wife was pregnant with our third . . ." he trailed off wringing his hands. "I should have been there for her."

"I don't understand, Captain," Jake said quietly, aware the captain was struggling. "Is that who she's talking to now? Mary Jane?"

"Yes," he said, shaking his head. "That's who she's talking to. That poor fucking kid. The details of the molestation were horrific enough but to add to it, the child had kept a diary of what her father had done to her from age ten to age twelve. It was detailed and heartbreaking and Charlie had to read and re-read every word of it in order to prepare the case for prosecution." Jake nodded in understanding.

"She has a good heart," Jake said, absent-mindedly, and then caught the captain's stare.

"Yes, Agent, she does. A heart of gold, a sharp mind, and the eyes of an angel. She's one of the most impressive police officers I have ever had the privilege of working with. I don't want to see her hurt. She's fragile. If you haven't picked up on that yet, you need to understand that. She's fragile."

"Are we still talking about the case?" Jake asked, flatly. The heat was starting to build in him as the captain confessed his admiration for Charlie. "She's tougher than you think Captain," Jake said defiantly, angry with

Charlie's captain for not giving her enough credit and becoming increasingly uncomfortable with the conversation. Jake shifted in his chair. He felt like he was about to hear an unsolicited confession.

"Oh, and you know her so much better than I do, Agent Adams?"

Jake didn't know what to expect next but he certainly didn't expect the captain to tear up and it threw him. "It's my fault. I should have been there for her. I don't want this to end a brilliant career so I have been covering for her, hoping it would pass."

"Captain, with all due respect what the fuck are you talking about here? Being with me is not going to ruin her career. She's single. I'm single and I'm in love with her."

The captain looked up from his desk where he had been focusing his misty eyes and leaned forward. "I suspected that," he said cryptically. "Charlie is very dear to me. That is why I'm telling you this story. You need to know."

Jake sat back in his chair and waited for the punch.

The captain found his resolve. He cleared his eyes, sat up straight, and continued. "In the months following the case, Mary Jane was put into foster care while her father was incarcerated. The mother overdosed and died." Jake nodded.

"Okay."

"It gets worse," the captain said gravely.

"Worse? How? Charlie told me about the case Captain. She said the father got sixty-five years and that Mary Jane didn't have to testify. She said that she made Virginia court history by using the girl's diary to convict the son-of-a-bitch."

The captain nodded. "It was unprecedented, but she didn't do it to spare Mary Jane from testifying. The kid couldn't testify."

"What do you mean?"

"Mary Jane committed suicide a month before the trial."

"What? I don't understand. What?"

"Mary Jane Klasky killed herself a month before the trial. She was thirteen years old."

"I don't . . . then who is Charlie . . . I don't . . ." Jake stammered.

"How did she die Captain? How did Mary Jane die?" Jake asked, already suspecting the answer.

"She threw herself in front of a freight train."

## Chapter 30
### He's Got a Knife

"Love Walked In" by Thunder pounded through the room, shaking the walls but not his resolve. It was still metal. Maybe it was the current wave of death coming to an end that was making him go soft. *Had this happened before?* He couldn't remember. There would be more. This he knew. It was inevitable. He had to savor this last meal like a prisoner on death row. The thought made him shudder but he quickly shut it down. He was too smart to ever be caught. The security that now surrounded his entrée, however, would make this execution the most difficult of all, however deserving. Then there would be nothing. The thought made him sad. It had taken years to cultivate this specially selected list of earned endings. He had never carried out a mission that included multiple winners, but it seemed the thing to do here. Or maybe he was getting greedy. There were so many others out there waiting for him and he would not disappoint them by getting himself caught. *What would become of the boy if he were caught?* He was in no shape to fend for himself and he couldn't count on brainless state workers to provide for his special needs. The thought of the child being on his own momentarily paralyzed him with fear. Perhaps a break was in order. The boy seemed happy here. In fact, he had never seen him so happy and that meant a great deal to him. Though he knew himself to be narcissistic and self-serving, he did in fact love the child.

"Alright, Clint, let's put it on the table," Charlie demanded. "I'm tired of fucking around."

"What's the point, Sarge? You're just going to defend him, but I'm telling you something is wrong here. I feel it in my gut. You know that part of me you used to trust," he added sarcastically.

After talking to Mary Jane, Charlie had decided to leave the station and head back to Clint's apartment. She wasn't at her desk when Jake bolted out of the captain's office and ran to her office looking for her, horrified by the information the captain had shared with him and desperate to protect her. Jake rang her cell phone but heard the barking dog that she had made his ringtone coming from her desk where she had left her cell. Frantic, he headed for her apartment.

"Clint, I can't believe the lengths you are willing to go to discredit Jake. This is insane. What do you have against him? Now I am not asking you, I am ordering you to tell me what you saw last night."

Clint rolled his eyes, unimpressed with her order but intimidated by green and gold flecks that lit up her eyes. She was on the edge. "I told you, I don't know for sure that it was him. There was no Fed Mobile in the parking lot but I do know that he did leave your apartment last night and he didn't go to his hotel."

"Why do you think it was him at Deborg's?"

"Instinct, timing, build, take your pick, Sarge."

"Did you call in the homicide, Clint?"

"What? Fuck no!" Clint said with a surprise Charlie felt was genuine. "Somebody called it in? Holy shit. Jesus, I didn't even know he was dead until I saw the uniforms rolling in this morning. Listen, once I got in the building I lost the guy I was tracking and I couldn't remember which floor Deborg lived on so I gave up. All of the sudden the whole premise seemed crazy so I walked back to my car, drove down the street, realized I was too lit to be driving, and pulled over and fell asleep. That's it. That's what happened."

"That's the first sensible thing you've said in the last 24 hours, dumbass," Charlie snapped. "You're damn right it was crazy. You are going to have to give a statement to Crammy, but how about you just report facts and not all your wild ass speculation?"

"Okay, I can do that. But what am I going to say I was doing on that side of town?"

"Tell the truth," she said, narrowing her eyes. "You were drunk."

Clint nodded. "How many days am I suspended for, Sarge? We have work to do before Crammy fucks this case up nine ways to Sunday."

"I know," Charlie sighed, exasperated. "I was going to make it one week, but I haven't turned in the paperwork yet so let's make it one day instead. So, get your ass back to work because I'm certain that the captain will be ordering a 24/7 surveillance on number six. Fucking freak. Jesus, I hate that we have to protect that horror of a human being."

Clint put his hand on Charlie's hand. He knew that number six had screwed with her more than any of the others besides Mary Jane, and he didn't need his beloved sergeant talking to anymore dead victims. He held his hand on hers, and she didn't try to pull away. "Make sure I'm on the stakeout roster, Charlie. I want in on this."

She nodded. "Okay, Night Rider. I'm sure it won't start until at least tomorrow night. There isn't enough time to put a schedule together before then."

"Maybe you and I could team up this time?" Clint asked hopefully.

"We'll see. It's the captain's call, Clint. Any luck on

AJ's IP address?" Charlie asked, changing the subject.

"Not yet, it's a ghost signal, bouncing from Landon to Timbuktu and back. My guy at VBPD has tracked it to five different states but he said he still doesn't have the actual origin." Not the information Charlie had been hoping for.

Charlie was distracted as she drove back to the station. Did Clint's information mean AJ wasn't overseas, or did that just confirm that he was in fact in a high security assignment and that's why he possessed the ability to bury his IP address?

As Charlie pulled back into the station she saw Jake sitting in his SUV in the parking lot so she took the parking space next to him. He looked upset. She hadn't left things very well with him this morning and she was grateful they were at the station where his icy stare was the most she had to fear. Jake jumped out of his SUV and was at her door in a hot second and pulling on the door handle. She opened the door and he grabbed her hand and pulled her from the seat wrapping his arms around her. "Jake. What's wrong?! You can't do this here. Tell me what's wrong?"

Jake was still reeling from the captain's confession that Charlie was routinely talking to a dead Mary Jane Klasky. *Jesus.* "Get in the car Charlie," he said opening the passenger door to the SUV and shoving her into the seat.

"Jake stop this! Tell me what is happening?" she demanded.

"Please, Charlie. Please trust me and come with me now," he pleaded. The look in his eyes told her to stop fighting. This wasn't arrogant, overbearing, scary Jake. This was rattled Jake and he needed her, now. Jake drove like a man possessed through the streets of Landon toward Charlie's apartment, neither of them saying a word as he crushed her hand with his. Once inside the apartment he led her to the bedroom where he sat her down on the bed and embraced her like he hadn't seen her for years. Then his eyes started to mist and made no effort to hide it. She didn't know what was happening, but she knew that he loved her and somehow it was hurting him.

She held him for what seemed like an hour before he finally spoke. "I love you Charlotte. I've never felt like this about anyone and it's overwhelming me. I'm sorry, I just feel like I'm losing control and I can't, I can't function like this. I know there is a lot to be done on this case. I'm sure the captain is wondering where you are but I had to hold you and I couldn't do that at the station. I . . . I need to protect you." He couldn't tell her the truth, that he was afraid for her sanity and afraid for his own. He had made the connection. He knew now why they were together and knew that they would never be able to part again.

"I'm where I need to be, Jake," she said. "I love you too and I'm right here. I will always be right here. Forever." She meant every word she was saying. This was real. At last . . . this was real. Forever wasn't a question. It was a statement of fact. She didn't understand it, but she believed it. She kissed him slowly, tasting his salty lips and taking his tongue deep. He quickly took control of the kiss and laid her on her back, his hands grabbing her breast in big handfuls and squeezing them forcefully, causing her to whimper in his mouth, igniting him. Jake pulled back from the kiss and stared into her eyes that had already begun to turn gold in the afternoon sun. She caught the flash in his right eye and was immediately both aroused and frightened. Kneeling beside her on the bed he pulled his clothes off, leaving his tie draped around his neck. Charlie rolled out of her suit jacket and started unbuttoning her shirt but Jake stopped her.

"Pray," he said in a voice she remembered from the hotel.

"What?" she whispered, so quietly she mostly just mouthed the words.

"Pray," he said again, producing a knife from his back pocket and exposing the blade with one touch.

"Jake," she whispered, her voice starting to tremble.

"Pray," he ordered again.

Charlie put her hands together in prayer and Jake put the knife between his teeth and pulled the tie from around his neck and used it to secure her wrists together before tying them to the headboard. Charlie was both breathless and terrified. It didn't occur to her for one second to resist, but that was the insane power Jake Adams had over her. Keeping the knife between his teeth, he slid her pants down and pulled off her shoes and socks, and left her red laced panties and sleeveless blouse in place. Charlie could feel the juices flowing between her legs as Jake took the knife into his hand and slid the tip of the knife across her covered breast, his stare locked with hers. One by one he sliced the buttons of her shirt off exposing her stomach and red push-up bra. Charlie closed her eyes in effort to embrace the ecstasy and shut out the terror building inside her.

He sliced the bra away from her skin, exposing her breasts, her hard nipples and releasing an audible growl from her captor. Next was her panties; two cuts. "Lie still," he commanded. She tensed and held her breath every time she felt the blade touch her skin, until she felt her panties fall away and heard the blade of the knife click closed. His mouth devoured her nipples and she came instantly from the sheer intensity of the scene he had created. The harder she came, the harder he bit down into her flesh. He mounted and thrust into her simultaneously and she thought he would rip her in two. He pounded away at her without mercy until her body, racked with orgasms, gave up and she lay limp like a rag dog while he continued to punish her. He finally collapsed on top of her, taking a nipple into his mouth and rolling them both on their sides while he gently sucked, his throbbing cock still unexpended on her aching thigh. He was disappointed that this level of intensity did not allow him to climax and he feared she was disappointed as well.

As she slowly regained awareness she realized her hands were tied to the bed but she couldn't fully remember how it happened. She remembered the knife though. Reading her thoughts, he reached up without releasing her nipple from his mouth and untied her hands. She rubbed her wrists and kissed his head while they both drifted in and out of an emotionally exhausted sleep.

It was the most intense sexual encounter she had ever had, read about, or imagined. It went far beyond the boundaries of anything deemed "normal" or "appropriate" and it sent her to a place to which she wanted to return again and again. She was disappointed he hadn't climaxed and started to understand why other women became frustrated. She vowed not to let this happen to her. There had to be something that would move him to orgasm and she would not stop until she found out what it was and surrendered it to him. She was fearful about what that might be but resolved to do whatever it took. She would do it for him. She would do it for them.

A half an hour later her phone rang, waking them both. Jake reached for the phone first and reared back to throw it across the room when Charlie's words stopped him. "Baby don't, it's going to be the captain," Jake handed her the phone and groaned "Fuck. Jesus, I feel like I've been drugged."

"Yes, Sir. I'm sorry, Sir, I left my phone at the office. Yes, we'll . . . I'll be there soon." She hung up the phone and winced, "We? I said we. Well that cat wasn't let out of the bag, it was yanked out."

Jake chuckled, "Fred Mertz."

"Oh my God I love you, Jake Adams!" she said, falling back into his arms completely enchanted. He rolled up on his elbow and studied her.

"Did I scare you?" he asked her with genuine concern. She shook her head no and his eyes narrowed.

"Okay, I was a little scared but I can take it," she said firmly. "I can take whatever you can dish out, Adams. Anything. I have never been this sexual or this satisfied in my life."

"Jesus Christ, Charlotte Cavanaugh. Where did you come from?" Jake sighed. "I can't believe that you aren't running for the nearest exit."

"I can't either," she purred.

"Maybe it's because you're as crazy as I am," he said sadly, pushing the hair out of her eyes.

"Maybe," she said, her eyes starting to mist. He pulled her into his arms and held her tight until she pulled away, her jaw squared. *Uh oh*, he thought.

"Can I ask you something Jake? It feels like . . . well, like maybe you are not always . . ." she shook her head and stood up. "This will have to wait, we have to get rolling. Cap wasn't pissed but he was annoyed that

he had to put together the surveillance without my help."
Jake nodded, relieved that she didn't finish her question.

Back at the station the captain was cranky. He was none too pleased with his favorite detective. "I have most of it covered, but of course nobody wants midnights so since you and Adams were MIA when this schedule was being put together, guess what? You two get the first three midnight shifts, starting tonight."

"Fair enough Cap," she smiled. "Sorry about that, it won't happen again."

"You're goddamn right it won't," he said, trying to sound stern.

"Can we switch the second night to me and Clint? I only put him on a one-day suspension but I'd like to keep him close." The captain nodded in understanding. He erased Jake's name and wrote in Clint's.

Charlie resisted the urge to skip back to her office, thrilled that she would be teamed up with Jake tonight and even more thrilled that there was a very good chance that she and Jake would be poised to catch the killer. She also knew Clint would be excited to get in on the stake-out. Thinking about Clint always brought her thoughts back to AJ. She wanted so much to tell AJ what was happening, but ever since she connected the dots that night at the bar with Clint, she no longer felt comfortable reaching out to him. She didn't really believe AJ was the killer but the coincidence was gnawing at her gut.

While Jake met with Cramlin to break down the Deborg homicide, Charlie dove into her inbox but was extremely distracted. She played the scene again in her mind, her stomach in knots while she played his words over and over, "I love you, Charlotte," then relived the feel of the fabric around her small wrists, the helplessness of being tied to the bed . . . *yes, she could handle this. She could so fucking handle this.*

Somewhere in between reading the reports, her mind wandered back to her mission. *If an afternoon as hot as she and Jake shared today didn't bring him to climax—what would?* She already knew the answer to that and she was determined to see it through.

She quickly caught up with her paperwork and impulsively pulled the pattern analysis at the bottom of the file to take one more look before she headed for the beach on a mission. She laid out the three news stories Clint had printed out, one of them still stained with spewed orange chicken from the Gay Dolphin.

### Molestation Victim Kills Tormentor

Howard Breuer, People Magazine, April 27, 2010
Fort Bragg, CA

*After Aaron Vargus endured years of sexual abuse, it seemed inevitable that something would finally have to give. One night in February 2009, he downed beers and vodka, drove to a mobile home in Fort Bragg, CA and shot the man he said was his tormentor once in the chest. "You're not going to hurt anyone again," Vargus, thirty-two, allegedly said as the sixty-three-year-old Darrell McNeill lay dying.*

*The fatal shooting in the quaint town flanked by redwood forests and spectacular coastal views has sparked a debate over whether Vargas should be treated like a hero for killing a man who many, including his own family, considered a danger to children, or a criminal for allegedly taking the law into his own hands.*

*Initially charged with murder, Vargas's attorney*

*Tom Hudson contended that the gun went off by accident during the scuffle, although his client was too drunk to remember how it happened. Prosecutors earlier this month agreed to a plea deal for voluntary manslaughter. They cited evidence that McNeill had molested Vargas as far back as when he was eleven years old, along with Vargas's clean record and the sentiments of McNeill's family who have come out in support of Vargas.*

### Serial Child Rapist Allegedly Killed by Molestation Victim in the Same Cell

By James Anderson Hampton Roads

*The sixty-four-year-old man had been locked up for much of the past four decades for sexually assaulting several teenagers in the South Hampton Roads. He tossed one boy in a ditch and abandoned another in a wooden box. Now, a man who himself was a childhood victim of sexual abuse is accused of killing Ausley.*

*Dewey K. "Frankie" Venable, twenty-four, had vowed in a letter to his grandmother that he would not let himself be raped in prison. He also had told family members that he had been disciplined for attacking inmates who were sex offenders.*

*"He had asked not to be stuck in a cell with a child molester, flat out, plain and simple," his aunt, Patricia Nelson, said in an interview. Venable told his family he did not commit the crime.*

*Department of Corrections officials would not talk about the pending criminal case or about information from inmate files. In an email response to the Virginia-Pilot, department spokesman Larry Traylor wrote that there are no policies specifically governing cell as-*

*signments for sex offenders or inmates who are known victims of child molestation.*

*Venable was molested at least once in the mid-1980s, when he was between the ages of four and seven, according to records in Norfolk Circuit Court.*

*In 1988, Dennis L. Sewell pleaded guilty to two counts of aggravated sexual battery for attacks on Venable and another child, court records show. Sewell received a suspended twenty-year prison sentence and ten years of probation.*

### Thirteen-Year-Old Boy Shoots Sexually Abusive Parents

Daniel August Jones, San Francisco Times October 17, 1989 Anaheim, CA

*A thirteen-year-old boy called 911 today at 5:00 a.m. to report that he had shot and killed both his parents. Police report the deceased as Gerard and Gwendolyn Jacobson of the Bay area. The 911 tapes reflect that Adam Homer Jacobson is the self-professed killer, though officials will not confirm this because the accused is a juvenile. Unofficial police sources confirm that the thirteen-year-old Jacobson allegedly shot his parents as they slept and then called police to turn himself in. Investigation into the scene and crime uncovered a wealthy and kinky lifestyle in which the Jacobson's only child was routinely "loaned" to "sexual swinging partners" at weekly parties given at the lavish Jacobson estate, complete with full BDSM sexual dungeon. Mark Jacobson, a businessman and sole heir to the Case Hard Steel Lock Empire, a multi-million-dollar corporation, lead a life of luxury and lascivious behavior. Neighbors re-*

*port numerous parties and neighborhood rumors of nude swims, wife swapping, and sexual deviance abound. The Jacobson's son has not been charged but is being held in "protective custody" according to Anaheim officials.*

Charlie: Hey handsome. I'm going to head home early and get ready for tonight. Want me to pick up some takeout from the Gay Dolphin and you come over at about 8:00?

Jake: Why are you texting me when you are ten feet away?

Charlie: Because if I walk the ten feet I can't call you handsome and because Crammy will place a Gay Dolphin order with me and I've already fed that cheap bastard once today.

Jake: Why don't we just go get a bite on the way? We have plenty of time.

Charlie: Because I need to run an errand and because I need a shower . . . I smell like . . . you. Purrrrrrr

Jake: I like marking you with my scent.

Charlie: )))))))))))))))))((((((((((((((((((

Jake: What's that, Baby?

Charlie: You make me shiver.

Jake: You can take a shower Baby, but there is no guarantee you won't be re-marked by the time we leave for the stakeout. What errand?

Charlie: I want to pick something up. MYOB

Jake: You are my business. I'll pick up dinner after I change. See you at 8:00 my love.

*My love.* Charlie sighed.

Charlie: Orange crusted chicken!

Jake: Yes love, I know. ☺

Charlie smiled and actually shivered remembering how Jake said he wanted to mark her at the beach. He was so fucking out there. *So what did that say about her that she was considering allowing him to mark her? Permanently?*

She didn't have a lot of time. She really did need a shower and she was hoping to get to her laptop before Jake arrived and try again to contact AJ, so Clint's contact could track the signal. She was determined to head to the beach and go through with her plan.

Charlie was sincere when she had asked Clint to try to pin down the origin of AJ without having to make it part of the case file, which they both felt was premature, but she had second thoughts about it almost immediately. While she had truly been wary when she shared with Clint that she had told AJ about her 2012 cases, she had also been shit-faced at the time. The whole idea was as crazy as Clint's accusation that Jake might somehow be involved.

When a case goes on for too long a detective has to resist the urge to reach too far in their desperation to catch a break, and Charlie felt like she had crossed that line in thinking that AJ was somehow connected to the case. She reached out to AJ but he didn't answer. Charlie showered quickly, paying special attention to her virgin and pristine nipples to ensure they were ready for the adventure she had planned for them. Then she pulled her wet hair into a ponytail and decided to try one more time before she headed to the beach.

VABlueAngel: AJ Please.

VABlueAngel: I know you said we had a shelf life, but I don't agree. I need to talk to you please. So much has happened.

**AJ101-789: Be careful tonight, Angel.**

*Chapter 31*
**Pierced**


Charlie drove to the beach in silence. No music, no news, just her and her thoughts, which were racing. AJ told her to be careful tonight but would not respond any further. *He knew. Did he know she was going to be on stakeout tonight, or was he just guessing? Or maybe fishing?* She needed to know where that IP address was coming from. *What if Clint's instincts were partially right and someone inside the department was somehow involved?* She shivered. Not the good kind.

She tried to clear her head. She would need a clear head for what she was about to do. It was crazy. She sped up, worried that she might lose her nerve. Thankfully, traffic was light and she caught mostly green lights when she hit the city line. She made her way to the strip and began to look for the shop. It seemed like these types of shops were staggered every fifty feet on the boardwalk but she didn't want just any shop. She wanted one particular shop, the one where he had confided to her how to win his trust forever. At last she came upon it. It was empty except for the pierced and tatted proprietor. "H-hi, I was interested. I mean I was wondering how . . ."

"Oh sweetheart! I know a virgin when I see one, doll!"

The fact that he was clearly and proudly gay somehow made her feel more comfortable. "Now don't tell me, don't tell me. I loooooove to guess!" Charlie giggled at his enthusiasm.

"I'm channeling my inner woman, and believe you me, she's in there! I'm thinking . . . you are not here for a tattoo."

"You're right," Charlie said, shyly.

"Oh, you are just too adorable! Now, are you doing this for a lucky man . . . or a lucky woman . . .? Don't tell me! Don't tell me! A lucky man!"

"Right again."

"Is he tall? Oh-My-God! I love tall men! Ooops, L-O-L, this isn't about me now is it?! I'm Alex by the way. If you come back on Saturday, I'll be Alexis," he winked.

Charlie was relaxing with every grand slur from this grand queen and she was so grateful to him. She touched his arm to shut him up and said, "He wants me to get my nipples pierced."

"Oh-My-God! That is so hot! And you're going to surprise him yes? Yes, you are! You little vixen! He is going to die! He's just going to die!"

*I don't want him to die. I want him to come*, she thought, her cheeks flushing.

Alex locked the front door and flipped the sign saying he would return soon. Charlie was comfortable with Alex but the cop in her told her that going to the back room of a tattoo and piercing shop with a man, well, almost a man, she didn't know and no witnesses was a terrible idea. She knew Jake would be upset with her for making a decision like that and had already decided that she would spare him the details. Alex led her to what looked like a dentist chair and activated a set of very bright lights. She felt as though she were in the lab of a mad scientist and could easily see Jake owning a store like this one. She wondered what kind of business his parents had been in that left him in such a comfortable financial position after all these years. She was surprised she hadn't asked him.

"Ahem! Ms. Thing! I will need your total attention for the next five minutes! You need to sign the release here and you need to choose a ring. Straight rod, c-ring with balls or c-ring with arrows. They all cost the same, it's just a personal preference thing. I'm partial to the straight rod, but that's no secret to anyone!" he laughed making a big sweep of his hand.

"Charlotte. My name is Charlotte. I'm sorry, Alex. I am really nervous. The arrows I guess. This is going to hurt isn't it?"

"Are your ears pierced, Ms. Charlotte?" he asked with an overemphasized Southern twang, "Same. Same. Now, here is a copy of your release and a care sheet. You have to clean them every day, twice a day for three months to ward off infection. No cheating. Infection is nothing to play around with got it?"

"Got it. Okay. What are those? They look like elec- trodes."

"No, no sweetie. These just allow us to do both nipples at once. Isn't that genius? Just like ear piercing! That'll be $90.00."

Charlotte paid in cash and began to relax. Ear pierc- ing was nothing.

"Okay, let's see my canvass," Alex chirped. She shot an uncomfortable glance at him. "Oh, don't worry honey. I wouldn't know what to do with them!" He said, making Charlotte laugh again. It felt very strange having another man handle her breasts. Even though Alex was as gay as Christmas at Bloomingdale's she felt like she was being disloyal to Jake. He buzzed around her breasts marking the future hole with a marker and attaching the electrode-looking apparatus while she shifted in the dentist chair.

"Okay all set. Now the way we do it is I'm going to count to . . . *ZAP*!!!"

"Ow!!!!!" she screamed. "Oh, my fucking God!! Ow! Ow! Ow! Jesus Christ! Ow!"

"Breathe, Ms. Charlotte. It's all over, it's done. Look."

She straightened her severely arched back and looked down at her freshly adorned nipples. "Oh my God, Alex. They're beautiful. Erotic. Oh my God. He's going to love them. I love them." Her nipples throbbed in objection.

"He's a lucky man," Alex winked. All flame was now gone from his voice. "They're beautiful. I'm sorry about that," he apologized. "I find that pretending I'm gay is the easiest way for women to relax. You should take some naproxen for a day or two."

Shocked, she nodded and looked at the floor. She understood, but it still made her uncomfortable that in her distraction she could be duped so easily. She was a lot of things, but naïve was not generally one of them. She quickly scampered out of the shop and headed back to her car.

Driving back to Landon, she couldn't stop grinning. She could feel them. Her nipples still throbbed but the pain was exquisite. She couldn't stop reaching up and outlining her little rings. A fire was burning in her groin. She couldn't wait to tell him. But when?

She arrived back at her apartment just as Jake was pulling up with the food. He shot her a cold stare. It had no effect on her. She was high from the rush and nothing could touch her.

"Where have you been, Charlotte?" he said in a demanding tone.

"Getting you a present my love. So, check that cold stare, Agent. I'm starving," she grinned.

Jake was annoyed but intrigued. This was definitely a different side of Charlie and it was arousing him. She was deliberately but not defiantly misbehaving. Jake unpacked the food while she changed for the stakeout and discreetly texted Clint, letting him know that he would be with her for the midnight shift stakeout the next night.

Clint:   Who's on tonight? Someone competent, I hope. I have a feeling.

Charlie: Jake and I. No worries, Night Rider.

She sat down at the kitchen counter dressed and ready to go and still grinning. She had it all worked out in her head. She decided she would tell him on the stakeout. She would wait until early morning, when the stakeout was starting to drag. Then she would tell him and he would have to wait until sunrise to actually see them, though she might let him trace the outside of them with his finger through her shirt.

"Where's your vest, Sergeant?" Jake asked.

She hadn't really thought that part through. She would be on a stakeout for the next three nights and would be unable to wear her vest due to the tenderness from her new nipple rings but there was nothing she could do about it now.

"No vest tonight, Agent. It's too uncomfortable while we are sitting all night. I'll bring it and if we see any action I'll strap in on over my shirt. Okay?"

"Not okay."

"Jake. It's okay. Honest. Work with me here."

"Not okay," he said again, his eyes starting to narrow. "What the hell are you grinning at, Cavanaugh? We are leaving here in ten minutes and you will be wearing a vest. Do you understand? I am not amused Charlotte. What the hell is going on with you tonight?"

"This is not how I wanted to do this. I wanted to surprise you in the morning," she grinned.

"Surprise me with what?" he asked, irritated.

"With these," she said, lifting her shirt and revealing her braless chest.

"Oh my God. Charlotte. Baby, they're beautiful. I can't believe you did this. Did it hurt? Can I touch them?" he asked wide-eyed. She lifted his hand to her ring and a shock pulsed through her body as he gently touched them. "You did this for me? Why?"

"Because I love you, Jake. You are the man of my dreams. I want to be the woman of yours."

*Chapter 32*
**The Train Has Left the Station**

"I'm not sure you thought this through, Sergeant," he grinned as they drove to the stakeout. "Tonight is not the night for us to be distracted and those are very distracting. I can't wait to feel them in my mouth." Charlie both shivered and grinned at the thought.

They picked up coffee and drove around the block several times to clear the area before agreeing on a good spot. Jake was arguing with her about the best location and she was perturbed about having to give in, but when he got that tone in his voice and that look in his eye, she knew arguing with him was futile.

"Does the target know?" he asked.

"No. Cap thought it would be best to stay the course and keep him in the dark on the off- chance he might be a suspect as well."

"A suspect?" Jake asked, suspiciously.

"I know it's a long shot but this has been a case of long shots and unexplained weirdness," she said with trepidation.

"What's on your mind, Sergeant?" he prodded.

"Why did you tell Clint that you and I were together the whole time the night of the Daniel Silver murder?" she asked, turning in her seat to look him directly in the eye.

"Why do think? To protect us."

"Protect us from what? I . . ."

"This conversation is over, Charlotte."

"Jake, I . . ."

"Over."

They sat in silence for over an hour, watching the house. Charlie's jaw was squared. She hated that Jake felt he could issue an order to her and she hated herself for following it. The house was busy with activity. Lights coming on in one room, going off in another, until the house was finally dark and still. The police radio quieted down as well and the tension was palatable. Her head was spinning over his refusal to discuss why he lied to Clint, over the pain from her aching nipples, and from the overwhelming physical ache she felt when she was sitting this close to him but not touching him. *To protect us. Why did we need protecting?*

"I'm going to go do a quick sweep of the property," he suddenly said, stepping out of the SUV.

"What? No wait. Why? Wait a second."

"Charlotte, the last time this happened, it happened with us sitting here," he said. "I'm just going to do a few sweeps tonight. I won't be gone long. You take point and stay put." He closed the door and didn't give her a chance to answer. The hatch to the back of the SUV popped causing Charlie to reach for her gun.

"Jesus Christ Adams," she whispered. "What the hell are you doing back there; you scared the shit out of me!"

"Getting my coat! Now pipe down! Eyes front!" he snapped.

When Jake returned some thirty minutes later, he explained that the house appeared secure and quiet but he didn't like how open it was. No fence or buffers. Then he slipped back into his sulky silence.

She stewed for over an hour but finally broke the spell by reaching for his hand and bringing it to her chest but he pulled away. "We have to stay focused, Charlie.

Tonight could be the night. I have a feeling."

That was twice. Clint had uttered those same words.

Ignoring him she again brought his hand to her chest. He closed his eyes and moaned and she shivered.

"Six more hours," she whispered.

"Six more hours," he repeated. "Jesus Charlie you're driving me out of my mind. Tell me about Thompson, your family, anything. Three nights of this is going to kill me!" She grinned, thrilled that she was tormenting him.

"No," she said firmly. "It's your turn. I want to know about you," she was stalling. She didn't want to tell Jake that Clint would be her partner tomorrow night instead of him.

"I've already told you my story," he said pushing her hair behind her ear.

"Tell me about your parents," she said, with genuine interest. "What did they do? What do your people do, as my grandmother used to say?"

"You haven't told me about your grandmother," he side-stepped her questions, again. "What was she like?"

She gave him her *Oh-no-you-fucking-don't face.* "What did your parents do?" she repeated.

"They entertained themselves," he said with disgust. "That's what my parents did."

Charlie remained quiet.

"They drank, they smoked weed, they traveled, and they partied. They did what you do when you live in California and you have money," he sighed.

She let the silence linger.

Jake took a deep breath. It was a risk, but he supposed it was inevitable. "My grandfather started a locksmith company when he was in his early twenties. He grew it into a lock manufacturing company, the largest one in the country at the time. By the time he was my age, he was a self-made millionaire. He was killed by the enraged father of a seventeen-year-old girl my grandfather was bedding when he was in his early fifties, and my father inherited everything. Immature prick that he was, he put my grandmother in an upscale nursing home 500 miles away, immediately sold the company and he and my mother spent their days and nights living a life of pleasure. My grandmother hired a lawyer and tried to fight him but the will my grandfather left was irrevocable.

"He did the same for me—an irrevocable trust which, if they hadn't died together, could have put my mother in the same position," he said, talking more to himself now. "God he was such a prick. My parents could have done anything with that money. They could have helped people, started a charity, or continued to build the business. But no, they were like two teenagers who had just been given the keys to the city. I hated them."

"Jake? What?" She placed a hand on his arm, as if to stop him from the shocking admission.

"This is why I don't like to talk about the past Charlie. My family was fucked up. My grandfather was fucked up. He fucked up my father and my parents fucked me up. It's not what you want the woman you want to marry to know about you. The good news is they're gone. All of them. They can't hurt me anymore and they can't hurt you."

"The earthquake."

"Yes. The earthquake."

Jake Adams knew how to redirect. He was a master at it.

"October 17th," she said.

She imagined that it was a date that would be with her forever because it was a date that was going to be with him forever. *Wait. What? The woman he wants to marry?*

"The woman you want to marry?"

"Yes Charlotte. This isn't exactly what I planned but yes, I want to marry you. I want to be with you every day for the rest of my life and I know you want to be with me."

Charlie teared up and brought his hand to her face. "I need to be with you," she said. "Want to be with you. Have to be with you. Oh my God. I love you Jake. I'm sorry this isn't how you planned it, but a stakeout is as romantic as it gets for cops, right?"

She was trying not to sound disappointed that this was the least romantic place she could think of for a proposal. He smiled sweetly, appreciative that she was trying to put a good spin on it. He decided that when he got a proper ring, he would do it the right way, on one knee at the beach, at the threshold of the ocean she loved so much. Reading his thoughts, she dropped his hand to her chest and said, "We already have the rings to seal the deal." He kissed her hand and willed the clock to move faster.

Clint watched from a nearby grove of crape myrtle trees trying to restrain his disgust for the woman for whom he cared and respected so deeply. It was not her fault, he decided. It was Jake's fault. He watched as the two of them laughed and talked and flirted and were even touching each other on the job. Oblivious to their surroundings; oblivious to the target, to the killer, and oblivious to him, in so many ways. Charlie would end up hating him for turning her into a girl. This he knew.

The night wore on. Neither Jake nor Charlie nor Clint got sleepy. All three were charged with the adrenalin from love, lust, and the search for a homicidal killer. They all could have skipped the coffee. At 0530 the radio finally chirped.  Jake drove with a purpose back to the apartment, neither of them speaking a word, Clint following from a distance.

Jake made the tail the second they turned off Wickermore Street and he grinned an evil grin at Clint's lame attempt at following him. He quickly dismissed Clint and turned his attention back to his prey. Clint McCallister was no match for him and never would be. After last night, he was certain Charlie was his and after the things he had in store for her this morning, there would be no turning back.

In the silence of the Fed Mobile each could hear the other's increased breathing. The sexual tension had been building all night, and in the homestretch it magnified exponentially. Charlie started to visibly shake, and Jake put a hand on her knee to steady her. "It's okay, Baby," he whispered. Jake was aware that she knew the intensity of their lovemaking was about to be taken up a notch and he knew she was frightened. Frightened and ready, an irresistible combination for Jake Adams. Charlie nodded, grateful for his reassurance. Beads of sweat had begun to form on her upper lip. Her heart was beating out of her shirt and discharge from her painful piercings was making her nipples erect and her shirt wet, like a lactating mother.

Once inside the apartment Jake pulled Charlie into an embrace that she instantly realized had changed. Embraces of the past were tainted with lust, desperation, and control. This was different. This was acceptance, trust, unconditional love, and a familiarity she had never known. Somehow, he had made her believe. She had made him believe. He picked her up and carried her to the bedroom where he laid her down and immediately raised her shirt to gaze at his treasure. He traced the rings, first with his finger, then with his tongue with no regard for their state of recovery. She tried to delay him, but it was futile. She whimpered in ecstasy and pain at his touch. His mouth enveloped her nipples and she could feel the steel against his teeth. She arched her back and gasped in response.

"Easy Jake," she begged. "Easy Baby. Please." It was too much. She was leaving the planet. Her nipples were aching. Her breasts were engorged from the long night of anticipation. The pain was intense and the sensation of the steel against his teeth triggered a violent orgasm. Jake's mouth latched on and he held her tight while she bucked and screamed as the morning sun filled the room. In her state of semi-consciousness, he took her. Her body limp; her mind gone. He whispered to her while he slowly entered her, "It's okay. I've got you. Let go."

She sighed in ecstasy, hearing him from a long distance away but responding by opening her legs to him, knowing she was loved, that she was safe. There would be no more trains. Jake's love would protect her.

He rode her slowly and rhythmically. "That's my good girl," he whispered softly. "Take it all. Take it." She responded by opening up further and whimpering with every completed stroke. "Open your eyes Charlotte," he commanded. She opened her tear-filled eyes and tried to bring him into focus. Jake was still Jake but didn't look the same except for his eyes which flashed, causing her to gasp and try to pull away. Her hands went to his face and neck as she tried to claw her way out from under him. He grasped both hands and pinned her tiny wrists easily with one hand. "Shhhhhh. It's okay Baby. It's okay," he whispered continuing to gently pump into her.

"Jake!" she gasped as her mind slammed back into reality with the force of a sledgehammer as another orgasm overtook her.

"Shhhh," he said, quieting her and stroking her hair while she tried to regain her bearings.

"Jake," she whispered looking around the room and taking in the sunlight from her windows.

"Are you ready my love?"

"Yes," she said breathlessly.

"Tell me."

"I want it Jake."

"Tell me," he repeated, his voice louder now, raining down on her.

"I love you. I want you to come."

"You first," he growled, pinning her arms above her head and slamming the full weight of his body into her. She screamed with every blow from his body. Faster. Faster. Harder.

"Jake!" she screamed.

"Now!" he commanded as she exploded into oblivion.

Caught off guard, his body betrayed his control and his orgasm was upon him before he knew it was happening. He cried out. Her nails clawed into his back as she realized it was happening. The pain of his tearing flesh pushed him over the edge and he unleashed everything he had into her.

He awoke hours later to her stroking his hair and

watching him sleep.

"Hi," his voice croaked.

"Hi there," she smiled.

"Did you get the number of that bus?" he said pulling her into his arms.

"The Charlotte Express," she smiled, "Lucky for you, you don't have to work tonight."

"What?" Jake sat up alarmed. "He hit? Did they catch him? Fuck!"

"Down boy. He didn't hit and they didn't catch him. The captain changed the stakeout schedule. Clint and I are on tonight, and you and I are back tomorrow night. I think he felt like he was taking advantage and monopolizing you," she lied. His face hardened. His eyes followed.

"Oh, come on, Adams, what was I supposed to say? 'No Captain, I'd rather work with my boyfriend.'"

"I guess that wouldn't have gone over very well," he pouted and flopped back onto the bed. *Way too easy*, she thought. She waited for the second wave but it never came. He pulled her back into his arms and cooed in her ear and snuggled her before remembering her gift to him. The rings. He jumped out of bed and ran to the bathroom.

"What are you doing?" she called to him. He returned with peroxide and cotton balls and gently cleaned her rings. Charlotte was in heaven. She had never been cared for with this combination of force and tenderness. It was the combination she had been looking for all her life.

They made dinner together and cuddled on the couch until Charlie finally pulled away and said she had to get ready. Clint had texted her and said he would pick her up at 8:30. "Why so early? Does he think this is a date?"

She shot him a look and then softened it.

"Clint and I have been working together for years. We are coworkers and friends. You have nothing to worry about. I will never ever be with or want to be with another man. Ever again," she said kissing him gently.

"I think you are going to need some help in the shower," he said grinning.

Clint arrived at 8:30 but when he saw Jake's vehicle he decided not to go up and texted her instead. Charlie kissed Jake goodbye and was surprised by how gut-wrenching it was to be leaving him. "Be careful, Love," he whispered pulling her close. "I will, Jake. I promise."

Once inside the cruiser with Clint, Charlie found his mood heavy and dark. "Hey, what's with the sourpuss, Night Rider? I thought you wanted in on this?"

"I do," he said and then returned to his silence. *Fucking moody men*, she thought. Clint chose the spot she tried to talk Jake into last night. "This is a good spot, Clint."

"It's a hell of a lot better than the spot you picked out last night," he snapped, regretting it as soon as he said it. Fire sparked in her eyes and he knew he had some quick explaining to do.

"What-the-fuck McCallister?"

"Easy Sarge. I wasn't spying on you, I just had a gut feeling that this thing was going to go down last night, and I wanted to make sure you had some backup and I didn't stay long. That's it. I swear."

"Without telling me and while you were on suspension? That is some incredibly poor judgment Clint. A whole shitload could have gone wrong with that plan, especially since we didn't know you were out here! What the hell is going on with you?"

"I just want to catch this fucker, okay?" he said, trying to sound contrite.

"Join the club pal," she chided back.

Another night of distraction and uncomfortable silence, just what she fucking needed. Jake texted her throughout and finally told her at one a.m. that he was going to bed. Clint let out an audible sigh with every chime of her phone until she said, "Put a sock in it, Clint." He was acting like a spoiled child and she was having none of it.

At two a.m. she got out of the cruiser and told him she was going to sweep the property and as was done to her the night before, she did not wait for an answer. Charlie was frustrated with herself and with her friend. It didn't have to be like this. She turned the corner of the house and was met with a punch to the face that took her by complete surprise. She fell backwards over some loose bricks and winced as her head hit the ground with a thud. "I'm sorry," was the last thing she heard before she lost consciousness and her attacker relieved her of her weapon.

*Chapter 33*
**Shots Fired Officer Down**

Charlie lay on the ground drifting in and out of con-sciousness, but unable to move or open her eyes. She was cold and she was scared. She didn't know what had happened, but she knew she was hurt and she knew she needed Jake. She heard a shot ring out and flinched but still could not open her eyes. She had been shot. *This is what being shot feels like*, she thought as her body grew colder and a white tunnel of fog carried her away. Char-lie could hear Clint, but he sounded a long way off.

"Oh my God! No! Charlie! Signal 13! Officer down! Shots fired!"

All she could manage to say was "Jake" and then ev-erything went black. She heard the sirens in the distance and briefly woke to the heroes cutting off her clothes. "Nooo," she protested, horrified that they were about to uncover her rings, but she slipped back into the darkness. "I'm here, Charlie," she heard Jake say.

There in the dim light Jake stood waiting for her. She walked slowly to him and he pulled her into his embrace and stroked her hair. She was unable to speak. Mary Jane stood in the corner smiling at her and giving her a thumbs-up. The light in the dark concrete hallway became blinding. She could no longer see either of them. "Jake!" she yelled.

"I'm here, Charlie," Jake said quietly, taking her hand. "I'm here."

"Cap! She's awake!" Clint yelled. "Charlie? Thatta girl. Time to wake up, Sarge," Clint said, taking her other hand.

"Okay, okay back up you two, give the doc some room to work here," the captain said as he came through the door. "You gave us a little scare there kiddo." The captain smiled warmly. Charlie tried to lift up her head and the pain caused her to cry out.

"I need you to lay still Sergeant Cavanaugh," the doctor instructed. "You've got quite a head wound there."

"What happened Cap? I was doing a sweep and bam, lights out. Was it the perp? Did we get him? Clint? What happened out there?"

"We'll give you all the details later, Charlie. Right now, you need to stay quiet and let the doctor do his doctor thing. Okay?" She nodded and immediately regretted it, crying out again. The doctor injected something into her IV line and told her she needed to rest. The next time she woke up it was daylight. Jake was perched on the edge of her bed holding her hand as Clint snored in the chair.

"Hi there, Beautiful," he said kissing her hand.

"Hi," she smiled back.

"I'm up! I'm up!" Clint said staggering to his feet. "Hey, there she is. About time you woke up. Do you have any idea how many dates I've had to cancel?" She laughed and brought her hand to her head when the pain pierced her head.

She felt the shaved spot and the stitches and her eyes widened. "Did I get shot? I thought I heard a shot?"

"You fell and landed in a pile of bricks and cracked your head like a coconut," Jake smiled weakly.

"I fell?"

"She fell? Then why does she have two black eyes Super Fed?" Clint challenged.

"Jake, could you give Charlie and me a minute

please?" Clint asked.

Jake looked at Clint and then narrowed his eyes at Charlie. She mouthed "please Baby" and Jake stepped away from the bed. "I'll be right outside this door," he said, mostly to Clint.

"Gee thanks, Agent Adams," Clint snapped. "Good to know."

Clint sat down on the bed and tried to take her hand but she pulled away. "Seriously, Clint? I'm lying here in a hospital bed and you're still going to stand there and try to measure dicks with this guy?"

"Why do men insist on measuring their dicks?" Clint said and grinned. *If there was any way to test Charlie for brain damage it would be with a movie line*, Clint thought.

"Jesus Clint. Tin Cup, Renee Russo said it."

"Her character's name?"

"Molly Griswold."

"Hey! Great! No brain damage!" Clint announced. "That's my girl and I'd win that measuring contest, in case there was any doubt in your mind."

Charlie's face turned serious. "I'm not your girl. I'm his girl. I'm your sergeant and at Hanican's, I was your partner, now what the hell happened out there? It's all so fuzzy."

Clint recounted the whole thing, "When you didn't come back, I went looking for you. As I got closer to the house, I heard the gunshot and I found you all bloody on the ground, so I called a Signal 13 and the cavalry came running. Your boyfriend out there appeared in seconds. Seconds, Charlie. He said he was parked nearby in case something went down. Yeah right!"

Charlie interrupted, "You mean like you were the

night before? Go on." Clint stared down at the sheets and shook his head 'no,' refusing to acknowledge that it was same thing.

"Once we got you out of there, we started our search. By the way, do you believe those fucking heroes staged a block away? Staged for an officer down!"

"It's standard operating procedure for them to wait until the scene is safe and makes perfect sense, they don't have weapons, you Thompson disciple," she said. "Go on."

"Anyway, the back door of the house was open, so we swept the house and it was empty. When K-9 got there, they immediately headed toward the back corner of the yard where we found Hanican DRT."

"Dead? Was it like the others? Plastic wrap around the head?" she asked, animated.

He shook his head 'no.' "Single gunshot wound to the head."

The door cracked open and Jake stuck his head inside. "Everything okay in here?" Jake asked.

"Fine, Agent." Clint said exasperated. "I was going to smother her with this pillow but now I've changed my mind." Charlie gave Jake an I'm sorry look and a thumbs-up and Jake closed the door.

"He was shot?"

"With your gun, Sarge," Clint said gravely.

"What?" she said in disbelief. "I shot Hanican? I don't even remember encountering him."

"Grecko is still combing through the crime scene, he's devastated that you were hurt, by the way. Jesus, I thought he was going to fucking cry."

"Sweet Clint," she said impatiently. "The gunshot wound?"

"There are a lot of theories out there but right now it looks like he found you unconscious and took your gun. I think that's bullshit. I think he knocked you unconscious and took your gun but wonder boy out there thinks you fell. He obviously thinks you're some kind of a klutz. I would never say that or think that of you. I mean, your driving sucks but you're no klutz."

"McCallister!"

"Oh, right. Sorry. Anyway, it looks like he offed himself with your weapon in the backyard. Grecko found a note in his pocked that said, "I'm sorry" and it had the addresses and names of the other five scumbags in the order they were taken out, each with a line through them."

Charlie screwed up her face.

"See! See! That's exactly what I'm saying! Too neat right? Too fucking big-red-bow right."

"Yea, it's kind of too easy. What else?" she prodded.

"Well, they found plastic wrap, a few Tyvek suits and chemicals in his unlocked shed but come on, anyone could have put those there. You could have put them there!"

"So that's your theory? I framed him?" she quipped. "You're only allowed to accuse me of a felony once every ten years McCallister."

"You know what I mean, Sarge. Come on! You're not buying this horseshit, are you? Because the captain sure as hell is and someone needs to talk some sense into him before he talks to the press and closes this case."

"Too late," Charlie said and pointed to the TV, where Captain Grisolm had a gaggle of microphones stuck in his face outside the hospital's main doors.

"So what do you think happened Clint? I want to

hear it," she said as Jake came in.

"The press conference is on," he said reaching for the remote and turning it up. The three of them stood there and listened to the captain's spin on how the people of Landon could rest easy tonight because the "Landon Police, the FBI, and a very brave Sergeant Cavanaugh, who is expected to recover from very serious injuries, solved the serial."

Clint rolled his eyes. "The Feds are getting part of the credit for this? Jesus, Adams, you weren't even supposed to be there last night."

"Nor were you the night before, Detective," Jake said glaring at Clint.

"How the hell did you know . . ."

"Take it easy Clint," Charlie interrupted.

"There is plenty of credit to go around. We all worked really hard on this," Jake said.

"I'm not sure we're done working on it, Agent. Charlie and I aren't buying this shit for a second," he said moving closer to Charlie's bed.

Charlie gave Clint the look. "Clint, when is the last time you slept? Shut your pie hole before the captain suspends you again. Go home and get some sleep. I should be out of here soon and we'll talk then okay?"

"Yea, okay. I am pretty beat and I do have a bed warmer at home waiting for me," he said raising his eyebrows.

"He means Chronic, his German Shepherd," Charlie said, rolling her eyes at Jake.

"Was that necessary? See, I'm thinking that was not necessary," Clint said, shaking his head as he left the room.

"Clint still spinning his conspiracy theories?" Jake

asked disinterested. She nodded.

"You?" she asked.

"This Hanican guy sounds, looks, and walks like a duck. He's a fucking duck. You ready to go home, Beautiful?"

*Chapter 34*
**Move the Dash**


Charlie chatted away into her cell phone, "Hey Clint, go ahead and bring me the case files. Yea, I'm going to do my supplements from home. This Nervous Nelly doctor isn't going to release me to full duty until the stiches come out in two fucking weeks . . . I know it's ridiculous. I told him I'm a desk jockey ninety percent of the time . . . Yeah okay, well not lately but usually," she laughed.

She hung up to find Jake giving her a disapproving look. "What part of off work did you not hear, Charlie?"

"Oh, come on. It's not going to hurt my head to get these reports out of the way. By the way Agent, have you finished yours yet?" she asked.

"No ma'am I have not. I have been too busy attending to your every need," he said, slyly.

"My needs . . . Yes, about that. My needs have not been met since I left the hospital. The doctor did not say we couldn't play. He just said to take it easy. Is that possible, Agent Adams?" she flirted.

"You're about to find out, Sergeant," he said taking her hand and trying to lead her to the bedroom. "Noooo," she protested. "Clint's on his way and he's bringing Gay Dolphin!"

"And that would be my cue!" he said, turning and heading toward the door.

"Jesus! Can't you two play nice?"

"We can, but we won't. I'm going to go to the hotel to shower and change and grab some fresh clothes suitable for two weeks of movies and lovemaking." He grinned.

"Here's your hat. What's your hurry?" she smiled.

Clint arrived with the case files and orange crusted chicken. They had a relaxed and easy visit. Charlie was relieved to find that though Clint still believed there was more work to be done on the case, he was starting to make room for the possibility that it was what it was. Though he reminded her that there were still some loose ends. Grecko did not have all of the forensics back, the ME's office still hadn't waved off on the puncture wounds, and his computer friend still had not been able to nail down AJ's IP address location. "He said the trail disappears almost as soon as he picks it up. This AJ guy really might be some kind of CIA spook. It would explain a lot."

"How would he have known about the stakeout though?" she pondered.

"I'm thinking something else," Clint said cryptically and Charlie raised an eyebrow. "I'm thinking your FBI buddy might not have as secure a communications link as he thinks. Or else he's sharing the info about our stakeouts with his fed buddies. You know how those assholes are."

"Clint."

"Sorry. I know. You're in love with him. I have to play nice. Yada yada."

"You missed a yada."

"How's your coconut, Sarge?"

"I'm okay. But my hair is fucked up."

"As pretty as you are, it won't matter," he said, locking onto her eyes which had softened as she gazed back.

"Hey, try to raise this AJ guy again," he suggested, trying to change the subject.

"Good idea!" she said, running to the bedroom for her laptop. Clint ran his fingers through his hair and tried to get his game face on.

VABlueAngel: AJ? You there?

VABlueAngel: Please AJ. Did you know that I was in the hospital? I'm guessing you knew.

VABlueAngel: I don't want to leave it like this AJ. Can't we at least say goodbye? Please?

**AJ101-789: I'm glad you're okay. I'll never forget you Charlotte. Goodbye Angel.**

"See if you can keep him talking. I'm calling Elahi over at VBPD." She tried to keep it going but there was no response from AJ. She felt sure it was the last time she would ever hear from him and it made her sad. She was sorry that she thought he might be involved when he clearly wasn't, sorry that she had hurt him, and sorry that she would never know if he was safe.

"Sorry, Clint, but I think this chapter of my life is closed," she said sadly. She didn't mean Clint, but that's what he heard. He tucked her hair behind her ear as Jake had done. His eyes were big and sad. "It doesn't matter. Elahi didn't pick up. I'll call him again later."

There was a knock at the door and Clint asked with his eyes if it was okay if he answered it and she nodded. It was Jake. "Oh, so now we knock huh?"

"Why are you still here McCallister?"

"Funny, I was just about to ask you the same thing."

"Knock it off you two," Charlie moaned.

"I'll see you later, Sarge," Clint said as he headed out, glaring at Jake as he went.

"That guy is a dick."

"No, he isn't," she said trying to look annoyed but finding it impossible looking at Jake. He was wearing worn jeans, sneakers, and a blue sweatshirt. It was a completely charming look for him and she wanted to crawl inside him.

"Are you hungry? There's plenty. He brought enough for you, too," she offered.

"Well, isn't he a fucking prince. Yes, I am hungry. Where were we?" he said, again taking her hand and leading her to the bedroom. Successfully this time.

It turns out it was possible for Jake Adams to make love slowly. He spent hours gently caressing her and teasing her as though she were made of glass. He spent most of his time gently stroking her rings with his tongue. Several times she tried to ignite the process but Jake was fully in control. He would move to her face, kiss her gently, and whisper in her in her ear, "Lie still, Baby." It was the longest, sweetest uninterrupted lovemaking session they had ever had. They were both wholly present and it was heaven. It ended unexpectedly with his climax rather than hers and she basked in it able to fully feel the rush inside her. It was the happiest Charlotte had ever been in her life. Bad hair and all.

She awoke to find that the sun had set and her phone was vibrating. Jake was sleeping peacefully beside her. It was Clint. She silenced the phone, it could wait. As she did she saw four other calls from him and three texts saying he was in the parking lot and needed to speak with her ASAP. She looked through a slit in the curtains and saw his green jeep so she quietly stepped out of the room with her phone and went to the kitchen.

He answered on the first ring. "Charlie! Jesus Christ I was about to break down the door," he slurred.

"Clint, what the hell is going on? Are you drunk?"

"Come down here now! I need to tell you something! Istsss very important."

"Clint. I am a patient supervisor and I am your friend but so help me God, I will fucking fire your ass. Stay put. I'm calling a cab for you and I want you to go home and sleep it off and we will talk tomorrow."

"Okay, you're right, of course you're right. I'm sorry, but I only had beer. I swear. Just too many. But this couldn't wait. It can't wait Charlie. I heard from Elahi. Please come down here!"

"It's the middle of the night and I am not coming down there McCallister. I told you this is over. The case is closed," she whispered, trying not to wake Jake.

"How can you say it's closed Charlie? This AJ guy could be the link to all six targets and he's not in in the Middle East. He's here. He's in fucking Landon! I told you something wasn't adding up. I told you," his slur becoming more pronounced with the addition of emotion.

"Clint I am not discussing this while you are drunk. I am calling a cab for you now." Charlie's hand shook as she dialed the cab company, the number programmed into her brain from calling cabs for so many other drunks. Clint's words rang in her ears. He's here. He's in fucking Landon. She wondered if she should wake Jake. "Hi Lenora, it's Sergeant Cavanaugh over at the PD. I've got one for you . . . Oh wow, bad news travels fast . . . yes I'm fine, thank you for asking, just a little banged up . . ." She gave Loose Lenora—her pet name from the guys in patrol—the address and vehicle description and ignored Clint trying to break into the call. She stood at the window watching for the cab. She couldn't see inside the Jeep but she knew Clint was looking up at her. *He's here. He's in fucking Landon.*

*Why didn't she want to know? Fucking Clint!* Her

world was perfect. The man she loved was sleeping in her bed, the case was solved, and she was being hailed a hero for tripping over a pile of bricks.

She glared down at the Jeep, cursing the taxi for not being there already. Then she saw the door open as Clint headed for her stairs. *Shit!* She met him on the second landing as the cab was pulling up. "Not one fucking word McCallister!" she ordered. "Cab! Now! Home!"

He lowered his head at her tone and then forcefully took her by the shoulders and got in her face. "He screwed up. He didn't cloak his last transmission. The last transmission from AJ101-789 came from the WIFI at the Landon Radisson," he said, searching her face for a reaction. "You still want me to go?"

"Yes," she said emotionless.

"Charlie . . ."

"Back the fuck off Clint. Go. Now."

She stood and watched as he tripped over the last step and made his way to the back seat of the cab. She didn't see him climb out the other side. Her stomach heaved as she made her way back up the stairs. Once inside she stood motionless, except for the shaking. She went to the refrigerator and opened a ginger ale in an attempt to bribe her heaving stomach into submission. The case folder lay on the countertop next to her laptop. It was high noon time, she and her case file staring each other down. She reached for it slowly, as though it were a snake and started flipping through the pages. She stopped at Clint's pattern analysis and then flipped to articles he had printed out.

*Thirteen-Year-Old Boy Shoots Sexually Abusive Parents*

*Daniel August Jones, San Francisco Times October*

*17, 1989 Anaheim, CA*

*A thirteen-year-old boy called 911 today at 5:00 a.m. to report that he had shot and killed both his parents. Police report the deceased as Gerard and Gwendolyn Jacobson of the Bay area. The 911 tapes reflect that Adam Homer Jacobson is the self-professed killer, though officials will not confirm this because the accused is a juvenile. Unofficial police sources confirm that the thirteen-year-old Jacobson allegedly shot his parents as they slept and then called police to turn himself in. Investigation into the scene and crime uncovered a wealthy and kinky lifestyle in which the Jacobson's only child was routinely "loaned" to "sexual swinging partners" at weekly parties given at the lavish Jacobson estate, complete with full BDSM sexual dungeon. Mark Jacobson, a business man and sole heir to the Case Hard Steel Lock empire, a multi-million-dollar corporation, lead a life of luxury and lascivious behavior. Neighbors report numerous parties and neighborhood rumors of nude swims, wife swapping, and sexual deviance abound. The Jacobson's son has not been charged but is being held in "protective custody" according to Anaheim officials.*

Nothing. No bells. No shiver. Was she was missing something or was this just another attempt by Clint to make her second guess Jake? She opened her laptop. Her conversation with AJ, still carelessly on the screen. She hoped Jake had not seen it. She hadn't discussed AJ with him and she caught a chill when she remembered how possessive he could be.

VABlueAngel: AJ? You there?

VABlueAngel: Please AJ. Did you know that I was in the hospital? I'm guessing you knew.

VABlueAngel: I don't want to leave it like this AJ. Can't we at least say goodbye? Please?

**AJ101-789: I'm glad you're okay. I'll never forget you Charlotte. Goodbye Angel.**

Nothing.

She glanced back at the article. Nothing. Then a spark caught. *Case Hard Steel Empire.* Jake had said his grandfather had started a lock manufacturing company. She Googled the name of the company. The first reference was the sale of the company in 1982 for a whopping sixty-eight million dollars. The second was a reference to the deceased owner and CEO Mark Jacobson, killed alongside his wife by their thirteen-year-old son Adam Jacobson, as they lay sleeping. She already knew this. There was no connection here. She tried to determine how old Adam Jacobson would be now. "He was thirteen at the time of the shooting" she mumbled "so that would make him . . ." She glanced back at the article date. October 17, 1989.

The blood drained from her face and the room began to spin. October 17, 1989.

She sat down on the bar stool to steady herself and typed in the Google search line

"Earthquake, California, 1989." Wikipedia spit it right out.

**1989 Loma Prieta Earthquake**

The Loma Prieta earthquake, also known as the Quake of '89 and the World Series Earthquake, struck the San Francisco Bay Area of California on October 17, 1989, at 5:04 p.m. local time. Caused by a slip along the San Andreas Fault, the quake lasted ten-fifteen seconds and measured 6.9 on both the moment magnitude scale (surface-wave magnitude 7.1) and on the open-ended Richter Scale. The quake killed sixty-three people throughout Northern California, injured 3,757 and left some 3,000–12,000 people homeless.

The earthquake occurred during the warm up practice for the third game of the 1989 World Series, featuring both of the Bay Area's Major League Baseball teams, the Oakland Athletics and the San Francisco Giants. Because of game-related sports coverage, this was the first major earthquake in the United States to have its initial jolt broadcast live on television.

She let out an audible sigh, unaware that she had been holding her breath. *Okay. Okay. There was an earthquake. His parents died in the earthquake. There is no connection,* she reassured herself. She flipped back to the AJ screen and picked up the Adam Jacobson shooting article. Her eyes went back and forth from the screen to the article and the screen to the article. She laid the article down and picked up a pen with shaking hands.

Smelling cheap cigar smoke, she looked up to see Thompson sitting on the other side of the breakfast bar. "Go ahead kid. Write it."

"I really don't feel well Thompson. I think I need to go back to bed."

"You need to be institutionalized. But not tonight. Tonight you need to write it."

*AJ*, she wrote.

*Adam Jacobson*

*Jake Adams*

She felt like she was stepping outside her body as under it she wrote.

*AJ101-789*

"Keep going," her ghost mentor prodded. Moses sat quietly watching them.

"Write it."

*AJ101-789*

"I did!" She snapped. She stared at the paper.

"Move the dash nitwit," Thompson said through cigar clenched teeth.

*AJ101-789*

*AJ 10-17-89*

*AJ October 17, 1989*

*Adam Jacobson October 17, 1989.*

*Landon Radisson*

She jumped when the bedroom door opened, quickly covering the paper and pushing it back into the file and closing her laptop.

"Baby, you're not doing your reports now?" Jake asked.

"The pain medication was upsetting my stomach so I got up to get a ginger ale."

"That's what I'm here for Love. I would have gotten it for you," he said pulling her into an embrace. "Sweetheart, you're shaking," he said alarmed.

"I'm trying to keep from throwing up," she said honestly.

"Back in bed now. I'm going to bring you some coke, works faster."

She shot a glance at the front door but the thought quickly left her as he hugged her from behind and gently pushed her toward the bedroom. She went to the bedroom, closed the door, laid down, and closed her eyes tightly. Jake caught her eyeballing the front door but did not react until the bedroom door was closed. Slowly he lifted the computer screen.

"Fuck, she knows," he said out loud.

"Fuck she knows," squawked Moses behind his cover. Jake started to feel himself slipping away, moving somewhere else in the same space, shifting.

His eyes went dark and he pursed his lips and nodded his head. "Well aren't we little Miss Clever," he said, grinning under his breath. He opened the case file and saw her handwriting.

*AJ*

*Adam Jacobson*

*Jacob Adams*

*AJ101-789*

*AJ 10-17-89*

*AJ October 17, 1989*

*Adam Jacobson October 17, 1989*

"Very good, little girl. A little late, but very good."

Moses lay dead in his cage. The night time cage cover would ensure that he wouldn't be discovered until morning. Jake felt bad about killing Charlie's bird and he knew it would upset the boy, but he didn't have a choice. He couldn't get Moses to stop saying "Fuck she knows." There were only so many clues Charlie could blatantly ignore. He was already questioning his decision to keep her alive, but the boy seemed to need her and wasn't that the whole purpose of Jake's existence; to protect Adam? The dichotomy added to the fucking. When Adam was doing his "sweet fucking" Jake could overcome him at will when he chose, biting her, making himself bigger so when he entered her all the way it hurt her so she would gasp and whimper, rolling her over and taking her from behind—pumping her while she cried until her orgasm exploded from her and she went limp. He loved fucking her until she passed out. Even while she was passed out.

He felt himself getting hard just thinking about it.

The only other possible solution was murder-suicide, because there was no way they would go on living without her. *Why not give the boy a break and roll the dice?* Jake thought. If he was wrong, a quick death for all of them was still an alternative, provided he wasn't incarcerated. The thought sent a shiver through his spine. *No. Never again. They would never go back. They would die first and take Charlie with them.*

The boy had spent five years in a maximum-security juvenile detention facility outside L.A. Had it not been for Jake he would never have survived it. Jake had been watching over the boy ever since the rapes. Jake was the one who pulled the trigger . . . twice. Those bastards deserved to die. Their own child. He grew angry as he thought about how the boy was restrained using plastic wrap so that there wouldn't be marks when he returned to school after a weekend of abuse. No. No one would ever be allowed to hurt the boy again. Jake would see to that.

He quietly crept back to bed. He searched for the song he needed and let it play quietly on the nightstand as he snuggled up behind Charlie, wrapping her in his arms and she sighed in her half sleepy state. *You let me violate you, you let me desecrate you . . .*

In the corner of the room, Mary Jane sat on a chair. Thompson stood behind her with his hand on Mary Jane's shoulder as Mary Jane let a single tear fall.

## Author Bio

**Patricia Harman** was born in Quantico, Virginia and was raised in nearby Stafford County and Prince William County with her six siblings. A police ride along at age 15 led her to a law enforcement career spanning four decades and culminating as a Police Chief. You can learn more about her by visiting authorpatriciaharman. com